The Invisible Wars

The Invisible Wars

How Nations Fight Without Firing Bullets

By

Helena Marković

Vij Books

New Delhi (India)

Published by

Vij Books
(Publishers, Distributors & Importers)
4836/24, 3rd Floor, Ansari Road
Delhi – 110 002
Phone: 91-11-43596460
Mobile: 98110 94883
e-mail: contact@vijpublishing.com
www.vijbooks.in

ISBN: 978-93-90349-02-9 (HB)

ISBN: 978-93-90349-09-8 (PB)

ISBN: 978-93-90349-45-6 (eBook)

This book was developed using advanced writing tools to support the drafting and ideation process. All content has been thoughtfully curated, refined, and reviewed to ensure quality and relevance.

Contents

Introduction

On a clear autumn morning, in a trading room high above the streets of New York, a single line of newswire text shaved billions off the market value of a European conglomerate. No missiles had been launched, no embassies stormed, no soldiers deployed. Yet the board of directors went into emergency session, supply contracts were frozen, and tens of thousands of workers across three continents suddenly found themselves facing uncertain futures. No crater marked the scene of impact. The weapon was not steel or fire, but information—an engineered narrative seeded, timed, and amplified with precision.

This is not an isolated vignette. A sanctions schedule drafted in Brussels can strangle an industry in Tehran. A rumour whispered into a journalist's ear in Washington can redirect capital flows from São Paulo to Singapore overnight. A lawsuit filed in The Hague can reorder the strategic calculus of an energy giant in Moscow. These are the new theatres of war: quiet, intricate, and devastating. The paradox of our age is that the most consequential wars leave no visible scars, and yet they shape the lives of billions with a force greater than many conventional battles.

We continue, however, to cling to an outdated grammar of power. The old reflexes persist: the idea that "real" war is fought with uniforms, tanks, and flags planted in conquered soil. But while we debate troop numbers and weapons procurement, the balance sheets, pipelines, data streams, and narratives that determine the fate of nations are contested in silence. Guns are bad at solving balance-sheet problems; artillery cannot compel the re-routing of global capital. Power has migrated into subtler forms, and yet we have not developed the language, let alone the literacy, to see it clearly. This book is an attempt to supply that missing grammar.

The Unseen Battlefield

Wars without bullets are not new. History is thick with embargoes, propaganda, espionage, and intrigue. What is new is their scale, speed, and systematic coordination. In the nineteenth century, a naval blockade might take months to constrict a nation's economy. Today, a single directive to a payment network can isolate a country in seconds. Propaganda once required posters, pamphlets, and costly distribution; now an algorithm can amplify a lie across millions of feeds before breakfast. Courts once settled disputes between individuals; now they are instruments of geopolitics, where a single ruling can shift the incentives of an entire industry.

This convergence of instruments—finance, law, logistics, narratives, code—is not accidental. It is engineered. Think-tanks issue memos that shape talking points; those talking points surface in media headlines; investors react to the headlines, moving markets; regulators, under pressure, craft rules that crystallise these market shifts into enduring constraints. What appears spontaneous is often designed. What looks like chaos is, in many cases, choreography. The aim of this book is to make that choreography visible, to teach causal literacy in an age deliberately arranged to obscure causation.

The stakes are not abstract. Citizens see prices rise and fall without explanation. Executives wake to find entire markets closed to them. Officials are confronted with policy shocks whose origins seem mysterious. In each case, what appears as an act of fate is, more often than not, an act of strategy. To act wisely—whether as voters, leaders, or participants in global markets—requires the ability to see through these invisible wars.

The Architecture of Non-Kinetic Conflict

What binds sanctions, cyber intrusions, disinformation campaigns, and legal offensives together is not merely their non-violent character, but their integration into campaign plans. These are not random tools deployed in isolation. They are instruments chosen, sequenced, and synchronised to achieve outcomes that tanks once sought. When the United States freezes access to the dollar system, when Russia seeds divisive narratives in foreign elections, when China leverages supply chains of rare earths, they are not improvising. They are executing engineered campaigns, designed to apply pressure in ways that avoid open war while extracting strategic concessions.

Why does this "grey zone" persist? Because it offers the benefits of war without the political costs of admitting it. A cyber operation that cripples a port can be disavowed. A sanctions package that devastates an economy can be described as "peaceful" pressure. Leaders can signal resolve to adversaries while assuring their own citizens that they remain at peace. This plausible deniability lowers the threshold for action and multiplies the frequency of conflict. The paradox is stark: the tools appear less violent, yet they may be used more recklessly precisely because they are seen as less grave.

Ethics in the Shadows

Any serious account of invisible war must grapple with its ethical terrain. It is tempting to see sanctions as harmless compared to bombs, or disinformation as trivial compared to massed armies. Yet when a nation's medicine supply is throttled by compliance delays, when food shipments stall due to overzealous banking restrictions, when public trust in institutions is corroded by engineered lies, the human consequences are profound. Civilians, far removed from decision centres, bear the brunt of measures framed as bloodless.

The moral calculus of invisible war demands fresh tools. Proportionality, necessity, discrimination—principles developed for kinetic war—must be adapted to peacetime instruments. Can we distinguish between targeted pressure on decision-makers and collective punishment of ordinary people? Can we evaluate the ethics of narrative manipulation that undermines trust not just in governments but in truth itself? These questions will recur throughout this book, not as abstract puzzles but as urgent dilemmas faced by policymakers, firms, and citizens alike.

Why This Book, and Why Now

This is not a book of alarmist warnings or sensationalist tales of hackers and spies. Nor is it a pundit's collection of breezy generalisations. It is meant as a manual for thinking: precise, comparative, and measurable. Each chapter dissects an instrument—sanctions, currencies, information operations, espionage, lawfare, cyber campaigns, psychological operations, supply chains—and treats it as part of a larger campaign system. The emphasis is on engineering: how these tools are designed, sequenced, and evaluated.

The reader will encounter field guides to instruments, case sketches tracing cause chains from memo to market move, ethical frameworks for assessing pressure, and measurement dashboards that clarify impact. The purpose is not to overwhelm with detail but to supply clarity and control. Citizens, executives, and officials alike will leave equipped with the literacy to see, to judge, and to act without being played.

The urgency is obvious. The wars of the future will not announce themselves with declarations or battle drums. They are already here, shaping our prices, our newsfeeds, our jobs, our elections. If we fail to see them, we will be at their mercy. If we learn to see them, we may still guide them toward outcomes that preserve stability and legitimacy.

The Road Ahead

The chapters that follow will move deliberately from definition to design, from field guide to framework. We begin by mapping the quiet theatre of war, defining what counts as non-kinetic conflict and how to detect its signatures. From there we proceed to sanctions, currencies, and narratives, tracing how they function as siege engines and perception controls. We turn to corporate espionage, lawfare, and cyber operations, before addressing psychological campaigns and the fragility of supply chains. We then take up the challenge of measurement, deterrence, and resilience, equipping readers not only to understand but to participate in defending institutions and communities.

Throughout, one motif recurs: the chain. Every action in invisible war is a link in a causal chain designed to be hidden. This book invites the reader to trace those chains, to see the connections between what looks like noise and what is, in truth, strategy. Whether one is a citizen confronting disinformation, a manager navigating sanctions, or a policymaker designing deterrence, the task is the same: to break the invisibility of these wars.

The closing chapters will not offer easy reassurance. Invisible wars will not vanish. They will intensify. But they can be managed with ethics, measurement, and resilience. A democracy that learns to detect campaigns early, to judge their proportionality, and to resist their corrosive effects can remain free even under pressure. A firm that trains itself to see dependencies and narratives can compete without being blindsided. And a citizenry that practises scepticism without surrendering to cynicism can defend the very fabric of trust on which institutions depend.

The invisible wars are here. They are being waged all around us, silently shaping the world we inhabit. The question is not whether they exist, but whether we will learn to see them, understand them, and act with the clarity that true power requires. This book is an invitation to begin.

Chapter 1

The Quiet Theatre of War

One winter's morning in 2010, a swarm of traders on three continents reacted to the sudden collapse of a major European bank's share price. The event appeared to erupt from nowhere—screens flashing red, analysts scrambling, investors fleeing. Yet the spark had been lit weeks earlier in a law firm's conference room, when a carefully crafted lawsuit questioned the bank's liquidity. A sympathetic journalist received a timely leak. Think-tank analysts issued a report amplifying the doubt. When regulators finally intervened, the damage was irreversible: billions erased, market confidence shattered, governments forced into hasty guarantees. No tanks rolled. No generals saluted. And yet, in retrospect, the choreography was unmistakable. A campaign had been waged in silence, leaving behind no craters, only balance sheets in ruins.

This is the essence of the quiet theatre of war. It is not fought in trenches or skies but in courts, currencies, cables, and narratives. It is the deliberate pursuit of strategic outcomes through means that stop short of formal combat yet far exceed ordinary competition. A cyber intrusion into an airport's scheduling system, timed to coincide with a diplomatic spat, sits in this grey zone. So does the sudden imposition of tariffs designed not for revenue but to coerce political concessions. These are not accidents of commerce; they are choices—calculated, sequenced, and often denied in public. They inhabit the threshold between peace and war, a zone of ambiguity where intent is clear to insiders but plausibly deniable to outsiders.

Why does this grey zone endure? The incentives are obvious. Launching a missile carries risk of retaliation; tightening a sanctions schedule often does not. Deploying divisions is costly and unpopular; deploying a narrative is cheap and politically safe. Leaders can act boldly abroad while assuring voters at home that no war is being waged. Cost asymmetry favours the strategist who masters these subtler instruments. A disinformation campaign costs little but can provoke billion-dollar defensive measures. A legal filing may be inexpensive yet alter the trajectory of an entire industry. It is no surprise, then, that the centre of gravity in modern conflict has shifted here, to the domain where outcomes are real but violence is hidden.

To grasp this theatre, we must confront a paradox: the effects are visible, but the causes remain obscure. The public sees fuel prices spike, elections tilt, or supply chains seize up. Rarely do they see the upstream manoeuvres—the think-tank memo, the backroom regulatory draft, the sudden media amplification—that set the chain in motion. The surface looks like fate; the reality is often design. Consider the rapid devaluation of a currency. To most citizens it appears as an act of markets, inscrutable and inevitable. Yet behind it may stand coordinated credit downgrades, timed data releases, and whispered doubts seeded by interested actors. To learn to see these causal chains is to reclaim agency. Without this literacy, we live as if under weather patterns we cannot influence, when in fact we are subject to campaigns engineered for advantage.

The inadequacy of traditional military tools becomes clear when measured against these new levers. Armies cannot compel a creditor to roll over debt. Aircraft carriers cannot alter the global standards of 5G technology. Divisions on parade do not frighten rare earth exporters into compliance. In an interdependent world, the decisive levers are balance-sheet power, legal authority, technological standards, and narrative control. Guns are bad at solving balance-sheet problems. That is why states reach first for economic restrictions, legal offensives, and information campaigns. Soldiers are still trained, but their deployment is often a last resort. The new "campaign plan" begins not with generals but with lawyers, coders, regulators, and analysts.

Yet the fact that these instruments are quieter does not absolve them of moral consequence. The rhetoric of "peaceful" pressure hides its distributive harm. Sanctions framed as tools of diplomacy can deny insulin to children thousands of miles from decision-makers. Information operations described as "messaging" corrode civic trust in societies that are not parties to the conflict. Legal offensives fought in prestigious courts can bankrupt small firms collateral to the dispute. The moral hazard is stark: tools designed for peace are turned toward wartime aims, but without the ethical scrutiny that armed conflict demands. This chapter therefore asks: how should we judge the proportionality of a sanctions list, the morality of a disinformation campaign, or the ethics of a legal offensive? The traditional laws of war have little to say; we must extend our calculus to this quieter theatre.

Before we can evaluate, however, we must map. The reader requires a field guide, a primer on the instruments of non-kinetic conflict. Sanctions and export controls, designed to constrict resources. Narrative shaping, aimed at influencing public opinion and elite choices. Capital controls, crafted to restrict financial flows. Cyber intrusions, both for espionage and disruption. Corporate espionage, targeting intellectual property and competitive advantage. Lawfare, in which courts and standards bodies become battlegrounds. Psychological operations, manipulating fear, pride, or doubt at scale. Each tool has its operators, signatures, and limitations. Alone, each is potent. Combined, they form campaigns as deliberate and coordinated as any military offensive.

The quiet theatre of war is not a metaphor. It is the daily reality of global politics and markets, felt in boardrooms, households, and ballot boxes. To understand it is to move from being a bystander to being a participant who can see the choreography behind the curtain. This chapter opens the door: it defines the battlefield, reveals its paradoxes, explores its moral terrain, and supplies the reader with a map. The journey ahead will dissect each instrument in depth, showing how they interlock into campaigns that shape the fate of nations. For now, the task is simple but urgent: to recognise that war today is not always loud, and that silence can be the most strategic weapon of all.

What counts as a war now

On a winter morning in 2007, Estonia—one of the most digitally connected societies in the world—suddenly found itself paralysed. Banks were inaccessible, ministries could not communicate, and news outlets were silenced. There was no invasion, no artillery, no soldiers crossing borders. The disruption came through code: a wave of cyberattacks, timed with protests over a disputed Soviet-era monument, that effectively shut down the nation's nervous system for weeks. Estonia remained formally at peace, yet its sovereignty was unmistakably under assault. The episode posed a question that has haunted strategists ever since: if a country can be crippled without a shot fired, what still counts as a war?

Traditional definitions falter in the face of such cases. The classical laws of war, built on the assumption of kinetic force, describe "armed attack" as the decisive threshold. A missile strike on a power station qualifies; a distributed denial-of-service attack that disables the same station does not. The problem is not academic. If a state responds militarily to a cyber intrusion, it risks escalation without legal cover. If it does not respond, it signals weakness and invites repetition. Between these poles lies the grey zone: actions more coercive than ordinary competition, yet not violent enough to trigger collective defence clauses or war powers legislation. It is in this zone that the twenty-first-century conflict increasingly resides.

The persistence of this ambiguity is no accident. Grey-zone operations thrive on plausible deniability. A trade embargo can be justified as regulatory enforcement; a sudden shortage of key components is attributed to "supply issues." Disinformation campaigns can be disavowed as the work of private trolls rather than state operatives. The absence of smoking guns—of uniforms, insignias, and declarations—allows aggressors to operate with confidence that retaliation will be slow, divided, or politically paralysed. Even when attribution is possible, the web of intermediaries, shell companies, and proxy groups muddies responsibility to the point where outrage dissipates into uncertainty.

Cost asymmetry compounds the temptation. To field an aircraft carrier requires billions; to manipulate an adversary's public debate may cost only a handful of salaries and server space. A sanctions package drafted by a finance ministry can, at negligible cost, shave points off an enemy's GDP, forcing them into years of adjustment. Cyber intrusions exploit existing infrastructure and can persist quietly for years before discovery. These tactics invert the cost-benefit ratio of traditional warfare: they impose steep burdens on the target while demanding little from the initiator. For leaders, it is a calculus too compelling to ignore.

Domestic politics provides the final reinforcement. War, in its conventional form, is unpopular, expensive, and dangerous to the careers of those who declare it. Non-kinetic measures, by contrast, can be presented as responsible, bloodless alternatives. A head of government can deny medicines through sanctions while insisting that "no war" has been launched. A state can harass foreign companies in its courts while maintaining the fiction of impartial legal process. Citizens, relieved not to see coffins returning home, are less likely to mobilise against such measures. Invisible wars, in this sense, are politically safer than visible ones.

Yet invisibility is not the same as insignificance. Market shocks that cost households their savings, election swings that reshape constitutions, regulatory storms that destroy industries—these are not marginal disturbances. They are strategic outcomes. To treat them as accidents of commerce or politics is to miss their orchestration. Think-tanks publish timely reports that feed into sympathetic media cycles. Headlines shift investor sentiment, sparking capital flight. Regulators, under pressure, adjust policy in ways that entrench the new status quo. To the casual observer, it looks like a coincidence. To the strategist, it is the visible outcome of an invisible chain.

The challenge, then, is not only to recognise these actions as warfare but to train ourselves to read their signatures. Timing irregularities—when a lawsuit, a news cycle, and a cyber intrusion converge suspiciously. Cross-domain synchronisation—when financial pressure coincides with narrative manipulation and legal filings. These are not the hallmarks of chance. They are the fingerprints of command intent. Just as military intelligence tracks troop movements and supply lines, citizens and policymakers must learn to track sanctions schedules, data leaks, and narrative arcs as interconnected elements of campaign design.

To think this way requires a shift in our conception of power itself. Guns, tanks, and ships remain potent symbols, but in interdependent economies their utility is often peripheral. What compels behaviour today are not artillery shells but balance sheets. Debt leverage dictates policy choices in debtor states more effectively than divisions massed at their borders. Commodity chokepoints—rare earth processing, microchip fabrication—offer more enduring leverage than temporary territorial occupation. International standards, once technical footnotes, now shape the trajectory of industries worth trillions. In this theatre, armies are spectators; the real battles are waged through contracts, tariffs, algorithms, and codes of law.

This is not to say that violence has disappeared, only that it has become the punctuation rather than the prose. Military force lingers as a threat in the background, a shadow that gives weight to quieter measures. But the grammar of strategy is increasingly written in other alphabets: legal briefs, financial directives, cyber code, media campaigns. To dismiss these as lesser forms of conflict is to misunderstand both their potency and their prevalence.

What counts as war now is not the clash of armies but the deliberate pursuit of strategic ends through instruments once dismissed as peripheral. The rules are uncertain, the boundaries contested, and the consequences profound. As long as ambiguity persists, states will continue to exploit the space between peace and war—pushing hard enough to wound, soft enough to deny. The rest of us must decide: do we cling to outdated definitions that comfort but mislead, or do we confront the quiet wars that shape our world with the seriousness they demand? The answer will determine whether we act with foresight or remain spectators to battles we cannot see.

The paradox of visible effects, invisible causes

On the night of 23 June 2016, when the Brexit referendum result became clear, sterling collapsed with a violence not seen in decades. Traders spoke of disbelief, of the market "teaching Britain a lesson." Yet the drama on the trading screens was only the final act of a play written elsewhere. Weeks earlier, think-tanks had circulated reports warning of catastrophic economic consequences. Newspaper front pages amplified those fears. Politicians, seizing on the narratives, framed them as inevitable outcomes rather than contested forecasts. By the time the vote tally tipped toward Leave, the groundwork had been laid: investor confidence had already been primed to shatter. The effect was visible to millions—the tumbling pound, the rising cost of imports, the nervous headlines. The cause was far less visible, hidden upstream in policy briefs, expert panels, and targeted media strategies.

This disjunction between what we see and where it comes from is the defining paradox of non-kinetic conflict. The public experiences shocks—currency collapses, sudden regulatory changes, electoral swings—as if they were earthquakes. But unlike tectonic movements, these events are rarely spontaneous. They are engineered by actors who understand that the visible stage of politics and markets is only the surface of a deeper machinery. The craft of modern conflict lies precisely in disguising deliberate orchestration as natural turbulence. To the untrained eye, it looks like chaos. To those versed in the patterns, it reveals design.

Consider the 1997 Asian financial crisis. To ordinary citizens in Thailand, Indonesia, or South Korea, the sudden evaporation of savings felt like an unstoppable act of fate. Yet capital flight was not simply "market panic." It was fuelled by strategic downgrades from rating agencies, amplified by commentary in influential Western outlets, and accelerated by hedge funds deploying speculative attacks. None of these actors needed to conspire explicitly; their synchronisation created the appearance of inevitability. The downstream effect was a visible catastrophe, the upstream causes cloaked in the technicalities of finance. The crisis became an opportunity for outside powers to demand structural reforms—proof that invisible chains of action could remake entire economies.

Elections offer similar lessons. When rumours of corruption in a candidate's circle appear in fringe blogs, leap into mainstream media, and then feed into televised debates, the visible effect is a swing in voter sentiment. The invisible chain, however, may have begun with a dossier prepared months earlier by a partisan research outfit or a foreign intelligence agency. What appears to the public as organic scandal is often the endpoint of a pipeline. The timing is rarely accidental. A leak too early fades from memory; too late and it lacks impact. Well-designed campaigns land precisely when they can tip a race. The paradox is cruel: citizens believe they are exercising free choice, while their perceptions have been conditioned by forces they cannot see.

Regulatory storms provide another illustration. A multinational corporation may suddenly face antitrust investigations in several jurisdictions at once. To the public, it looks as if regulators simply woke up to a long-standing problem. Yet closer inspection often reveals lobbying by competitors, carefully placed investigative journalism, and coordinated legal filings. Each element alone might be dismissed as coincidence. Together, they form a synchronised assault. The effect is the public spectacle of accountability; the cause is the invisible convergence of interests upstream.

Learning to read these hidden chains requires new habits of attention. Timing irregularities are one signal. If a damaging media story, a sudden cyber intrusion, and a hostile regulatory action occur within the same week, the odds of coincidence diminish. Cross-domain synchronisation is another. When legal, financial, and informational levers are pulled in sequence, the presence of strategic intent becomes plausible. These patterns are not always definitive proof—after all, noise abounds in complex systems—but they are cues that merit scrutiny. Just as epidemiologists trace outbreaks back to patient zero, citizens and analysts can train themselves to trace shocks back to their origins.

The difficulty lies in our cognitive bias toward the visible. Humans are narratively wired: we assign causes to what we see in front of us. A market crash must be the fault of reckless traders; an election result the product of voters' sudden change of heart. Rarely do we pause to ask who planted the doubts, who shaped the headlines, who nudged the regulatory agenda months in advance. This blindness is not accidental—it is cultivated. Campaign designers rely on the natural opacity of complex systems to conceal their fingerprints. Their aim is not only to achieve outcomes but to ensure that those outcomes appear self-generated.

Philosophically, the paradox raises troubling questions about agency and responsibility. If the causes of visible events are deliberately hidden, how can citizens hold anyone accountable? How does one assign blame for a currency collapse triggered by coordinated rumours, when each rumour is individually defensible as free speech? How should courts evaluate a wave of lawsuits filed in multiple jurisdictions, each legal on its own terms but collectively designed to overwhelm? The paradox corrodes not just perception but the very possibility of moral judgement.

Yet recognising the paradox also equips us with tools of resistance. Causal literacy—the discipline of tracing outcomes back to upstream interventions—can be cultivated. Analysts who compare cross-sector timelines, journalists who question the synchrony of events, citizens who resist the allure of simple explanations all contribute to narrowing the gap between effect and cause. The challenge is to do so without succumbing to paranoia, to distinguish between genuine synchronisation and the human tendency to see patterns everywhere. The reward is greater resilience: a society less easily swayed by engineered storms.

The paradox of visible effects and invisible causes is not confined to politics or finance. It is a structural feature of interdependence. In a world where markets, media, law, and technology interlock, the site of action is almost always upstream of the site of impact. The visible is downstream; the decisive is hidden. To ignore this is to live at the mercy of shocks. To confront it is to reclaim some measure of agency, however incomplete.

The hardest question remains unresolved: how much of what we experience as spontaneous life—our elections, our prices, our news—is in fact the residue of invisible campaigns? The answer may be unsettling. Yet only by asking can we begin to see through the fog. And only by seeing can we decide whether to remain spectators of these invisible wars or participants capable of discernment. The next crisis, the next sudden swing, the next regulatory storm will come. The question is whether we will mistake its visible effects for its true cause—or whether we will finally learn to look upstream.

Why guns are bad at solving balance-sheet problems

In 1956, Britain, France, and Israel launched a military operation to seize back control of the Suez Canal after Egypt nationalised it. Their forces moved with overwhelming superiority, swiftly overwhelming Egyptian positions. On the battlefield, the operation was a success. Yet within days, the victors found themselves strategically defeated—not by tanks or aircraft, but by balance sheets. The United States, alarmed by the risk of Soviet intervention, threatened to dump sterling bonds and cut financial support. Facing the prospect of a currency collapse and economic crisis, Britain had no choice but to retreat. Guns had secured the canal; balance sheets had lost it.

This episode illustrates a hard truth: in an interdependent world, military force often struggles to achieve what financial leverage can decide in an afternoon. The command of divisions, frigates, or aircraft carriers still matters in certain theatres, but the determinants of global power increasingly lie elsewhere—in debt obligations, commodity flows, and the governance of technical standards. To treat war as if it were still reducible to physical destruction is to miss the terrain on which nations now gain or lose.

Material power is visible and familiar: armies parading, fleets deployed, weapons tested. Balance-sheet power is quieter, less theatrical, but often more decisive. A creditor can compel reforms that no occupying force could enforce without enormous resistance. A supplier of a critical commodity can hold entire industries hostage without firing a shot. The standard-setting committee in Geneva or Brussels can determine which nation captures a trillion-dollar market by embedding its preferred protocols into the global system. These instruments lack the drama of tanks crossing borders, but they shape outcomes with precision and permanence.

Debt leverage is perhaps the most underappreciated of these instruments. Sovereign debt markets give creditors subtle yet immense influence over debtor states. When Argentina defaulted in 2001, the consequences reverberated for more than a decade. Courts in New York, where bonds were issued, effectively dictated Argentina's access to international finance. The state could not simply "resist"; its fiscal capacity was constrained by legal and financial architecture beyond its borders. No invasion was required. The very infrastructure of global finance ensured compliance. Contrast this with Iraq in 2003: the United States deployed hundreds of thousands of troops at vast expense, only to find itself mired in insurgency and unable to impose stable governance. One creditor with the right jurisdiction exerted more enduring control over Argentina than a superpower army did over Iraq.

Commodity chokepoints function in a similar way. The Strait of Hormuz, through which nearly a fifth of global oil passes, can be disrupted by a few well-placed mines or patrol boats. Rare earth processing, concentrated overwhelmingly in China, gives Beijing leverage over industries from smartphones to fighter jets. During the 2010 dispute with Japan, Beijing quietly restricted rare earth exports, sending shockwaves through supply chains. No warships fired, no formal declarations were made, but the message was unmistakable: control over a material chokepoint can tilt negotiations more effectively than a show of force. Compare that to the immense cost of securing oil flows through decades of military presence in the Gulf. Balance-sheet power achieves in silence what material power struggles to hold at immense expense.

Standards-setting may seem still more prosaic, but it too determines the winners of the future. The contest over 5G telecommunications protocols was not fought with soldiers but with lobbying at standards bodies, patent filings, and influence over regulatory agencies. Whoever secures dominance in standards locks in royalty streams, shapes the trajectory of innovation, and embeds dependence on their technological ecosystem. Divisions and frigates have nothing to contribute to this contest. The victors are those who can mobilise firms, engineers, and diplomats to shape the invisible architecture of interoperability.

Why, then, do states increasingly reach first for economic, legal, and informational instruments? Because they operate below the threshold of open war, exploit asymmetries of cost, and preserve domestic political safety. A sanctions package can be framed as "measured pressure," even when it devastates an adversary's economy. A regulatory ruling can be presented as impartial enforcement, even when designed to tilt a strategic contest. Narrative campaigns can be cloaked in free speech, cyber intrusions in criminal activity, legal offensives in routine litigation. These tools offer strategic effect without the political liability of declaring war. In democratic states especially, leaders find them attractive: they can act forcefully abroad while assuring voters that peace prevails.

The mental model that emerges is not of battlefields and frontlines but of campaigns orchestrated across domains. A modern campaign may begin with a legal filing that delegitimises an adversary firm, followed by media coverage amplifying reputational doubt, then a regulatory investigation triggered by the outcry, and finally a wave of capital flight punishing the target. At no stage are soldiers deployed. Yet the cumulative effect may equal or surpass that of a successful military strike. The campaign plan without soldiers is not hypothetical; it is already the modus operandi of great powers.

This shift does not mean material force is obsolete. Military power still underwrites deterrence and provides the shadow of coercion behind subtler measures. But in many contests, the gun is a blunt instrument where a balance sheet is a scalpel. A state can occupy territory but cannot compel investors to finance it, or force engineers to adopt its standards. Guns can seize assets, but cannot guarantee their value in a global market. Balance-sheet power operates not through destruction but through integration: it exploits the very interdependence that ties nations together.

The tension is unresolved. States still pour resources into weapons systems even as the decisive levers of power migrate into other arenas. Military prestige, domestic politics, and habit all play their part. Yet the mismatch grows sharper with each crisis, where markets, laws, and narratives dictate outcomes while armies stand idle. The question, therefore, is not whether guns retain a role—they always will—but whether we are prepared to acknowledge that many of the most decisive battles of our time are being fought on ledgers, not landscapes. And if balance-sheet power so often prevails, what does it mean for nations still obsessed with the theatre of force, while neglecting the quieter campaigns that truly shape their fate?

The Ethics of Fighting in Peacetime

In 1997, the United Nations tightened sanctions on Iraq in an effort to weaken Saddam Hussein's regime. The measures were framed as humane alternatives to war, designed to apply pressure without bloodshed. Yet within a few years, reports began to document a different reality: hospitals running out of essential medicines, infant mortality rates climbing, and ordinary families forced into destitution. The sanctions had starved the regime of resources but had also starved civilians of dignity, health, and life itself. The paradox was stark. What was presented as a "peaceful" instrument became, in practice, a tool of mass suffering.

This is the moral hazard of non-kinetic warfare: the ability to wage campaigns under the banner of peace while inflicting damage comparable to conventional conflict. The public face of these measures is often cloaked in humanitarian rhetoric—targeted sanctions, calibrated restrictions, or regulatory enforcement. Yet their distributive impact is rarely neat. The burdens fall not on decision-makers in palaces or parliaments but on civilians far removed from the levers of power. The invisibility of the suffering—no bombed-out buildings, no televised carnage—only compounds the problem. Pain is dispersed, statistics replace stories, and the architects of pressure can claim innocence.

The ethical question is not whether states will use these instruments—they will—but whether we have the vocabulary and courage to judge them with the seriousness they demand. Traditional just war theory gives us concepts such as *proportionality*, *necessity*, and *discrimination*—principles designed to restrain violence. But what happens when the weapons are sanctions, cyber campaigns, or narrative manipulation? The legal frameworks are thin, the moral analysis often absent. Yet the stakes are no less profound, for the ability to deny a population electricity, medicine, or truth is no less consequential than the ability to drop bombs.

Take financial sanctions. A central bank can be cut off from international payment systems in a stroke. The official justification may be to punish elite decision-makers, yet the effects cascade downwards. Local businesses lose access to credit, workers lose jobs, pensioners lose savings. Supermarket shelves thin out, not because of direct prohibition of food imports but because logistics systems and insurers retreat under the shadow of compliance risk. The target is political leaders; the collateral is millions of households. Can we really describe this as "bloodless pressure"?

Cyber operations carry similar dilemmas. A well-placed intrusion might disable a power grid or disrupt a hospital's scheduling system. The operator may intend to signal capability or to rattle a government's resolve. But the patients waiting for surgery, the elderly stuck in overheated apartments, the students missing critical exams—these are the ones who feel the immediate consequences. The invisibility of their suffering to those who launched the attack does not lessen its weight. In fact, it raises a deeper question: does distance from harm make ethical reflection harder, or should it compel greater restraint?

Even narrative campaigns, which seem at first glance less tangible, impose ethical costs. Disinformation designed to delegitimise institutions corrodes civic trust, leaving citizens unable to distinguish fact from fabrication. The long-term effect is not only political instability but psychological harm: the sense that one cannot rely on any source of authority, that reality itself is contested ground. To destabilise another society in this way may yield short-term gains, but it leaves behind communities fractured in ways that no quick treaty can repair. The harm is not measured in casualties but in the erosion of social cohesion.

How, then, might we judge proportionality in non-kinetic campaigns? A starting point is to evaluate whether the burden falls primarily on decision-makers or on those without agency. Targeting elite assets—luxury property, offshore accounts, business licences—may be ethically defensible in ways that blanket trade restrictions are not. Similarly, cyber intrusions that reveal corruption may pass a different moral test than those that disable hospitals. Information campaigns that expose truths, however uncomfortable, differ from those that fabricate lies. The test is whether the measure aligns harm with responsibility, or whether it displaces suffering onto the innocent.

A second criterion is reversibility. Bombs destroy irreversibly; sanctions, in principle, can be lifted. Yet in practice, the damage from prolonged sanctions—lost schooling, chronic malnutrition, broken supply chains—often endures long after restrictions are eased. Ethical assessment requires attention not just to the immediate burden but to the long tail of consequences. If a measure leaves behind generational scars, its proportionality must be doubted.

A third is transparency. Many non-kinetic campaigns operate under layers of deniability. Sanctions are enforced through opaque compliance systems; cyber intrusions are attributed with ambiguity; disinformation campaigns hide behind proxies. The lack of transparency not only hinders accountability but also corrupts the possibility of public debate. A society cannot judge the ethics of its actions if it cannot see them. Designing measures with clearer visibility—naming targets, acknowledging collateral risks, providing exit strategies—strengthens legitimacy even when the measures themselves are harsh.

Underlying these criteria is a larger philosophical tension. War, in its classical form, forced societies to confront the horror of violence directly. Cities saw the damage, families buried the dead, publics demanded justification. Non-kinetic war, by contrast, hides its human costs beneath layers of abstraction—compliance codes, data dashboards, economic forecasts. The very invisibility that makes these tools politically convenient makes them morally treacherous. We risk becoming societies that inflict suffering without ever witnessing it, confident in the illusion that we are "at peace."

The question is whether citizens, executives, and officials are prepared to pierce this illusion. To ask: who pays when a currency is frozen? Who suffers when a rumour destabilises markets? Whose lives are narrowed when narratives corrode trust? Without such questions, the ethics of peacetime conflict remain unexamined, and the rhetoric of humanitarian restraint becomes a mask for harm.

There is no simple resolution. States will continue to wield non-kinetic instruments because they are effective, deniable, and politically safer than open war. Yet if we fail to judge them with a sharper moral calculus, we drift into a world where immense suffering is inflicted without acknowledgement. The true hazard of fighting in peacetime is not just the harm it causes, but the blindness it cultivates—the capacity to believe we are acting humanely while quietly waging war. The next time a measure is described as "harmless pressure," the real test will be whether we can see past the rhetoric to the lives reshaped in its shadow.

A field guide to the instruments

In early 2022, as Russian tanks rolled into Ukraine, something striking happened: the fiercest blows did not fall from artillery but from balance sheets. Overnight, Russian banks were cut off from global payment systems, exports of advanced semiconductors were halted, corporate assets were frozen, and oligarchs' yachts were seized in foreign harbours. Flights were banned, media outlets blocked, athletes disqualified. The composite campaign unfolded in days, demonstrating how quickly the modern arsenal of non-kinetic tools can be mobilised. It was war without declaration, fought with instruments more varied than missiles—sanctions, export bans, narrative offensives, capital controls, cyber disruptions, and legal manoeuvres. Each tool had its own character, but together they created an integrated siege.

The modern strategist does not rely on one instrument alone. Just as a general co-ordinates infantry, armour, and artillery, non-kinetic campaigns integrate financial, legal, informational, and technological tools. Understanding their purpose, operators, and signatures is essential for anyone who wishes to read the choreography behind today's crises. What follows is a primer—a map of the instruments most often used in invisible wars, sketched here before later chapters deepen the detail.

Sanctions are the bluntest and most visible of the non-kinetic tools. Their purpose is straightforward: deny an adversary access to capital, markets, or goods until they change behaviour. Operated mainly by states and multilateral institutions, they come in flavours ranging from targeted asset freezes to comprehensive embargoes. Their signatures are immediate—announcements in official registers, sudden currency swings, and public lists of prohibited entities. But their true power lies in secondary effects: compliance officers at banks, insurers, and logistics firms over-enforce to avoid risk, creating a ripple far larger than the initial prohibition. The sanctioned state may proclaim resilience, but its citizens feel the tightening grip in inflation and shortages.

Export controls work more surgically. Where sanctions attack the financial bloodstream, export controls strike at the arteries of technology. Their purpose is to choke the supply of critical inputs—semiconductors, aerospace components, advanced software—thereby slowing or derailing strategic industries. Typical operators are commerce ministries, licensing agencies, and industry regulators, often co-ordinating across alliances. Their signature is less dramatic than sanctions: long technical annexes specifying which chips, codes, or machines may not be shipped. Yet their effect is profound. Without lithography machines, an aspiring chip industry stalls; without dual-use chemicals, a missile programme falters. Unlike the drama of embargoes, export controls operate like slow poison—hard to notice at first, decisive over time.

Narrative shaping is older than either but more pervasive. Its purpose is not to starve or delay but to frame: to persuade publics, elites, and investors to see the world in ways favourable to the campaigner. Operated by governments, media outlets, think-tanks, and increasingly influencers and bots, it works by repetition, selection, and timing. The signatures are subtle: sudden amplification of a story across platforms, oddly synchronised talking points, or a disproportionate focus on one controversy at the expense of others. Narratives, once seeded, influence elections, policy debates, and investor confidence. Unlike sanctions or controls, they leave no ledger entry. Their currency is belief.

Capital controls are more defensive, though no less potent. States use them to prevent capital flight, to redirect flows, or to punish adversaries by excluding them from settlement systems. Operators here are central banks and finance ministries, wielding tools from transaction bans to currency pegs. Their signatures include sudden restrictions on withdrawals, spikes in parallel market rates, and the creation of "friendly" alternative payment corridors. Capital controls rarely appear alone; they usually accompany sanctions or crises, acting as both shield and sword. For the citizen, they are felt in queues at ATMs and the silent devaluation of savings.

Cyber intrusions represent the most modern addition to the toolkit. Their purpose ranges from espionage and data theft to sabotage of infrastructure. Operators vary from state intelligence agencies to proxies and criminal groups acting with tacit blessing. Their signatures are often invisible until revealed by investigators: anomalous traffic, compromised servers, or leaked databases. At times, the effect is spectacular—the Stuxnet worm physically damaging Iranian centrifuges; at others, it is the slow accumulation of stolen designs and pre-positioned access. The ambiguity of attribution is their greatest asset. Unlike a missile strike, a cyber intrusion can be denied, disavowed, or blamed on rogue actors.

Corporate espionage blurs the line between state and firm. Its purpose is to capture intellectual property, strategic plans, or competitive advantage. Operated by intelligence services, private contractors, or rival corporations, it thrives on supply-chain vulnerabilities and insider recruitment. Its signatures are quiet: a sudden competitor leapfrogging in technology, an unexplained leak of proprietary data, or a lawsuit exposing stolen code. Though less visible than sanctions or cyberattacks, corporate espionage can tilt entire industries. A stolen design for an aircraft engine or pharmaceutical compound reshapes markets more decisively than years of open competition.

Lawfare—the strategic use of courts and legal systems—is the weapon of those who master rules as battlefields. Its purpose is to impose costs, set precedents, and delegitimise adversaries under the guise of legality. Operators range from states and NGOs to corporations funding proxy litigation. Its signatures include sudden waves of lawsuits, forum shopping across sympathetic jurisdictions, and the coupling of legal filings with media campaigns. Lawfare can tie adversaries in knots of compliance, drain resources through prolonged litigation, or shape international norms in ways that endure for decades. Unlike armed force, its victories are disguised as justice served.

Psychological operations, or psyops, target not infrastructure but minds. Their purpose is to shape perceptions, morale, and behaviour directly. They may be used to sap confidence in a government, to fracture alliances, or to rally support for a cause. Operators are military units, intelligence services, and increasingly data-driven firms contracted for influence campaigns. Their signatures are emotional rather than material: surges of fear, anger, or pride at precisely timed moments. A meme spreading virally, a rumour igniting protests, a manipulated video circulating before an election—each is a psyop in miniature. Their power lies not in the message alone but in the orchestration of context, repetition, and amplification.

Taken separately, each of these instruments is formidable. Taken together, they form campaigns of extraordinary subtlety and reach. Sanctions may weaken an economy while narratives shift blame, lawfare entangles firms, and cyber intrusions sow uncertainty. Export controls can slow an adversary's industry while corporate espionage accelerates one's own. Psychological operations ensure that populations doubt their leaders at precisely the moment pressure bites. The art of the modern strategist is to integrate these tools, sequencing them like movements in a symphony—each distinct, yet reinforcing the others.

The field guide sketched here is only the beginning. In later chapters, each instrument will be examined in detail, with case studies and measurement tools. But even this brief survey makes clear a sobering truth: the arsenal of modern conflict is vast, varied, and mostly invisible to the public eye. Wars are now fought through lists, leaks, laws, and lines of code. To navigate this world, one must first learn to recognise the instruments, to read their signatures, and to see how they combine into campaigns. The question that follows—whether we can regulate, restrain, or resist them—remains open. And it is a question we can no longer afford to ignore.

Chapter 2

Sanctions as Siege Engines

In the winter of 1914, as German armies pushed through Belgium and France, Britain struck from an unexpected angle. It imposed a blockade, not just on ports but on credit, insurance, and the maritime arteries that sustained German trade. No battle was fought on the high seas; instead, ledgers and manifests were seized, ships diverted, and neutral carriers pressured. By the war's end, malnutrition and scarcity had weakened Germany as surely as any artillery barrage. The blockade showed that economic measures could achieve strategic effects equal to—or even greater than—conventional force. Yet it also raised questions that remain unresolved: who suffers when nations are besieged without bombs, and what does it mean to weaponise commerce itself?

More than a century later, sanctions are still treated in popular discourse as a polite alternative to war, a means of "doing something" without bloodshed. Yet to policymakers and adversaries alike, they are recognised as siege engines—capable of constricting economies, fracturing alliances, and eroding regimes. They operate in escalation ladders: symbolic listings intended to signal disapproval, targeted restrictions aimed at sectors, and systemic measures designed to strangle entire financial circulations. Their power lies not in isolated prohibitions but in how they are engineered. Breadth, extraterritorial reach, and the licensing of exceptions can tilt the balance between inconvenience and devastation.

Consider Iran in 2012, when multilateral sanctions targeted its oil exports and financial transactions. The breadth was such that insurers, shippers, and banks worldwide had to choose between compliance and exclusion from Western markets. Within months, Iran's currency collapsed, inflation soared, and the government faced unprecedented pressure. Yet the same tool applied to Cuba for decades produced far less change, in part because enforcement was inconsistent, allies were divided, and the target adapted. Sanctions are not moral gestures; they are systems whose design and cohesion determine whether they achieve tactical pressure or strategic failure.

But every blockade invites evasion. Behind each announcement of "comprehensive restrictions" lies a cat-and-mouse game of leakage and loopholes. Ships perform evasive manoeuvres—disabling transponders, renaming vessels, conducting transfers in shadowy waters. Front companies appear overnight in distant jurisdictions, masking true ownership behind layers of shell structures. Insurance markets sprout grey providers willing to underwrite the risky voyages at inflated premiums. Enforcement becomes an operational art in itself: tracing beneficial ownership through obscure filings, matching cargo manifests against improbable routes, or detecting anomalies in maritime AIS signals. Where the pressure is partial, intermediaries can grow rich, skimming rents from those desperate enough to pay.

The ethics of these measures cannot be sidestepped. Sanctions are announced with humanitarian exemptions, but real-world frictions mean that food, medicine, and other essentials often stall in transit. Banks over-comply rather than risk penalties, halting even legal trade. The human cost is measured not in explosions but in shortages, untreated illnesses, and wasted years of education. Political blowback follows: domestic populations rally around sanctioned regimes, allies grow weary of carrying the economic burden, and carefully constructed coalitions fray. A sanction meant to weaken a government may inadvertently consolidate its legitimacy, reframed as an external siege against which citizens must unite.

The reach of sanctions has also expanded beyond traditional borders. Secondary sanctions allow one state's decisions to bind the behaviour of firms and banks worldwide. Dollar primacy, correspondent banking networks, and the plumbing of settlement systems give the United States, in particular, unparalleled leverage. A bank in Singapore or Zurich may refuse to deal with a sanctioned entity not because of domestic law, but because it cannot risk exclusion from dollar clearing. For allies and neutrals, this raises sovereignty dilemmas: does compliance mean capitulation to another state's policy, or a pragmatic recognition of financial reality? Contestation moves from politics into law, with challenges in the World Trade Organization, arbitration tribunals, and national courts.

Yet the story is not merely of blunt instruments wielded carelessly. Sanctions can be engineered with sophistication. Targeting architectures rather than populations—specific networks, enablers, and technological nodes—can maximise pressure while minimising collateral damage. Building sunset clauses and humanitarian corridors can create off-ramps that preserve legitimacy. Measurement is essential: monitoring price spreads, customs anomalies, and inventory signals helps distinguish between propaganda and genuine effect. Loud rhetoric often exaggerates impact, but careful engineering, backed by credible monitoring, can turn sanctions into tools of precision rather than instruments of attrition.

Sanctions are thus best understood as part of a larger grammar of invisible conflict: neither harmless nor secondary, but central to how nations contest power without conventional war. They blur the line between diplomacy and coercion, between law enforcement and siege. Their effects are uneven, their morality contested, their success contingent on enforcement and cohesion. As this chapter will show, to read sanctions as systems—engineered, adaptive, and interdependent—is to see how they truly function. The question that follows is not simply whether sanctions work, but how they might be designed to pressure without breaking, to constrain without immiserating, and to deter without destroying. The answers are far from settled, but the stakes could hardly be higher.

From protest to pressure to siege

In 1989, following the Tiananmen Square crackdown, Western governments scrambled for a response that could register moral outrage without provoking outright confrontation with China. They chose sanctions. The measures were mostly symbolic: arms embargoes, travel bans on a handful of officials, and suspensions of certain loans. Factories kept running, ports kept trading, and Beijing weathered the storm with little more than reputational bruising. Yet the choice was telling. Sanctions had become the go-to instrument for states wishing to signal disapproval, a halfway house between words and war. But what begins as protest can evolve into pressure—and, in the right configuration, into siege.

Sanctions follow a ladder of escalation. At the lowest rung lie symbolic listings: asset freezes or travel bans imposed on individuals or small entities. These are often crafted less to damage than to demonstrate resolve. The aim is reputational: to stigmatise, to send a warning, to affirm solidarity with victims. Their effectiveness is limited in material terms—an oligarch barred from holidaying in Europe is an inconvenience, not a crisis—but they mark the first turn of the screw. They serve as the entry point for escalation, easily announced, quickly adjusted, and politically useful for leaders needing to "do something."

The next rung involves sectoral restrictions: measures targeting industries central to an adversary's economic health. Energy exports, financial services, aviation, shipping—sectors that serve as arteries of revenue and influence. When the European Union restricted technology exports to Russia's oil industry in 2014, the goal was not to collapse the economy overnight but to erode capacity over time, raising costs and delaying projects. Such sanctions are designed to sting, to signal seriousness, and to create bargaining leverage. They bite harder than symbolic listings but still leave the adversary breathing.

At the highest rung is systemic strangulation: sanctions designed to isolate an entire economy from global networks of finance, trade, and technology. These go beyond protest and pressure, seeking instead to suffocate. Cutting Iran from the SWIFT payment network in 2012, or freezing Afghanistan's central bank reserves in 2021, were moves of this order. They aim to deny a state the oxygen of external finance, to cripple its ability to import essentials, and to force leaders into concessions under the weight of domestic collapse. At this level, sanctions are siege engines—designed not to send a message but to break resistance.

Design choices make the difference between irritation and devastation. Breadth determines scope: are sanctions focused narrowly on luxury goods, or do they encompass vital commodities such as oil and gas? Extraterritoriality extends reach: do restrictions bind only domestic actors, or do they threaten penalties on foreign firms that transact with the target? Licensing determines permeability: are there exemptions for medicine, food, or humanitarian supplies, and how are they administered? Each choice translates into macro effects. A broad, extraterritorial regime with tight licensing can collapse currencies and drain reserves within weeks; a narrow, symbolic regime may be little more than a gesture.

History shows both the potency and the pitfalls of this ladder. South Africa in the 1980s provides one of the most cited success stories: sustained multilateral sanctions, combined with internal resistance and economic malaise, contributed to the apartheid regime's eventual collapse. By contrast, Cuba endured decades of American sanctions with its leadership intact, in part because measures lacked broad multilateral support and because the regime weaponised the siege narrative to consolidate control. In Rhodesia, sanctions imposed by Britain and the United Nations in the 1960s were undermined by South African and Portuguese evasion, limiting their effectiveness. The lesson is clear: cohesion among enforcers matters as much as severity of design.

Yet sanctions are not static. They are iterative systems, adapted in response to evasion and countermeasures. Iran developed elaborate barter networks and shadow fleets to move oil despite embargoes. North Korea has long relied on front companies, illicit transfers, and cyber theft to sustain itself under near-total isolation. Enforcement agencies in sanctioning states respond in turn, tightening rules, refining analytics, and targeting facilitators. What begins as a symbolic protest can evolve into an enduring campaign of adaptation and counter-adaptation.

The ladder metaphor captures not only escalation but entrapment. Once sanctions are imposed, they are politically difficult to unwind. Leaders risk appearing weak if they lift measures without dramatic concessions from the adversary. Domestic lobbies, humanitarian groups, and affected industries push in opposing directions. As a result, sanctions often linger long after their initial rationale has faded, ossifying into permanent sieges whose humanitarian impact outlasts their strategic purpose. The protest becomes pressure; the pressure becomes siege; the siege becomes routine.

This raises deeper questions. If sanctions are engineered systems rather than moral gestures, who engineers them, and to what end? Are they designed with clear metrics of success, or simply with political optics in mind? Do they weigh proportionality against unintended suffering, or are those burdens displaced onto unseen populations? As tools of invisible war, sanctions demand the same scrutiny as bombs and bullets, for their capacity to alter lives is no less profound.

The paradox is stark: what begins as a symbolic act of disapproval can, through design, escalation, and persistence, become an instrument of strangulation. To understand sanctions is to see not just the ladder of measures but the architecture of systems, the politics of enforcement, and the human costs that accompany every rung. The next question is whether states can learn to wield these siege engines with precision and restraint—or whether, in the pursuit of pressure, they will continue to slide from protest into siege without ever pausing to ask what is left standing inside the walls.

Leakage, loopholes, and the offshore maze

In late 2022, as Western governments tightened restrictions on Russian oil exports, satellite images revealed a curious sight: tankers meeting in mid-ocean, often in the shadow of clouds, their transponders suddenly switching off. Hours later, they would part ways, one carrying crude to Asia, the other returning "empty." The paperwork suggested routine voyages; the reality was ship-to-ship transfers conducted to obscure the cargo's origin. Despite unprecedented sanctions, Russian oil continued to flow, discounted but hardly blocked. The sanctions had bitten, but they had not broken. Instead, they had created a shadow fleet of ageing tankers, opaque ownership structures, and opportunistic middlemen—an entire offshore maze of evasion.

This pattern is not new. Sanctions are rarely absolute; they are porous by design and practice. The success of a sanctions regime depends less on the severity of its legal text than on the rigour and imagination of its enforcement. Without that, measures meant to starve regimes of resources mutate into subsidies for the nimble and the unscrupulous. Partial enforcement can, perversely, enrich intermediaries who specialise in exploiting cracks: shell companies that mask ownership, brokers who arrange circuitous routes, insurers who price in the risk of defiance. What was intended as strangulation becomes an opportunity for those positioned to play both sides.

At the centre of this dance lie *front companies*. Registered in permissive jurisdictions, often with minimal disclosure requirements, they serve as cut-outs to disguise true ownership. A sanctioned shipping firm may reappear within weeks as a new entity with nominally different directors, operating the same vessels under a different flag. Layers of incorporation across Panama, the Marshall Islands, or obscure Caribbean islands create chains that frustrate regulators and investigators. Beneficial ownership registries exist in theory, but the opacity of trust structures and nominee directors keeps the ultimate beneficiaries safely hidden. Analysts must comb through filings, leaks, and anomalies to connect the dots, a painstaking process that adversaries exploit through sheer volume of entities.

Maritime evasion has grown into its own art. Automatic Identification System (AIS) transponders, designed for safety, are routinely switched off in what regulators call "dark activity." Vessels may conduct ship-to-ship transfers in international waters, mixing sanctioned cargo with legitimate consignments. Flags of convenience are swapped with ease, allowing tankers to reappear under the registry of states with limited capacity to monitor compliance. The result is a global shell game: each ship a moving puzzle, each cargo a challenge to trace. Analysts have begun to deploy machine learning to detect anomalies—vessels "travelling" implausible routes or loitering in suspicious areas—but the scale is daunting. Thousands of ships ply the seas daily; even with advanced analytics, enforcement remains uneven.

Insurance adds another layer of complexity. Legitimate insurers in London or New York withdraw from covering sanctioned cargoes, but the vacuum is filled by grey-market insurers based in jurisdictions less sensitive to reputational risk. These providers charge premiums well above market rates, effectively monetising the sanctions. Thus, partial enforcement shifts revenue from established firms to shadow markets, without necessarily reducing the flow of goods. The sanctioned state still earns export revenue; the intermediaries pocket windfall profits. What was meant to increase costs for the target spreads costs across the system, often in ways that advantage opportunists.

Even when sanctions bite hard, leakage can dull their edge. Consider North Korea. Despite some of the strictest sanctions ever imposed, the regime has sustained itself through networks of traders in China and Southeast Asia, smuggling coal and importing fuel in defiance of UN resolutions. The trade is modest compared to legal commerce, but sufficient to keep the regime afloat. Enforcement requires costly monitoring of ports, cargo inspections, and diplomatic pressure on third states. Yet the incentives for local traders and officials often point the other way: profits from sanctions evasion are high, and accountability is weak. The result is a regime that survives in the space between rules and enforcement.

Compliance, then, is less about issuing prohibitions than about designing enforcement as operational art. Data matching across customs declarations, corporate registries, and shipping logs can reveal suspicious patterns. Beneficial ownership analytics, integrating leaks such as the Panama Papers with open corporate filings, can unmask hidden networks. Maritime monitoring, using satellite imagery and AIS analysis, can detect anomalous behaviour. But even with these tools, capacity is finite. Each new sanction creates investigative burdens; each evasive tactic requires fresh adaptation. Enforcement agencies are locked in a perpetual race against adversaries who can innovate faster and take more risks.

The paradox of partial enforcement is that it can create perverse incentives. Instead of crippling the sanctioned state, it shifts trade into opaque channels where margins widen and accountability shrinks. Middlemen in Dubai, Istanbul, or Singapore thrive on arranging transactions that others fear to touch. Flags of convenience benefit from registry fees. Grey insurers pocket risk premiums. The system adjusts, redistributes, and survives. For ordinary citizens, the impact is felt in rising costs and shortages; for elites and well-connected intermediaries, it may even be profitable. Sanctions become not just instruments of pressure but engines of inequality and corruption.

Yet the offshore maze is not impenetrable. Multilateral cohesion can narrow the avenues of evasion, as when coordinated sanctions against Libya in the 1990s limited the regime's ability to find alternative buyers. Innovations in transparency, such as public beneficial ownership registries and stricter maritime reporting standards, can raise the cost of deception. But these require political will and sustained investment—resources often scarce once the initial drama of a sanctions announcement fades. Enforcement fatigue sets in, coalitions fracture, and the maze grows back.

The larger lesson is sobering. To speak of sanctions as if they were clean instruments of pressure is to miss the reality of their execution. Enforcement is messy, uneven, and riddled with incentives for evasion. The shadow fleets, front companies, and grey insurers are not marginal; they are central to how sanctions actually operate in the world. Every measure creates a countermeasure, every prohibition a market for circumvention.

What remains unresolved is whether sanctioning states can ever truly keep pace with the creativity of those determined to evade. Can technology, transparency, and multilateral pressure outstrip the adaptability of shadow networks, or will the offshore maze always expand to meet the challenge? The answer will determine not only the effectiveness of future sanctions but also the legitimacy of wielding them as engines of strategy in a world where every wall seems to produce a door.

Collateral damage and political blowback

When the United Nations imposed sweeping sanctions on Iraq in the 1990s, the stated intent was clear: weaken Saddam Hussein's regime, deprive it of resources for weapons programmes, and pressure it into compliance. What followed instead was one of the most devastating humanitarian crises of the late twentieth century. Medicine shipments stalled in customs warehouses for months. Malnutrition spread among children, and once-ordinary ailments became life-threatening as hospitals ran out of basic supplies. The architects of the sanctions insisted on humanitarian exemptions, yet the machinery of enforcement—slow licensing, wary banks, over-compliance by firms fearing penalties—meant exemptions existed more on paper than in practice. The result was stark: a measure designed to constrain a dictator instead hollowed out the lives of ordinary citizens, while Saddam himself maintained his grip on power.

This paradox remains central to the ethics and politics of sanctions. Humanitarian exemptions are standard in sanction regimes, carefully worded to reassure publics and allies that the measures are targeted, not indiscriminate. Yet the realities of implementation often turn those assurances hollow. Banks, insurers, and shipping firms, faced with legal ambiguity and reputational risk, adopt a posture of "de-risking," refusing transactions altogether rather than parsing which are permissible. Food shipments are delayed, medical devices sit idle at borders, and humanitarian agencies struggle to navigate compliance systems. The intent may be to spare civilians; the effect is frequently to trap them in bureaucratic choke points created thousands of miles away.

The human costs are only part of the story. Sanctions also reshape political psychology in ways that often run counter to their architects' intentions. Pressure that is meant to fracture regimes can instead consolidate them. Citizens who resent their rulers may rally around them when confronted with what feels like collective punishment from foreign powers. Identity threat—when a community perceives its survival or dignity under attack—can override grievances against leaders, redirecting anger outward rather than upward. Iran offers repeated illustrations: waves of sanctions have devastated purchasing power and fuelled protests, yet they have also provided hardliners with a narrative of resistance, casting compliance as betrayal and suffering as sacrifice for sovereignty.

This rally-round-the-flag effect is not limited to authoritarian regimes. Democracies, too, can respond defensively when their citizens perceive sanctions as unfair impositions on national dignity. During the 1997 Asian financial crisis, IMF conditionality—strict reform packages often equated with externally imposed sanctions—sparked resentment across affected countries. Governments complied reluctantly, but domestic politics hardened against Western institutions, leaving a legacy of scepticism that endures in policy debates today. Measures framed as technocratic necessity were experienced as humiliation, fuelling nationalist sentiment and diminishing the moral authority of those imposing them.

Allied fatigue is another underappreciated dynamic. Sanctions are most effective when multilateral, but sustaining cohesion over years requires managing the political and economic costs borne unevenly across coalition members. European states, heavily dependent on Russian energy in the early 2020s, bore steeper short-term costs from embargoes than partners further afield. As winters grew colder and energy prices rose, domestic pressures mounted to soften measures. In such cases, the strain of collateral damage is not just on the target state but on the sanctioning alliance itself. Political will frays, compliance weakens, and adversaries exploit divisions.

Sanctions can also backfire by creating new domestic stakeholders with incentives to perpetuate the very regimes they aim to weaken. Black markets and grey economies flourish under restrictions, empowering actors who profit from scarcity and smuggling. In Venezuela, military elites gained control over food distribution networks during years of sanctions and shortages. Far from undermining the regime, this dynamic deepened elite loyalty, binding their fortunes to the survival of the system. Sanctions meant to erode power instead reconfigured it, redistributing rents in ways that stabilised the ruling coalition.

To understand these effects, one must look beyond the surface mechanics of trade flows and financial restrictions to the narratives woven around them. Sanctions are rarely experienced in the abstract; they are mediated through propaganda, media frames, and collective memory. Leaders under pressure recast sanctions as evidence of external hostility, integrating them into national stories of resistance. Civilians do not weigh sanctions in terms of balance sheets; they interpret them through the lens of fairness, dignity, and belonging. The political psychology of sanctions is therefore inseparable from their material effects. A package that looks elegant on paper may, in lived reality, galvanise precisely the unity it was meant to fracture.

Comparative history underscores the stakes. Sanctions against apartheid South Africa contributed to regime change, in part because they aligned with internal resistance movements and resonated with global moral consensus. By contrast, sanctions on Cuba, maintained for decades, entrenched the Castro regime by feeding its narrative of heroic survival against imperial siege. In both cases, the mechanics of trade restrictions mattered less than the interaction between external pressure and internal political culture. Where sanctions amplified existing fractures, they proved effective; where they smoothed over divisions, they prolonged the status quo.

This duality raises an uncomfortable question for policymakers: how to calibrate sanctions so that they weaken elites without crushing civilians or consolidating regimes. Humanitarian exemptions are not enough if they remain trapped in red tape. Targeting elite assets and networks may be more precise, but the leakage into wider society is difficult to control. Designing sanctions as blunt instruments risks political blowback; designing them as surgical strikes risks ineffectiveness. The tension is not easily resolved.

Ultimately, collateral damage and political blowback are not side effects of sanctions; they are central dynamics that determine success or failure. To imagine that sanctions can be engineered as cost-free moral gestures is to indulge in dangerous illusion. Every restriction creates ripple effects—economic, humanitarian, psychological—that shape political outcomes in unpredictable ways. The challenge lies in anticipating which ripples will fracture a regime and which will reinforce it.

And so the question persists: when states deploy sanctions as siege engines, are they truly weakening their adversaries, or are they fortifying the very walls they seek to breach? The answer lies not in the intent of policymakers but in the lived experiences of those caught in the middle—and in the stories that transform scarcity into either rage against rulers or defiance against outsiders. The calculus is as moral as it is strategic, and its outcomes remain stubbornly beyond the neat confines of policy design.

Secondary sanctions and sovereignty

In 2014, a small European bank found itself in the crosshairs of American regulators. Its "crime" was not financing terrorism or laundering money for cartels, but facilitating transactions for Iranian companies that were, at the time, subject to United States sanctions. The bank operated entirely within the laws of its own country. Yet the mere fact that its business touched the dollar system—routing payments through New York for clearing—brought it under Washington's reach. The penalty ran into hundreds of millions of dollars. For the bank's managers, the message was unmistakable: sovereignty stopped at the water's edge of the dollar.

This is the essence of secondary sanctions. Unlike primary sanctions, which forbid a state's own citizens and firms from dealing with designated entities, secondary sanctions extend the prohibition outward, threatening penalties on third parties—foreign banks, companies, or even governments—that continue business with the target. It is power exercised not by tanks or treaties but by the architecture of financial networks. In a world where most trade is invoiced in dollars, and where banks rely on correspondent relationships that eventually run through New York, few actors can avoid entanglement. The United States does not need to patrol every harbour or monitor every cargo; it needs only to guard the pipes through which money flows.

Banking *de-risking* is the first ripple effect. Faced with the possibility of billion-dollar fines and exclusion from dollar markets, financial institutions often withdraw from entire regions or sectors deemed high-risk. The calculus is simple: the revenue from handling transactions with, say, Sudan or Venezuela is tiny compared to the potential liability. As a result, perfectly legal commerce—food exports, humanitarian aid—struggles to find channels. Firms cannot secure financing or insurance, not because their activities are forbidden, but because banks have pre-emptively chosen to sever ties. Risk aversion metastasises into economic isolation, far beyond the intent of formal sanctions policy.

Correspondent banking networks act as chokepoints. A small bank in West Africa may handle payments for local businesses, but to send dollars abroad it must rely on a correspondent bank in New York or London. If that correspondent cuts ties, the smaller bank is effectively cut off from global finance. This is not an abstract vulnerability: countless institutions in the Global South have found themselves "de-risked" out of existence, victims not of formal blacklists but of the chilling effect created by secondary sanctions. The sanctioning state wields power not only directly but through the caution of private actors, each guarding its access to the central arteries of finance.

At the core of this system lies *dollar primacy*. The dollar is not just a currency; it is the medium through which oil is priced, commodities are traded, and reserves are stored. The ubiquity of the dollar gives American sanctions extraordinary extraterritorial reach. Even transactions that never involve a US company directly can be pulled into jurisdiction because they are settled in dollars, routed through US clearinghouses, or involve software licensed by American firms. Power rides on plumbing: the invisible infrastructure of finance that states and firms rely upon every day.

This reach is not uncontested. Allies have bristled at being compelled to enforce measures they did not design or support. The European Union, angered by US withdrawal from the Iran nuclear deal in 2018, attempted to construct a special-purpose vehicle—INSTEX—to enable trade with Iran outside the dollar system. It was technically ingenious but politically fragile, never moving significant volumes before being abandoned. China and Russia have sought to build alternatives to SWIFT, the global messaging system for banks, and to settle more trade in roubles or yuan. Yet these efforts highlight the difficulty of escaping entrenched networks: plumbing is not easily replaced, and trust takes decades to build.

Legal contestation has followed. Companies and governments have challenged secondary sanctions at the World Trade Organization and in national courts, arguing that extraterritorial measures violate principles of sovereignty and international law. Canada, the EU, and others maintain "blocking statutes" that prohibit their firms from complying with certain foreign sanctions. Yet the effectiveness of such countermeasures is limited. When the choice is between obeying local law and preserving access to the US financial system, most firms choose the latter. The sheer weight of the dollar bends legal arguments into submission.

The paradox is stark: secondary sanctions claim to defend international order, yet they erode the sovereignty of allies and neutrals. A European firm trading lawfully under EU rules may still find itself punished by Washington. A Turkish bank conducting business with Tehran may be fined not by its own regulators but by foreign ones. In the name of punishing adversaries, secondary sanctions risk alienating partners. They transform economic interdependence into a tool of hierarchy, reinforcing perceptions that rules apply selectively, according to who controls the chokepoints.

For smaller states, the lesson is sobering. Participation in global markets comes with hidden vulnerabilities, rooted in the wiring of finance. Access to dollars, correspondent banking, and international clearing systems can be weaponised at short notice, regardless of local law. This asymmetry alters not just policy choices but national strategies. Governments weigh whether to build reserves in gold, diversify into alternative payment systems, or align more closely with sanctioning powers to avoid exclusion. Sovereignty becomes contingent on the tolerance of distant regulators and compliance officers in financial capitals.

Yet secondary sanctions also invite a longer-term backlash. Overuse risks pushing states to accelerate de-dollarisation, building alternative systems even at high initial cost. Already, central banks from Moscow to Brasília experiment with digital currencies and bilateral swap lines designed to bypass the dollar. Their success remains uncertain, but the intent is clear: to escape the vulnerability revealed by secondary sanctions. If power rides on plumbing, then rivals will seek to lay new pipes.

What remains unresolved is whether the sanctioning state can calibrate its use of this power without eroding the very system that makes it effective. Every penalty imposed on an ally's bank strengthens the argument for alternatives. Every act of extraterritorial reach chips away at the legitimacy of a shared order. The question is not whether the dollar will remain dominant—it almost certainly will for years to come—but whether its dominance will be sustained by consent or corroded by compulsion.

And so we arrive at the central tension: can a tool designed to discipline adversaries be used without alienating allies? Secondary sanctions extend power far beyond borders, but in doing so they blur the line between influence and coercion, between partnership and subordination. The very infrastructure that gives them force may, over time, be undermined by the resentment they generate. Whether the world accepts or resists this extraterritorial reach will shape not only the future of sanctions but the deeper question of how sovereignty is defined in a global economy wired through common pipes.

Designing smarter sanctions

In 1991, the images from Baghdad were not of burning tanks but of empty shelves. After the Gulf War, sanctions designed to punish Saddam Hussein's regime instead strangled ordinary Iraqis. Hospitals lacked antibiotics, children grew up stunted, and yet the political leadership remained insulated. The international community had found a weapon that was devastating—but devastating in the wrong way. That episode haunts sanction architects to this day. It showed that poorly designed economic sieges can hollow out societies without shifting the decisions of the ruling elite. The challenge, then, is not whether sanctions should exist but whether they can be *engineered* with precision, discipline, and a sense of moral responsibility.

To treat sanctions as engineering rather than theatre is to reject the temptation of symbolism. Politicians love sweeping bans and loud announcements; the cameras reward them. But sweeping measures often collapse under their own bluntness. They either punish populations indiscriminately or create black markets that enrich the very actors they were meant to weaken. Smart sanctions begin with a simple principle: target *architecture*, not *populations*. Instead of embargoing whole economies, focus on nodes—critical firms, chokepoint technologies, banking rails, licensing authorities—where pressure can be applied with leverage but minimal collateral harm. This requires technical mapping: tracing who owns what, who controls which bottlenecks, and how flows of capital, commodities, and information intersect. It is slow work, invisible to television crews, but it is the difference between a measure that changes decisions and one that merely generates suffering.

Consider the contrast between comprehensive embargoes on Cuba, which entrenched the Castro regime for decades, and the surgical restrictions on semiconductor exports to specific Chinese firms, which aim to slow capacity growth without triggering wholesale economic collapse. The former broadcast moral posture while creating humanitarian hardship; the latter attempts to engineer strategic friction. Neither is perfect, but the contrast illustrates the direction of evolution: away from mass punishment, towards systems design.

The second principle is to build *sunset pathways*. One of the great weaknesses of sanctions is that they too often become permanent, detached from the behaviours they were meant to change. Leaders lose the political courage to remove them, fearing accusations of weakness. This transforms sanctions into indefinite blockades with no incentive structure left intact. Smart sanctions are different. They are designed with expiry points—automatic review clauses, conditional rollbacks, and measurable benchmarks. This gives targets a rational pathway out, preserving the coercive force while reducing the risk of endless stalemate. Sunset pathways also discipline the sanctioning coalition itself, forcing regular evaluation of whether measures are still fit for purpose.

Humanitarian corridors are the third element. Every sanctions regime claims to exempt food, medicine, and basic goods. Yet in practice, bureaucratic frictions and over-compliance by banks often make such exemptions meaningless. A shipping firm, fearing regulatory entanglement, may refuse to carry wheat even if it is technically authorised. Pharmacies in sanctioned states report life-saving drugs rotting at ports because payment channels collapsed. To avoid these outcomes, humanitarian corridors must be *pre-committed* and *operationalised*: dedicated banking channels, licensed insurers, and monitored logistics pipelines that function in practice, not just on paper. The Red Cross and UN agencies should not have to negotiate ad hoc every time. Smarter sanctions engineer humanitarian protection into the very design, recognising that legitimacy is not a decorative concern but a strategic asset.

Measurement underpins all of this. Without feedback loops, sanctions are blunt instruments. Too often, policymakers mistake the size of a sanction package for its effectiveness. Yet the critical question is not how many firms are listed, but whether the pressure alters behaviour at the top. Price spreads between official and black-market exchange rates, unusual fluctuations in inventories, customs anomalies, shifts in shipping insurance premiums—these are the subtle metrics that reveal whether pressure is biting. Monitoring them requires technical capacity and analytic discipline, but without them sanctions risk drifting into ritual: a performance of toughness with little strategic yield.

Case studies underline the point. Sanctions on apartheid South Africa in the 1980s combined symbolic boycotts with targeted financial restrictions. The latter proved more effective because they created liquidity crises in banks connected to the regime. In contrast, broad restrictions on Iraq during the 1990s devastated civilians while leaving the Ba'ath Party apparatus intact. In recent years, North Korea has shown how poorly monitored sanctions generate unintended rents: elites profit from smuggling networks that thrive precisely because formal trade is blocked. The lesson is clear: engineering without measurement is negligence, but measurement without design is empty numerology. Both must work in tandem.

Designing smarter sanctions also demands multilateral cohesion. A sanction designed in Washington but ignored in Dubai or Hong Kong is little more than an inconvenience. Conversely, even a modest restriction can bite hard if enforced consistently by a coalition. Here, engineering extends beyond technical targeting to alliance management: aligning incentives among states, coordinating enforcement capacity, and sustaining political will over time. Rhetoric will not hold a coalition together; shared measurement and transparent pathways to review might.

Critics may object that such engineering is naïve—that power politics demands blunt tools, not carefully tuned mechanisms. Yet history shows otherwise. Blunt sanctions entrench regimes, corrode legitimacy, and sow resentment among allies. Precision, by contrast, builds credibility. It signals seriousness without recklessness. It avoids the trap of appearing simultaneously cruel and ineffective. Smarter sanctions are not about moral perfection but about strategic efficiency: maximising pressure on decision-makers while minimising unintended fallout.

The paradox, of course, is that the very discipline required for smarter sanctions makes them less attractive to political leaders hungry for spectacle. Symbolism sells; engineering is invisible. But it is precisely in the quiet discipline of mapping nodes, measuring effects, and sustaining humanitarian corridors that sanctions can become something more than noisy gestures. They can become tools of statecraft that shift adversaries' calculations while sustaining the legitimacy of the international order itself.

The unresolved question is whether leaders and publics can be persuaded to value efficacy over theatre. Can policymakers resist the urge to announce "the toughest sanctions ever" and instead commit to designs that may look modest but work better? Can electorates learn to judge pressure by outcomes rather than headlines? If sanctions are to remain credible instruments in the invisible wars of the twenty-first century, they must be treated not as political slogans but as systems to be engineered. Whether states rise to that challenge will determine whether sanctions remain a weapon of consequence—or a hollow ritual that corrodes its own foundations.

Chapter 3

Currency as a Weapon

In the spring of 2012, Iran attempted to pay for wheat shipments through a European bank. The cargo was ready, contracts signed, ships waiting in port. But the payment never cleared. The bank, fearing secondary sanctions from Washington, froze the transfer. The ships remained docked, the wheat rotted, and Tehran discovered that it was not the possession of gold, oil, or willing trading partners that mattered, but access to the invisible wiring of finance. Food had been turned into leverage without a single soldier or ship deployed.

This episode is emblematic of the new battleground: the financial system itself. Nations no longer need to seize territory or blockade ports to exert power. They can weaponise the pipes through which money flows—messaging networks, correspondent banks, settlement systems—and exclude adversaries at the flip of a switch. To be outside these systems is not simply inconvenient; it is existential. No currency in reserve, no access to clearing, no ability to transact: the modern state suffocates quietly, not with explosions but with declined payments.

The paradox is stark. Coins and notes, the symbols of money, matter far less than the rails on which money moves. What a state issues domestically is less significant than what it can clear internationally. Control of standards, of protocols, of who is "in" and who is "out"—these determine which economies thrive and which falter. The US dollar's supremacy does not rest merely on faith in Washington's solvency but on the entrenchment of its payment infrastructure across the globe. It is plumbing disguised as neutrality, politics dressed up as routine settlement.

Currency, then, is not merely a medium of exchange but a theatre of coercion. Exchange rate shocks can be engineered through credit ratings, targeted leaks, or orchestrated rumours. Capital flight can be induced not by tanks but by compliance officers withdrawing credit lines. A whisper from a ratings agency can prove as destabilising as a missile. This is the grey power of finance: it strikes invisibly, but with consequences that ripple through households, firms, and governments alike.

The scope of this chapter is to map those levers of monetary coercion. We will explore how payment rails themselves have become battlefields, how the exclusion of a single bank or the redefinition of a standard can alter national strategies overnight. We will analyse how foreign exchange markets, often presented as the epitome of spontaneous order, can in fact be nudged or jolted by coordinated campaigns of narrative and signal. We will consider the human cost of financial warfare: the small businesses cut off from credit because banks fear the shadow of sanctions, the workers laid off not because of local mismanagement but because a correspondent bank thousands of miles away severed ties.

Yet we will also evaluate the counterclaims: that digital money, central bank digital currencies, and new regional payment arrangements promise escape from these chokepoints. Are these truly solutions, or merely illusions wrapped in technical jargon? Can regional swap lines or commodity-based invoicing provide resilience against coercion, or do they simply reveal how difficult it is to build alternatives to entrenched systems?

Measurement, finally, will be critical. For too long, debates on currency weaponisation have been shaped by rhetoric rather than evidence. This chapter will propose concrete indicators—basis spreads, onshore-offshore gaps, anomalies in customs and settlements—that allow us to distinguish between noise and signal, between symbolic pressure and systemic coercion. By grounding discussion in metrics, we can assess campaigns for what they are: engineered systems of influence, not moral gestures.

The stakes are immense. Monetary coercion reshapes sovereignty itself, not by redrawing borders but by dictating who can pay and who cannot. The tools are silent, but their effects reverberate in protests, unemployment queues, and election outcomes. As states grow more interdependent, the temptation to weaponise finance will only intensify. The question, therefore, is not whether currency can be used as a weapon—it already is—but how societies should understand its deployment, measure its effects, and weigh its legitimacy.

The battlefield of money is here, pulsing beneath the surface of everyday transactions. The challenge is to see it clearly, to strip away the neutrality of infrastructure and expose the power embedded within it. Only then can we judge whether the use of currency as a weapon strengthens or corrodes the very order it claims to defend. The following pages will open that debate.

Payment rails as battlefields

In 2012, when Iranian banks were disconnected from SWIFT, the Brussels-based messaging system that underpins most of the world's cross-border payments, it was as if a nation had been severed from its oxygen supply. Oil could still be pumped, contracts still written, and willing buyers still existed. But the ability to settle those trades collapsed overnight. Tankers idled in port, revenues evaporated, and Tehran learned that the battlefield was not the Strait of Hormuz, but the data cables and settlement ledgers humming invisibly beneath financial markets.

This was not an isolated episode. When Russia invaded Ukraine in 2022, exclusion from SWIFT and the freezing of central bank reserves inflicted a shock greater than many military analysts thought possible. It was not the seizure of territory that rattled Moscow but the sudden inability to access hundreds of billions in foreign assets, to pay foreign suppliers, or to receive income from exports through normal channels. Currency reserves that had been painstakingly accumulated over decades were rendered inert at the stroke of a keyboard. The lesson was blunt: in the twenty-first century, control over *rails*—the infrastructure that carries value—matters more than the physical possession of coins, notes, or even commodities.

The paradox is that money itself has become less about substance and more about systems. The power lies not in what is held but in how transactions are transmitted, verified, and cleared. Messaging networks such as SWIFT, settlement systems like CHIPS in the United States or TARGET2 in Europe, and the web of correspondent banking relationships form a hidden architecture of global finance. Control over these arteries allows states and coalitions to decide who remains plugged in and who is left to improvise.

Messaging networks: the nervous system of finance
At first glance, SWIFT appears technical and banal—a cooperative providing secure messages between banks. Yet its significance lies precisely in that neutrality. By establishing a single global standard for payment instructions, SWIFT became indispensable. To exclude an institution is not merely to make its life inconvenient but to render its transactions suspect, forcing counter-parties to spend more, risk more, and often walk away. The very standardisation that makes modern finance efficient also makes it coercible.

Settlement systems: the moment of truth

If SWIFT is the nervous system, settlement systems are the beating heart. These platforms—where final transfer of funds occurs—are chokepoints of immense strategic value. The US CHIPS network, clearing dollar payments, and Europe's TARGET2, clearing euros, act as guarantors of trust. Delay a payment, and firms miss shipments. Exclude an entity, and it becomes radioactive to the market. The mechanics are simple; the consequences are profound. What matters here is not the rhetoric of diplomacy but the cold fact of whose balances are recognised and whose are ignored.

Correspondent banking: power by diffusion

Beyond formal systems, much of global commerce still relies on the old architecture of correspondent banking: institutions holding accounts with one another to process transactions in foreign currencies. This web is dense but fragile. Fear of regulatory penalties has led to widespread "de-risking," where banks cut ties with clients or entire jurisdictions deemed risky. The effect can be devastating. Small states find themselves locked out of the financial mainstream not through overt sanction but through the cumulative caution of institutions unwilling to risk scrutiny.

Case studies illustrate the leverage. When North Korea was cut off from its main correspondent accounts in Macau in 2005, its access to the dollar economy collapsed almost instantly. The move was not a comprehensive embargo but a targeted strike against a single financial node—enough to paralyse Pyongyang's external trade. Similarly, Venezuelan banks have struggled not only with formal sanctions but with counterparties worldwide unwilling to touch payments for fear of secondary exposure. The effect is exile by hesitation, as crippling as any official decree.

The broader political economy reveals why reserve currency status is less about prestige and more about infrastructure. The dollar dominates not simply because it is trusted, but because the plumbing of finance—the messaging standards, the settlement platforms, the correspondent links—is built around it. Eurodollars, offshore dollar deposits, thrive because liquidity is deepest where rails are most established. Alternatives exist in theory: the euro, the renminbi, regional payment systems. Yet without the same density of correspondent networks, the same universality of standards, they remain auxiliary.

The coercive potential flows from this imbalance. Exclusion from dollar rails magnifies risk, raises transaction costs, and ultimately constrains sovereignty. This explains why states invest heavily in hedging strategies: building currency swap lines, experimenting with central bank digital currencies, or settling trade in commodities. But even these efforts run up against the entrenched dominance of the established rails. The physical analogy is apt: building a parallel railway across a continent is costly, time-consuming, and often politically unfeasible. The incumbents control not just the track but the standards of gauge, signalling, and safety.

This brings us to the philosophical core: power today lies not in visible stockpiles but in the invisible choreography of flows. The capacity to delay, to exclude, to redefine standards is more decisive than the ability to mint coins. Monetary power no longer looks like a mint or a vault; it looks like a server farm in Virginia, a clearinghouse in New York, a central switch in Brussels.

Yet this raises unsettling questions. If financial rails can be turned into battlefields, what does this mean for the idea of neutral commerce? How resilient are societies whose prosperity depends on uninterrupted access to these systems? And how sustainable is a global order where one or two powers can, with technical switches, determine the fates of entire nations?

The answers are contested, and the alternatives uncertain. But the reality is clear: the pipes of finance are no longer neutral infrastructure. They are contested terrain, and the battles fought upon them may shape the century as decisively as wars once fought for land or sea.

FX shocks and narrative catalysts

In August 1997, a single announcement from Thailand's central bank—the decision to float the baht—set off a chain reaction that toppled currencies across Asia. Stock markets plunged, IMF officials scrambled, and governments fell. Yet beneath the headlines, the most destabilising forces were not tanks rolling across borders but words: the declarations of rating agencies, the warnings of investment banks, the whispers that reserves were evaporating. It was a reminder that exchange rates can be broken not just by deficits or debt, but by stories amplified at the right moment.

The paradox of modern currency markets is that they are both vast and fragile. Daily trading exceeds six trillion dollars, dwarfing any single state's reserves. Yet a rumour, downgrade, or data release can send a national currency tumbling in hours. What appears to the public as an inevitable market verdict often reflects careful orchestration upstream. Exchange rates are not just mirrors of fundamentals; they are battlegrounds where perception is weaponised.

Consider how credit rating agencies—nominally independent arbiters—can trigger cascades. A downgrade by Moody's or S&P narrows the pool of investors permitted to hold a sovereign's debt, forcing sales that depress currency value. But the *timing* of such downgrades can align suspiciously with political negotiations. In 2011, the United States' AAA downgrade came amid congressional brinkmanship over the debt ceiling, sharpening pressure on policymakers. In emerging markets, downgrades have often arrived just as governments sought loans from international institutions, tilting bargaining power towards creditors.

Think tanks and research houses play a subtler role. A report hinting at unsustainable current account deficits, or warning of "capital flight risks," can prime investors to exit positions pre-emptively. These analyses rarely operate in isolation. When coupled with leaks from ministries, central bank minutes, or orchestrated op-eds, they form a campaign of narrative pressure. A market accustomed to scanning for signals can be steered into self-fulfilling moves.

Leaked data or deliberately timed releases offer another lever. A surprise inflation figure, an unexpectedly high unemployment rate, or hints of dwindling reserves can send currencies spiralling. Yet such numbers are rarely neutral. They can be delayed, massaged, or selectively disclosed. The manipulation lies less in falsification than in choreography: deciding *when* and *how* information reaches markets. The Argentine peso, for instance, has repeatedly swung not only on fiscal data but on the credibility of those who released it.

At the sharp end of this machinery lie orchestrated shocks. Coordinated statements by finance ministries, central banks, and international institutions can overwhelm markets by sheer unanimity. When the G7 declared in 1985 that the dollar was overvalued and pledged joint action—the Plaza Accord—the effect was immediate. Traders knew they were not facing a diffuse market but a concentrated coalition with both intent and capacity. The dollar weakened, and the narrative of inevitable decline reinforced the momentum.

Yet manufactured volatility carries risks. If investors suspect coordination, trust in market neutrality erodes. Sovereigns that appear to "game" data or pressure agencies risk longer-term costs: higher borrowing rates, demands for greater transparency, and scepticism of future reforms. This tension makes the management of narrative catalysts both art and gamble. What succeeds in the short run may corrode credibility in the long run.

Philosophically, the phenomenon raises unsettling questions. If currencies can be driven by stories as much as by substance, what does sovereignty mean in a world of instantaneous flows? For citizens, the impact is tangible: sudden spikes in import prices, vanishing savings, and rising unemployment. For governments, the dilemma is acute: defend credibility by conceding to external pressure, or resist and risk deeper isolation.

The task for analysts and citizens alike is to cultivate *causal literacy*. A violent swing in an exchange rate is not always the spontaneous outcome of markets finding equilibrium. It may be the climax of a carefully managed information cascade. Timing irregularities—downgrades coinciding with negotiations, reports aligning across institutions, data drops that cluster around political events—are signals that shocks may be manufactured. Recognising the fingerprints of narrative catalysts is essential in distinguishing between structural weakness and strategic attack.

The deeper lesson is that money today is not merely arithmetic but argument. Currencies move not only with deficits and surpluses but with the stories told about them. The battle for credibility is fought in press releases, research notes, and television studios as much as in trading rooms. The pipes of global finance may be technical, but the pressure within them is often rhetorical.

The question that lingers is whether societies can insulate themselves from these orchestrated storms. Can transparency, diversified reserves, or regional cooperation shield economies from volatility engineered abroad? Or must nations accept that in a world where narratives move markets, sovereignty is always contingent on someone else's story? The answer remains uncertain—but the stakes could not be higher.

De-risking, capital flight, and the social tax

In a small East African city, a women's cooperative once thrived on exporting handmade textiles to buyers in Europe. The business depended on modest cross-border payments—two or three thousand dollars at a time—routed through local banks to cover raw materials and transport. But after international sanctions touched a neighbouring country, those banks quietly closed their correspondent accounts, fearing exposure to compliance risk. Overnight, the cooperative found itself unable to pay suppliers or receive funds from customers. The women were not sanctioned.

Their country was not sanctioned. Yet their livelihoods vanished because bankers, faced with the cost of verifying every transaction, chose the safest option: cut the cord.

This is the paradox of modern financial warfare: measures aimed at regimes and elites often cascade downwards, starving small enterprises and households of credit. De-risking—the withdrawal of financial services from customers or regions perceived as high-risk—becomes a blunt instrument. What begins as an effort to tighten compliance morphs into widespread exclusion. When banks over-comply to shield themselves from penalties, they amplify harm far beyond the original intent of policymakers. The casualties are not oligarchs or generals, but shopkeepers, migrant workers, and families trying to wire tuition fees.

Fear drives this cycle. A single compliance failure can expose an international bank to fines running into billions, as BNP Paribas discovered in 2014 when penalised nearly nine billion dollars for violating U.S. sanctions. Faced with such existential threats, financial institutions err on the side of retreat. They sever ties with whole sectors—remittance firms, charities, agricultural traders—rather than risk inadvertently processing a prohibited payment. Each severed link pushes legitimate money flows into the shadows, where costs rise and trust erodes.

The feedback loop is punishing. Once mainstream banks exit, alternative channels surge: informal hawala networks, cash couriers, lightly regulated fintechs. These substitutes carry higher costs and less protection for ordinary users. At the same time, their growth reinforces banks' reluctance to return, since regulators view such ecosystems as inherently suspicious. A vicious circle emerges: fear of sanctions fuels over-compliance; over-compliance fuels capital flight; capital flight entrenches risk perceptions that justify continued withdrawal.

The macroeconomic effects are severe. Small and medium-sized enterprises, already constrained by limited access to credit, see lines of finance evaporate. Importers struggle to pay suppliers abroad; exporters cannot repatriate earnings. Investment dries up, not because fundamentals are weak, but because the payment plumbing is fractured. The result is unemployment, currency depreciation, and a silent tax on growth. Where sovereigns may weather sanctions through reserves or political resilience, local businesses and households absorb the brunt of disruption.

The social tax imposed by de-risking is often invisible to those designing the measures. Humanitarian exemptions, written into sanction regimes with great fanfare, rarely translate into smooth operations on the ground. A pharmaceutical importer may technically be authorised to ship medicine, but if insurers refuse coverage, ships will not sail. If banks decline to clear payments, invoices go unpaid. Shelves empty while officials in capital cities insist exemptions exist. The gap between legal carve-outs and operational reality is where human cost accumulates.

Psychology matters here as much as policy. Banks, regulators, and governments inhabit an atmosphere of suspicion, where the penalty for leniency is ruin and the reward for over-caution is safety. In this climate, reputational risk is treated as more dangerous than economic loss. A single media headline about lax oversight can sink share prices more swiftly than missed lending opportunities can raise them. Thus, the rational choice for institutions becomes over-withdrawal—a rationality that is socially destructive.

There is also a distributional injustice embedded in this dynamic. Wealthy elites, with offshore accounts and access to complex intermediaries, can often bypass restrictions. It is the smaller firms and poorer households that face exclusion, unable to absorb higher costs or hire legal teams to navigate compliance. A farmer needing fertiliser imports, a student needing remittance flows, a charity delivering food aid: these become the collateral casualties of a compliance culture designed to intimidate the powerful. The irony is sharp—those least implicated in the behaviours targeted by sanctions are often those most exposed to their fallout.

The consequences extend beyond economics into politics. As citizens experience shortages and unemployment, they may attribute blame not to their government but to foreign powers imposing or enforcing sanctions. This "rally-round-the-flag" effect strengthens authoritarian regimes, who exploit the narrative of victimhood. By over-compliance, international banks inadvertently become participants in a political theatre where sanctions consolidate rather than destabilise power. Financial warfare thus risks undercutting its own strategic rationale.

The philosophical question is whether financial coercion can ever be justified without a full accounting of these distributive harms. War has long been subject to debates over proportionality and civilian immunity. Should non-kinetic measures be exempt? If the intent of sanctions is to alter elite behaviour, but the reality is mass exclusion of ordinary people from the circuits of finance, then proportionality has been breached. Invisible weapons still wound, and responsibility cannot be evaded by pointing to the absence of bombs.

Recognising the social tax of de-risking forces a recalibration of strategy. Sanctions need more than legal carve-outs—they require active enforcement of humanitarian corridors, support for correspondent relationships, and investment in compliance technologies that can distinguish illicit from legitimate flows. Without such measures, financial warfare becomes indistinguishable from collective punishment.

The unresolved tension is stark. States will continue to weaponise finance, and banks will continue to fear penalties. But can a global system built on risk aversion be recalibrated to serve justice as well as strategy? Or must societies accept that in the invisible wars of finance, the burdens will always fall heaviest on those least able to bear them? The answer remains open, and its implications are as much moral as they are economic.

Digital money, CBDCs, and sanctions resistance

When Russia's invasion of Ukraine in 2022 triggered sweeping financial sanctions, officials in Moscow did not rush to tanks or troops for relief—they looked to payments architecture. Talk turned quickly to the rouble's digitalisation, to alternative rails with China, to bypasses around the dollar's choke points. Commentators speculated about central bank digital currencies (CBDCs) ending Western dominance of finance. For a moment, the narrative was intoxicating: code, rather than cannons, would rewrite the balance of power. Yet beneath the headlines lay a more prosaic truth: while technology can rewire payment flows, the underlying constraints of liquidity, trust, and governance remain stubbornly in place.

The allure of digital money in sanctions resistance is easy to understand. The digital yuan, the eNaira in Nigeria, or experiments in the Bahamas promise sovereign control over payments without reliance on foreign intermediaries. In theory, if a sanctioned state could transact entirely in CBDCs across friendly borders, Western sanctions would lose their teeth. But theory often ignores plumbing. Payments are not just messages between wallets; they are promises embedded in a system of settlement, foreign exchange, and correspondent relationships. Without interoperability, a CBDC becomes little more than a domestic convenience, unable to carry weight in the global marketplace.

Take China's e-CNY, often touted as a geopolitical game-changer. Domestically, it is a controlled experiment in digital finance. Internationally, its reach is modest, limited by capital controls and by the absence of partners willing to settle trade entirely outside the dollar and euro systems. Even when bilateral swaps are arranged—say, between Beijing and Moscow—the question of liquidity intervenes. How many suppliers of oil, wheat, or microchips are willing to hold balances in roubles or yuan when dollar clearing remains cheaper, deeper, and more secure? Digital form does not solve this fundamental demand problem.

Interoperability is another barrier. For CBDCs to neutralise sanctions, they must cross borders smoothly. Yet linking payment systems requires not just technical APIs but political trust. Shared standards raise questions of surveillance, data sovereignty, and dispute resolution. Which regulator arbitrates fraud? Which court adjudicates contract breaches? The political economy of reserve currencies rests on credible governance, not merely on coding protocols. Without predictable legal frameworks, traders and investors will not migrate en masse to alternative systems.

Liquidity, meanwhile, dictates hierarchy. The dollar's strength is not simply a matter of political will; it is a reflection of vast, deep markets in Treasury securities, backed by enforceable property rights and an independent central bank. A digital rouble or lira cannot conjure liquidity out of thin air. Without secondary markets and credible convertibility, such currencies will remain niche instruments, tolerated at best for bilateral barter-like exchanges but incapable of scaling to global dominance.

That is not to say digitalisation is irrelevant. New tools allow states to explore hedges against coercion. Bilateral swap lines, for example, provide a liquidity buffer for trade partners willing to hold each other's currencies. Commodity invoicing in roubles, yuan, or rupees creates partial shields, reducing reliance on Western banks. Regional nets, such as the Cross-Border Interbank Payment System (CIPS) in China or the Pan-African Payment and Settlement System (PAPSS), aim to keep value circulating within trusted blocs. Yet each of these is better understood as a supplement than a substitute: an extra layer of resilience rather than an outright escape from dollar primacy.

The hype around cryptocurrencies as sanctions busters illustrates the same gap between narrative and reality. In theory, decentralised networks could route around centralised chokepoints. In practice, liquidity bottlenecks and compliance overlays remain decisive. Exchanges that provide on- and off-ramps into fiat are themselves subject to regulation. Attempts by sanctioned actors to move large sums through crypto markets trigger price anomalies visible to analysts and regulators alike. Far from anonymity, the blockchain ledger often proves an open book for forensic investigators.

There is also the problem of scale. While the global daily turnover of foreign exchange exceeds six trillion dollars, the liquidity of crypto markets—even in their most exuberant phases—has been a fraction of that. No serious economy can finance sustained imports of food, medicine, or machinery through thinly traded digital tokens without absorbing intolerable volatility. For households in inflationary economies, stablecoins may provide temporary shelter; for sovereigns under sanctions, they are inadequate armour.

The deeper lesson is that financial coercion does not rest solely on technology but on architecture. Payment systems are embedded in hierarchies of trust: central banks, legal regimes, and credible institutions. A CBDC is not, in itself, a revolution. It is a digitised claim whose value still depends on the stability of the issuing state and the willingness of others to accept it. Without the political economy of reserve backing, digital form cannot transform weak currencies into strong ones.

Still, the experiments matter because they reveal intent. States exploring CBDCs or regional nets are not seeking to topple the dollar overnight but to carve out margin: room for manoeuvre, insulation against shocks, bargaining chips in negotiations. For smaller states, digital money promises inclusion in regional ecosystems where correspondent banking has withered. For larger powers, it is an insurance policy against the weaponisation of the existing system. These motives are pragmatic, not utopian, and their success will depend less on rhetoric than on engineering details of liquidity management, FX conversion, and governance.

The unresolved question is whether digitalisation will fragment the global financial order or merely add new layers to it. Will we see genuine multipolarity in payments, with blocs transacting in regional CBDCs? Or will the gravitational pull of dollar liquidity continue to centralise power, relegating alternatives to niche roles? The answer may hinge not on technology itself but on geopolitics: whether states can build enough trust to pool sovereignty around new rails. For now, the promise of sanctions resistance through digital money remains more aspiration than achievement—an ambition caught between the friction of pipes and the allure of code.

Measuring monetary coercion

When Argentina's peso collapsed in 2018, traders and politicians alike scrambled to assign blame. Some spoke of reckless domestic policy, others of speculative attacks, others still of capital fleeing towards the safety of dollars. Yet amid the noise, one truth became evident: without reliable measures of stress, every interpretation was possible, and none could be conclusively proved. In the theatre of monetary coercion, perception can be weaponised as effectively as policy. That is why measurement matters. Without tools to distinguish natural turbulence from engineered pressure, citizens and leaders alike are left vulnerable to narrative manipulation.

The paradox is clear. Financial coercion works precisely because its effects appear organic: a sudden widening of spreads, an unexpected currency dip, an unexplained rerouting of trade settlements. But in the absence of careful tracking, these movements are mistaken for spontaneous market reactions. Just as a doctor relies on vital signs to separate infection from exhaustion, analysts must build dashboards of financial indicators to diagnose whether volatility is the result of structure or strategy. Without such instruments, coercion can be overstated, understated, or entirely misread.

One starting point lies in *basis spreads*—the price gap between borrowing dollars in one market and swapping into them in another. When sanctions or capital controls distort access to liquidity, these spreads widen. For example, Japanese banks once paid significantly more than their U.S. counterparts for dollar funding, a discrepancy tied not only to demand but also to shifts in regulatory and geopolitical pressure. Such gaps serve as early warning lights: when they widen abruptly, it may suggest that access to the dominant currency has been constricted, intentionally or otherwise.

Closely related are *offshore-onshore gaps*. Consider the Chinese yuan, which trades both domestically in Beijing and offshore in Hong Kong. When confidence falters, the offshore rate diverges from the controlled onshore benchmark. If sanctions or political signalling restrict inflows, the offshore market becomes a pressure gauge, revealing strains that the domestic system conceals. The magnitude of that divergence offers a quantifiable measure of coercion, one that can be tracked daily by any attentive observer.

Settlement flows tell another story. When correspondent banks refuse to clear transactions, or when networks such as SWIFT exclude targeted entities, payments do not vanish—they reroute. Trade that once settled in New York may detour through Dubai or Singapore. These reroutes leave traces: longer processing times, higher costs, anomalous spikes in traffic at secondary hubs. By mapping such anomalies, analysts can infer when sanctions or financial blockades are reshaping global commerce. Each reroute is not just a logistical inconvenience but a measurable indicator of coercive impact.

Invoicing currency shares add a subtler dimension. The proportion of global trade denominated in dollars, euros, or yuan is not static. Shifts in those shares reflect not only market preference but also the pressure of policy. When Russia began invoicing oil in roubles and yuan after 2022, it was more than symbolic: it signalled an attempt to erode the coercive reach of the dollar system. Monitoring these shifts provides insight into whether coercive measures are driving diversification—or whether the gravitational pull of liquidity continues to override political resistance.

To turn these scattered signals into usable intelligence, one must build a dashboard. This need not be proprietary or arcane. Public data—basis spreads from market feeds, currency gaps from Bloomberg or Refinitiv, settlement lags visible in customs records, invoicing currency shares reported by central banks—can be combined. The aim is not to achieve perfect attribution but to establish baselines and detect anomalies. Just as meteorologists cannot stop storms but can track their severity, policymakers can use such dashboards to calibrate responses, separating transient weather from deliberate disruption.

This emphasis on measurement also deters exaggeration. Governments under pressure may claim every fluctuation is a foreign attack, while their adversaries may trumpet success without evidence. Dashboards cut through rhetoric by grounding analysis in observable signals. A widening spread or rerouted settlement can be debated, but it is harder to dismiss than a vague accusation of manipulation. Numbers do not end the argument, but they discipline it.

Philosophically, the act of measurement forces clarity on responsibility. If coercion is truly invisible, it invites conspiracy thinking, where every downturn is seen as sabotage. But if it is measurable, it can be challenged, constrained, and ultimately governed. The ability to quantify does not make coercion benign, but it allows societies to weigh its costs against alternatives. Just as civilian casualties are counted to inform debates on kinetic war, financial casualties—job losses from credit withdrawal, inflation from currency shocks—require metrics to hold power accountable.

The challenge, of course, is that indicators can be gamed. A state wishing to mask its vulnerability may intervene to narrow offshore–onshore gaps or pump liquidity into basis spreads. Conversely, an adversary may amplify panic by leaking selective data or by framing anomalies as catastrophic. Measurement is therefore not neutral: it becomes part of the contest. But even here, transparency matters. A well-informed public is harder to mislead.

The unresolved question is whether dashboards can ever keep pace with the ingenuity of coercion. Financial engineers constantly invent new instruments, and coercers constantly probe for unseen chokepoints. Will measurement always lag a step behind, chasing shadows? Or can the discipline of tracking itself change the calculus, making coercion less invisible, less deniable, and therefore less potent? What is certain is that without measurement, societies fight blind in a war that depends above all on obscurity.

Chapter 4

Information Cascades and Perception Control

In October 2010, a single tweet from an obscure account claimed that an explosion had rocked a Saudi oil facility. Within minutes, commodity traders in London noticed a spike in chatter; futures markets twitched upward, driven not by confirmed fact but by the echo of a claim. The rumour was false. Yet for several hours, billions of dollars moved on the back of a sentence no more verifiable than a whisper in a marketplace. What mattered was not the truth of the statement, but the speed at which it travelled, the authority it borrowed through repetition, and the decisions it compelled before verification could catch up.

This is the terrain of modern conflict: not shells but signals, not armies but algorithms. Narratives today can cross from the fringe to the mainstream in hours, propelled by influencer networks, automated amplification, and selective coverage. A phrase voiced on a blog, amplified by a handful of bots, picked up by sympathetic commentators, and cited in a briefing memo can reshape expectations in policy rooms and trading floors alike. By the time a correction arrives, the damage—or the desired effect—has already been done.

The paradox is stark. Never before has so much information been available to so many, and never before have so few actors been able to manipulate collective perception at scale. Control rarely comes in the form of outright falsehood. More often, it is exercised through the architecture of framing: which numbers are emphasised, which images are cropped, which baselines are chosen. A chart can be technically accurate yet profoundly misleading if its denominators are adjusted to amplify or obscure trends. The sophistication of such techniques makes detection difficult, especially when the human mind, primed for pattern and story, craves coherence over precision.

The stakes are immense. Perceptions move markets, shape elections, and condition whether societies accept or resist foreign policy. A downgrade by a ratings agency framed as sober analysis can trigger capital flight, yet the very timing of its release may serve geopolitical strategy. A think-tank report, funded by undisclosed interests, can tilt the policy debate in one capital while fuelling media talking points across continents. In such a world, attention itself functions as currency, with outrage and virality traded like commodities on exchanges of influence.

The chapter you are about to enter dissects this ecosystem with surgical precision. It shows how information moves through pipelines as tangible as those carrying oil or gas. From the mechanics of amplification—botnets, aligned media outlets, choreographed influencers—to the subtler techniques of propaganda without posters, it reveals how narratives are crafted, repackaged, and weaponised. Case studies from public health campaigns to energy disputes to armed conflicts will illustrate how the same playbook adapts across domains.

Yet the analysis does not stop at content. It turns to the economics of the disinformation market itself: who pays, who profits, and who is caught in the crossfire. We examine how media capture and self-censorship, whether through ownership concentration, advertising dependence, or legal intimidation, create invisible fences around public discourse. Even before a story reaches the newsroom, it can be killed by the quiet arithmetic of risk and revenue.

Perhaps most importantly, this chapter equips you with tools—both personal and institutional—for resisting manipulation. Simple protocols like cross-sourcing, time-delayed decision-making, and dissent memos may appear modest, but they form the building blocks of resilience. In the same way that handwashing transformed public health in the nineteenth century, these hygiene practices can inoculate organisations and individuals against infection by narrative contagion.

But the ultimate tension remains unresolved. If narratives are supply chains of belief, can transparency alone restore agency? Or will ever more sophisticated techniques of perception control continue to outrun our defences, ensuring that by the time truth emerges, the market, the vote, or the battlefield has already shifted? The pages that follow do not offer comfort, but they do offer clarity—and in a world where perception can be engineered, clarity may be the last form of power still within reach.

From message to market move

In May 2019, an anonymous post appeared on a niche financial blog suggesting that Chinese authorities were preparing to dump their holdings of US Treasury bonds in retaliation for tariff escalations. Within hours, the story had been picked up by regional news outlets, amplified by Twitter accounts with tens of thousands of followers, and cited on a major cable business channel. By the next morning, yields on long-term Treasuries had jumped and commentators were warning of financial warfare. Later investigations revealed no evidence of any such Chinese plan. Yet the damage was done: billions of dollars had shifted, portfolios had been reshuffled, and investor sentiment had darkened—all triggered by a chain of repetition in which each stage lent credibility to the last.

This is how power moves in the twenty-first century: not solely through armies, treaties, or tariffs, but through the architecture of attention. A fragment of information—accurate, distorted, or fabricated—can cascade from obscurity to policy relevance in the space of a trading session. The potency lies less in the content of the message than in the way it is carried: who echoes it, how it is framed, and at what moment it arrives. The medium is not just the message, but the multiplier.

To grasp the dynamics of such cascades, one must view information as having its own logistics chain, as real as that of oil or grain. It passes through intermediaries—bloggers, influencers, bot networks, aligned media outlets—each adding a layer of validation or urgency. Just as a container passes from port to truck to warehouse, a narrative travels from fringe forums to mainstream broadcasts to government briefings. The handoffs matter. A statement that would be dismissed as speculation when voiced by an unknown blogger acquires gravitas once quoted by a recognised think-tank analyst or an investment bank report. The repetition itself creates plausibility; the echo suggests substance.

The architecture of amplification is neither accidental nor evenly distributed. States and private actors alike cultivate networks of amplification with deliberate intent. Russia's Internet Research Agency infamously orchestrated botnets to push divisive narratives during electoral cycles, while corporate interests fund influencer partnerships that blur the line between sponsored content and independent commentary. What unites these diverse strategies is their reliance on the human tendency to mistake repetition for truth and correlation for causation. The cascade does not need to persuade everyone;

it only needs to nudge enough decision-makers at critical nodes—traders, journalists, policymakers—who shape the environment for others.

Consider the 1997 Asian financial crisis, when rumours of a devaluation in Thailand's baht—circulated in analyst notes and amplified by wire services—preceded the very policy moves they described. Investors, reading that others expected collapse, rushed to hedge or exit positions, thereby hastening the collapse itself. A whisper became a prophecy, the prophecy a trigger, and the trigger a self-fulfilling outcome. The supply chain of belief created the reality it claimed to observe.

How then can observers regain agency in this environment? The first step is causal auditing: a disciplined practice of asking three deceptively simple questions—*who benefits, who repeats, and when*. A sudden surge of stories about food shortages, for example, may benefit grain exporters or destabilisers of a regime. If the same talking points appear simultaneously across think-tank briefs, television commentary, and social media threads, one should ask whether this is organic convergence or orchestrated release. Timing adds a further clue: narratives often surface at moments calibrated to coincide with summits, sanctions announcements, or market expiries. Tracing these alignments exposes intent that content alone conceals.

This method does not require specialised technology. It requires attentiveness to incentives and sequencing. For instance, when a leak about credit downgrades appears a week before the scheduled review, one must consider not only the credibility of the leak but also the market advantage conferred on those who moved early. Similarly, when a fringe claim migrates seamlessly to mainstream op-eds, the identities of the amplifiers may reveal institutional pathways of influence.

The significance of these dynamics extends beyond financial markets. In democratic societies, cascades shape electoral outcomes by embedding frames—crime surges, migration crises, cultural panics—that structure voter perception. In authoritarian contexts, cascades provide the illusion of consent by creating the sense that "everyone" believes a particular line. In both cases, the same mechanics are at play: a message, strategically repeated, reconfigures the cognitive landscape in which decisions are made.

Yet there is also an irony worth dwelling on. The very abundance of channels that promises pluralism and freedom of speech creates vulnerabilities to manipulation. Where once a government had to control printing presses or radio stations, today influence can be purchased cheaply in the form of bot armies or algorithmic boosts. The barriers to entry are low, the returns high. But this also means that defensive literacy—understanding amplification as a process—becomes more feasible for ordinary citizens. The complexity of global finance or geopolitics may elude casual observers, but the pattern of a rumour's spread is increasingly trackable to anyone with curiosity and a critical eye.

The challenge is that cascades often operate faster than verification. By the time a correction circulates, market moves have settled, policy debates have shifted, or social unrest has flared. Truth arrives late to the battlefield, after positions are entrenched. This asymmetry places a premium on anticipatory scepticism: the ability to withhold immediate assent, to map amplification chains before reacting, to resist the reflex of treating repetition as reliability.

The deeper question is whether societies can institutionalise this form of scepticism without collapsing into cynicism. If every claim is dismissed as propaganda, trust erodes, leaving fertile ground for manipulation by those who thrive in chaos. If every cascade is accepted at face value, collective agency is ceded to those who engineer perception. The balance lies in cultivating habits of causal auditing—not to reject information outright, but to slow down enough to trace its lineage and ask who stands to gain.

And yet, even with such awareness, one must confront the possibility that some cascades are designed precisely to overwhelm the capacity for scrutiny. Flooding the zone with noise—dozens of conflicting stories, partial truths, and staged leaks—can exhaust attention and push observers to disengage. In such cases, the victory lies not in persuading but in paralysing. What then becomes the fate of agency when exhaustion itself is the weapon? That unresolved tension frames the chapters to come, where the mechanics of narrative warfare reveal not only how cascades are built, but how societies might resist—or succumb—to them.

Propaganda without posters

In the Second World War, propaganda was a matter of posters in the street, newsreels in the cinema, and speeches on the radio. It was loud, visible, and unmistakable. The citizen knew when they were being addressed and could recognise the hand of the state in the message. Today, the landscape looks radically different. The most persuasive propaganda rarely declares itself as such. It seeps into our assumptions not by shouting falsehoods but by shaping what is counted, what is shown, and how numbers or images are arranged on the page.

The paradox of our time is that propaganda thrives not because of a deficit of information but because of its abundance. The very tools designed to democratise knowledge—social platforms, open datasets, satellite feeds—have enabled more sophisticated methods of manipulation. No need to invent a blatant lie when a simple crop of a graph, a carefully chosen baseline, or a shift in denominators can alter the story while retaining a veneer of objectivity. These subtler tactics pass under the radar precisely because they look like data rather than opinion.

Take the example of public health statistics during the COVID-19 pandemic. In some countries, infection rates were plotted with a logarithmic scale that made exponential growth look deceptively tame; in others, denominators were switched between "per capita" and "absolute numbers" depending on whether the comparison favoured or embarrassed the government. Both charts contained "true" data points, yet their framing led to radically different interpretations. Citizens were not lied to; they were guided toward conclusions by the hidden hand of selection and presentation.

Energy debates offer another case. In the run-up to the European winter of 2022, charts circulated showing soaring natural gas imports from Russia to certain states. What many of these visuals concealed was the baseline: the previous year's data had been selected to make increases look more dramatic, ignoring that total volumes were still falling relative to pre-war norms. Meanwhile, other charts shifted the frame of reference to "share of energy mix" rather than raw volumes, making a minor increase in one sector appear existential. Each version told a different story, both anchored in reality, yet each shaped to support a political line.

Conflict reporting shows similar patterns. During the 2014 Ukraine crisis, casualty figures were sometimes expressed as "percentage of the population affected," minimising apparent impact, while rival outlets presented them as "total casualties per day," amplifying urgency. Even photographic evidence is not immune. Cropped images can exclude surrounding context: a protest crowd may look vast when the frame cuts out empty space, or it may look thin when the angle hides density. Both pictures can be technically accurate while narratively misleading.

What unites these practices is that they work not by inventing content but by exploiting cognitive shortcuts. Humans are wired to trust numbers, charts, and visuals as neutral. Few pause to interrogate why one baseline was chosen over another, or what lies outside the frame of a cropped photo.

The effect is insidious: propaganda becomes invisible precisely because it wears the clothes of analysis.

This does not mean intent is always malicious. Journalists under deadline may unconsciously select the chart that looks most dramatic. Politicians may emphasise a denominator that resonates with voters. Corporations may foreground metrics that please shareholders. But once these choices accumulate, the public is not engaging with an objective picture of reality but with a curated version—one that consistently leans in certain directions.

The key, then, is not to chase each claim individually but to learn to spot the *craft*. Ask why a baseline begins where it does. Consider what would change if the denominator shifted. Compare graphs side by side to see whether scale manipulation alters the apparent story. These small acts of scrutiny transform the reader from passive consumer to active auditor. They do not require advanced statistical training; they require awareness of the techniques that give propaganda its quiet force.

There is also a deeper philosophical lesson. Propaganda without posters shows that control today lies not in the blunt imposition of ideology but in the calibration of perception. Whoever frames the data frames the debate. Whoever decides what enters the denominator decides who counts. In such an environment, truth is not abolished but bent, not through grand lies but through subtle steering.

Yet this sophistication creates its own fragility. The more propaganda relies on the authority of numbers and graphs, the more it risks exposure once the mechanics are revealed. A citizenry trained to question baselines and crops can puncture narratives more effectively than one fixated on debating raw claims. The contest, then, is not over facts alone but over literacy in the *forms* facts take.

And here lies the unresolved tension. Can societies cultivate such literacy broadly, or will it remain confined to specialists and sceptics? If only elites can detect denominator tricks, manipulation retains its power over the wider public. But if everyday readers develop the habit of interrogating framing, the quiet machinery of propaganda loses much of its leverage. The outcome will determine whether the age of subtle manipulation entrenches itself—or whether, by learning to see the craft, citizens can reclaim the agency that posters once sought so blatantly to deny them.

Disinformation markets

In 2017, a Macedonian town called Veles briefly became the centre of global politics. Hundreds of teenagers and small entrepreneurs discovered that fabricating sensational headlines about the American election could earn them more from Google advertising than any local job. Articles like "Pope Endorses Candidate X" or "Secret Emails Reveal Conspiracy Y" were churned out by the dozen, spread through Facebook groups, and monetised through clicks. What looked like a spontaneous flood of falsehoods was, at its core, a business model. Disinformation had become not merely a political tool but a market—one where attention was the traded commodity and outrage the currency of choice.

The paradox is that while states and intelligence agencies often receive the blame for orchestrated falsehoods, the real accelerants are commercial. Platforms optimise for engagement because it drives advertising revenue. Influencers amplify extreme claims because controversy grows their audience. Brokers—ranging from data analytics firms to viral marketing shops—package outrage in ways that can be purchased off the shelf. What emerges is not a traditional command system of propaganda but a decentralised ecosystem of buyers and sellers, each pursuing profit or influence but collectively producing distortions with geopolitical consequence.

At the heart of this market lies a simple mechanism: *virality arbitrage*. The cost of producing a piece of content—an article, a meme, a short video—can be negligible. The potential return, in attention, advertising dollars, or political leverage, can be vast if the content happens to catch a wave. This asymmetry explains why small amounts of money can produce large policy shifts. A modest spend on targeted ads or influencer partnerships can seed a narrative that, once picked up by aligned media or amplified by bot networks, travels far beyond its origin. Political operatives have long understood this leverage. Today, they can outsource much of the work to the commercial infrastructure of digital marketing.

Consider the Russian Internet Research Agency's campaigns around the 2016 US election. Much of its effectiveness did not come from fabricating new positions but from amplifying existing social cleavages—racial tensions, gun rights, immigration fears. With relatively modest budgets, the agency achieved reach comparable to established news outlets, because the market rewarded polarisation. Attention was captured not by sober analysis but by content designed to provoke anger, fear, or triumph. What looked like state propaganda was in practice a shrewd exploitation of the existing economics of outrage.

But disinformation markets are not solely the domain of foreign adversaries. Domestic actors—political campaigns, activist groups, even corporations—play within the same structures. Credit rating downgrades, think-tank "research" reports, or selective leaks can all function as instruments of narrative trading, influencing investor sentiment or regulatory agendas. In each case, the question is not whether the information is wholly true or false but whether its timing, framing, and amplification are designed to move markets of belief. Just as financial traders exploit volatility, narrative entrepreneurs exploit cognitive volatility: moments when the public, investors, or policymakers are primed to react.

Philosophically, this invites us to rethink the metaphor of information as speech. The more apt comparison is information as a commodity traded in markets. Supply can be manufactured cheaply, intermediaries profit from volume, and demand is shaped by cognitive biases that make humans particularly susceptible to emotionally charged stories. In such a market, regulating content alone—policing each falsehood or correcting each rumour—is akin to chasing counterfeit coins while the minting presses run unchecked. The more consequential lever is the *design of the market itself*: the incentives platforms set, the revenue models that reward virality, and the amplification infrastructures that determine what scales and what withers.

This shift in perspective also clarifies why disinformation campaigns can appear unstoppable. Traditional censorship assumes a top-down adversary that can be blocked or silenced. But in markets, supply is fluid and adaptable. Shut down one account, and another emerges. Close one domain, and content migrates to another. The barrier to entry is so low that supply is effectively infinite. What matters is not the elimination of bad content but the rebalancing of incentives so that outrage is no longer the most profitable good on offer.

There is a further dimension: the buyers. States may invest in influence campaigns, but so too do corporations seeking to soften regulatory scrutiny or amplify consumer demand. Media outlets, in pursuit of traffic, may become unwitting amplifiers. Even individuals, motivated by social capital, act as micro-brokers when they share sensational material that confirms group identity. In this sense, disinformation markets blur the line between manipulation and participation. Citizens are not just victims; they are actors whose clicks, shares, and endorsements form the currency of the system.

Case studies illustrate how quickly modest investments can cascade into systemic effects. A coordinated burst of tweets, timed with a favourable think-tank report and a friendly news cycle, can generate not only a temporary spike in belief but concrete policy outcomes: cancelled trade agreements, delayed infrastructure projects, or shifts in diplomatic posture. The actual cost may be a few hundred thousand dollars—a trivial sum compared with the billions spent on conventional military campaigns. Yet the return on investment can alter alliances, redirect budgets, and fracture social cohesion.

The implication is unsettling but liberating. If disinformation is a market, it can be studied, mapped, and potentially redesigned. Analysts can track brokers, identify repeat buyers, and measure price signals such as the cost of trending a hashtag or sustaining a botnet. Citizens can cultivate literacy in spotting when outrage is being packaged for sale. Policymakers can consider interventions not just in terms of censorship but in terms of competition policy, advertising regulation, and transparency of sponsorship. The battlefield of belief is not only ideological but economic.

Still, the question remains: can markets of attention ever be "reformed" when their fundamental product is human emotion? Outrage sells because it resonates with deep-seated instincts of identity and belonging. Virality follows the pathways of human psychology as much as algorithms. To reshape disinformation markets, therefore, is not only to alter platform incentives but to confront the social demand that keeps the commodity profitable. And here lies the enduring tension. Even if supply is disciplined, the appetite for sensationalism may prove inexhaustible. The future of political stability may rest not only on regulating sellers but on cultivating citizens willing to resist the allure of cheap outrage—a task far harder than any content takedown or technical fix.

Media capture and self-censorship

In 2011, a team of investigative journalists in a Central European country uncovered evidence of systematic tax fraud implicating one of the nation's largest conglomerates. The documents were solid, the story watertight. Yet the article never saw daylight. Within days of the pitch, editors quietly shelved it. The reason was not a flaw in the reporting but a phone call from the conglomerate's legal counsel, paired with a reminder that the company was among the newspaper's biggest advertisers. The journalists were left with a bitter lesson: censorship today often does not arrive in the form of state diktats or blue pencils. It is administered through subtler, quieter levers—ownership, money, and fear of litigation.

This is the paradox of the modern information economy. Societies pride themselves on freedom of the press, yet vast swathes of what might matter never reach public consciousness. Stories die before birth not because journalists lack the will to write them but because invisible fences—economic dependence, political ties, reputational risk—narrow the corridors of permissible reporting. The very outlets celebrated as watchdogs often sit inside cages built not by censors in uniform but by shareholders, advertisers, and lawyers.

Ownership is the most obvious fence. In many countries, media empires are concentrated in the hands of a few families or conglomerates with sprawling business interests. A television network owned by a construction magnate may hesitate to expose corruption in public contracts. A newspaper tied to an energy conglomerate may tread carefully on climate coverage. Even where there is no explicit directive, the culture of the newsroom evolves to avoid inconvenient truths. The absence of an order does not mean the absence of influence; silence can be the product of anticipation.

Advertising dependence creates another choke point. The migration of revenue from subscriptions to digital advertising has made media outlets beholden to corporate sponsors and platform algorithms. A car manufacturer unhappy with a safety exposé may quietly pull millions in advertising, sending a message that editors cannot ignore. In some cases, advertisers do not even need to issue threats—the fear of losing scarce revenue is sufficient to shape editorial choices. This dependence introduces an insidious bias: stories that anger power are softened, while those that flatter consumer or investor sentiment are prioritised.

Legal frameworks add a further dimension. Libel laws, particularly when weaponised by wealthy individuals and corporations, can deter even robust reporting. Strategic lawsuits against public participation (SLAPPs) need not succeed in court to succeed in practice; the mere cost of litigation can bankrupt small outlets or consume the bandwidth of larger ones. Journalists learn quickly which names and topics come with prohibitive risk. The chilling effect is cumulative: entire areas of inquiry become no-go zones.

Comparative analysis reveals how these dynamics play out differently across systems. In the United States, the First Amendment provides strong protections, yet the reliance on advertising and shareholder ownership still skews coverage. In parts of Europe, state broadcasters offer stability but are vulnerable to political appointments and budgetary pressure. In Asia and Africa, where press freedom is more fragile, a combination of ownership monopolies, advertising scarcity, and legal intimidation often produces self-censorship as potent as outright bans. Each system bears its unique vulnerabilities, but the structural patterns rhyme.

The effect is not merely academic. When investigative journalism withers, corruption flourishes, citizens are left uninformed, and democratic accountability erodes. The silence around certain issues is itself a political act. Readers who consume media uncritically often assume that what is reported represents the universe of what is knowable. Yet the most consequential stories may be precisely those that never appear, strangled by the invisible hand of capture.

Interviews with working journalists often surface the same refrain: the decision to kill a story is rarely dramatic. It comes as a quiet editorial suggestion to "hold off," or a subtle nudge to redirect focus to safer ground. Over time, self-censorship becomes internalised. Reporters learn not to pitch sensitive stories at all, protecting their careers and their employers' balance sheets. The result is a gradual narrowing of the Overton window, with public debate shaped as much by absence as by presence.

Evaluating source independence, therefore, requires more than reading the label. A news outlet may brand itself as independent, but if its revenue model relies heavily on a handful of advertisers or its ownership ties it to political power, independence is compromised in practice. Transparency registers, ownership databases, and financial disclosures can help readers probe beneath the surface. Yet the burden also falls on readers to cultivate scepticism: asking whose interests are served by the silence as well as by the speech.

The philosophical stakes are profound. Freedom of the press is often defended as a binary—censorship exists or it does not. The reality is spectrum and gradient. Influence does not always announce itself; it often manifests as what is left unsaid. Understanding media capture requires us to attend to the silences, the recurring absences, the suspicious uniformity across outlets that otherwise compete fiercely. Silence, too, is a message.

The tension that remains unresolved is how to protect media ecosystems without rendering them dependent on new patrons, whether state or corporate. Public funding risks politicisation, while pure market models invite commercial capture. Hybrid solutions—trusts, reader-supported models, diversified revenue—offer partial answers but not panaceas. The question persists: in a world where stories can be suffocated before they breathe, how can societies ensure that what needs to be told is told? And perhaps more pointedly—are we prepared to recognise that the greatest threats to free expression may come not from overt suppression but from the quiet collusion of money, ownership, and fear?

Building personal and institutional hygiene

In 2003, a single dossier about weapons of mass destruction, built on thinly sourced claims, helped justify the invasion of Iraq. Years later, after inquiries and recriminations, one truth stood out: it was not the absence of intelligence but the absence of rigorous checking, of disciplined scepticism, that allowed shaky narratives to harden into policy. Institutions with some of the finest analytical capabilities in the world failed not because they lacked information, but because they lacked hygiene.

The lesson endures. In an age of accelerated information flows, the enemy is rarely total ignorance; it is contamination, distortion, and the unchecked spread of plausible untruths. The hygiene metaphor matters because, like hand-washing, small, habitual practices can avert large-scale disasters. The most effective defences against manipulation are not heroic interventions but routines—protocols for questioning, verifying, and slowing down decisions when speed would otherwise amplify error.

At the personal level, hygiene begins with verification. Simple cross-sourcing—checking whether a claim survives contact with multiple independent outlets—immediately filters noise from substance. Tools abound, from reverse image searches to public registries, yet the more crucial step is cultural: cultivating the reflex to pause before passing information along. A healthy scepticism asks not only *is this true?* but also *why am I being shown this now, and by whom?* That second layer transforms fact-checking into context-checking.

Time-delay decision-making extends this ethic. Much of disinformation thrives on urgency—"act now," "share before it's deleted," "markets will collapse tomorrow." By creating a deliberate buffer, whether hours or days, decision-makers deprive manipulative narratives of their intended tempo. For individuals, this may mean waiting before forwarding a sensational story. For institutions, it may mean resisting the 24-hour news cycle when formulating strategy. Delay is not indecision; it is inoculation.

Institutional hygiene deepens these habits into structured practices. Red teams, for example, provide formal dissent by stress-testing prevailing assumptions. When military planners or corporate boards invite a designated group to argue the opposite case, blind spots surface before they metastasise into failures. Dissent memos, too, prevent premature consensus. By allowing staff to lodge objections in writing, even if the majority disagrees, organisations create an archive of alternative perspectives—an insurance policy against groupthink.

Narrative inventories represent a newer tool. Just as companies keep track of financial liabilities, institutions can log the narratives circulating around their operations: which stories gain traction, who repeats them, and which audiences they reach. By mapping these flows, leaders distinguish between isolated rumours and coordinated campaigns. More importantly, they restore agency: understanding the supply chain of belief turns noise into something traceable, and therefore manageable.

These micro-practices ripple outward into macro-resilience. A government that cross-sources intelligence before launching policy avoids costly missteps. A newsroom that embeds dissent memos produces journalism less prone to capture or spin. A business that maintains narrative inventories can anticipate reputational risks before they erupt. Hygiene at the level of individuals and teams aggregates into sturdier institutions, and sturdier institutions in turn reinforce democratic and economic stability.

Yet the cultivation of hygiene carries a philosophical challenge: how to foster scepticism without tipping into cynicism. Excessive doubt corrodes trust, paralyses decision-making, and leaves societies vulnerable to nihilism—the very goal of disinformation campaigns. Hygiene, properly understood, is not the rejection of trust but its careful rationing. We wash our hands not because the world is wholly poisonous, but because we know contamination exists and vigilance protects us.

Case studies illustrate the stakes. During the COVID-19 pandemic, countries with transparent verification practices—regular disclosure of data sources, open scientific debates, acknowledgement of uncertainty—faced lower levels of public disorientation. In contrast, where officials rushed to enforce singular narratives and suppressed dissenting memos, trust collapsed, fuelling conspiracy theories and vaccine hesitancy. Hygiene does not guarantee compliance, but its absence guarantees suspicion.

The economic domain offers similar lessons. Banks that established red teams to model stress scenarios ahead of the 2008 financial crisis fared better than those who clung to consensus forecasts. Hygiene, in these cases, meant refusing to believe in the permanence of rising housing prices simply because everyone else did. It meant institutionalising doubt, not as paralysing scepticism but as structured curiosity.

There is also a moral dimension. In societies saturated with propaganda and disinformation, the act of maintaining hygiene is a civic duty. Verification before amplification is no longer optional; it is the price of participating responsibly in public discourse. Institutions, likewise, bear responsibility not only to their shareholders or constituencies but to the informational commons itself. Hygiene practices reduce collateral harm, much as environmental protocols reduce pollution.

Still, unresolved tensions remain. Hygiene takes time and resources, and in competitive environments—whether in politics, markets, or media—the temptation to cut corners is constant. A newsroom that pauses for a second source risks being scooped; a policymaker who waits for dissenting views may lose tactical momentum. The paradox is that hygiene often feels like a handicap in the short term, yet proves to be the ultimate advantage in the long run.

The question that lingers, then, is whether societies under strain will value hygiene enough to build it into their institutions, or whether speed, spectacle, and certainty will continue to crowd it out. If hygiene is boring, invisible, and slow, can it compete with the adrenaline of instant response? The answer will determine not only the resilience of our information systems but also the integrity of our collective decisions in the years ahead.

Chapter 5

Corporate Espionage in the Age of Platforms

In the summer of 2019, a major software firm awoke to find one of its flagship products abruptly delisted from a dominant app store. No hack had been detected, no database breached, no code stolen in the night. Instead, a quiet policy shift by the platform—nudged, some suspected, by a rival's lobbying and opaque review rules—erased billions from its market value overnight. It was espionage without infiltration, sabotage without break-ins: a new theatre of conflict where control of access and visibility proved more decisive than any stolen trade secret.

For centuries, corporate espionage conjured images of stolen blueprints and briefcases exchanged in dimly lit hotels. Today, the battlefield has migrated into platforms that were never built with security politics in mind: cloud consoles that monitor every process, advertising exchanges that record behavioural telemetry, and app stores whose approvals act as gatekeepers of global commerce. The paradox is striking. The very infrastructures designed to enable innovation now double as surveillance vantage points. Competitors, regulators, or hostile states can exploit these levers to tilt competition, making the governance of platforms a question not just of commerce but of sovereignty.

This chapter asks readers to reconsider what espionage means when market access itself becomes an intelligence asset. Trade secrets still matter, but they are increasingly entangled with the permissioned vantage points that platforms provide. Telemetry—once a mere engineering tool—can serve as a compass pointing to a competitor's strategy. Policy toggles buried in administrative dashboards can decide whether one firm's updates reach users or languish in limbo. The line between operational friction and covert sabotage is deliberately blurred, and only those who understand the mechanics can tell the difference.

The threat is not confined to outsiders. Insider risk and supply-chain ingress remain persistent, and the stakes have multiplied in an interconnected economy. A poisoned update or compromised build server can cascade across industries with devastating speed. Behind many of these incidents lie ordinary pressures—debt, ideology, personal grievance—that transform employees or contractors into vectors of compromise. The question is not whether insiders exist but how their pathways into sensitive systems are mapped, monitored, and constrained. In this respect, espionage is not an exotic anomaly but an extension of everyday incentive structures.

Beyond infiltration, data brokerage has matured into a shadow industry of its own. Open-source intelligence, scraped datasets, and commercial brokers can reconstruct a competitor's intent with remarkable accuracy. A single dataset may reveal little; triangulated across sources, it forms a mosaic sharper than most leaks. Here the ethical line becomes critical: what counts as legitimate reconnaissance in a competitive marketplace, and when does it cross into intrusion? The ambiguity itself is weaponised, as firms exploit grey zones to justify aggressive collection or to tar rivals as aggressors.

The legal domain compounds this ambiguity. Litigation, once a forum for redressing grievances, increasingly serves as a stage for discovery fishing. By filing suits, companies can force rivals into disclosing sensitive documents, delaying launches, or signalling regulators. Protective orders and cross-border discovery rules turn into tools of strategy as much as of justice. This legal theatre does not replace technical espionage; it complements it. For the well-resourced, courts become another channel for intelligence gathering, one whose legitimacy makes it harder to contest.

Counterintelligence for firms, then, must evolve beyond firewalls and nondisclosure agreements. It requires asset inventories that treat not only patents and source code but also platform dependencies and access rights as targets worth defending. Compartmentation, rotating access, and anomaly hunts help reduce exposure, but the deeper work lies in culture: creating shame-free environments where reporting suspicious behaviour is encouraged, not punished. Firms that fail to build this resilience quietly erode their own competitiveness, no matter how brilliant their innovations.

The broader stakes are national. As economies consolidate around a few global platforms, vulnerabilities at the corporate level translate into risks at the geopolitical level. Espionage once undermined individual firms; now it can distort entire markets or tilt regulatory regimes. The governance of platforms thus becomes a matter of national security, and the maturity of corporate counterintelligence a component of national competitiveness.

What follows in this chapter is not a catalogue of threats but a reframing of espionage itself. In an age where platforms mediate commerce, communication, and computation, the act of protecting a firm is inseparable from protecting a nation's economic sovereignty. The reader will encounter case sketches of policy toggles used as weapons, poisoned updates that paralysed supply chains, lawsuits wielded as intelligence traps, and cultural practices that shield or expose firms to compromise. Each example is chosen to show not only how espionage has changed, but why ignoring its new forms risks ceding advantage before the contest has even begun.

The open question—the one that shadows every page—is whether firms and states can adapt quickly enough. If platforms are the new battlefields, can governance keep pace with the ingenuity of exploitation? Or will the silent power of permissioned vantage points outstrip the slow machinery of regulation and defence? The answer will shape not just corporate fortunes but the balance of global power itself.

From trade secrets to platform leverage

In 2020, a popular mobile application vanished from a leading app store without warning. The official explanation was a vague breach of terms of service; insiders whispered of a quiet complaint from a rival, delivered through opaque review channels. Overnight, a billion-dollar company found itself cut off from users, its revenue collapsing not because its code was stolen or its engineers defected, but because access to a gatekeeper had been withdrawn. This was not industrial espionage in the classical sense—there were no stolen blueprints or midnight data extractions. Instead, the battlefield had shifted to the levers of platform governance, where a toggle buried in a console had more destructive impact than any stolen trade secret.

The paradox of the platform era is that control increasingly matters more than theft. In the industrial age, espionage was about extracting secrets: chemical formulas, aeronautical designs, proprietary algorithms. In the platform economy, however, the power lies less in possessing knowledge than in shaping flows: who is visible, who is throttled, who is denied. Platforms such as cloud service consoles, app stores, and advertising exchanges have become surveillance and coercion infrastructures. Their custodians, intentionally or not, occupy the vantage points from which competitors can be observed, markets tilted, and rivals sidelined.

Consider cloud infrastructure. Providers see not only the data stored but also metadata—patterns of compute demand, deployment regions, or unusual spikes in bandwidth. To a savvy observer, these are not trivial technical details but signals of strategic intent. A sudden cluster of GPU reservations may hint at an AI breakthrough. A shift in regional deployment may betray an entry into a new market. What was once innocuous telemetry has become a form of reconnaissance, blurring the line between service provision and intelligence gathering. Even when providers pledge neutrality, the temptation for competitors or governments to press for access lingers.

App stores magnify the problem by embedding editorial discretion within technical infrastructure. Policies that govern which apps are discoverable, how rankings are determined, and which updates are approved are framed as neutral safeguards. Yet they can be weaponised—sometimes subtly, sometimes openly. A delay in approving a critical update can cost a start-up its momentum. A quiet adjustment in ranking algorithms can funnel attention away from one player towards another. These are not spectacular acts of hacking but slow-burn distortions, whose legitimacy is obscured by the language of trust and safety.

Advertising exchanges illustrate how platform leverage extends into the very currency of attention. By controlling which data is shared with advertisers, how audiences are segmented, and which bidding rules apply, exchanges effectively decide which firms can reach which markets. A small tweak in access privileges or latency parameters can determine whether an advertising campaign thrives or flounders. For competitors, the effect may be indistinguishable from sabotage, though cloaked in the plausible deniability of "technical adjustments." In a world where markets hinge on visibility, opacity in exchange mechanics is itself a strategic weapon.

These are not isolated concerns but systemic risks. Traditional espionage focused on breaching walls and stealing secrets; platform leverage allows competitors to rearrange the terrain entirely. The implications extend beyond corporate rivalries into national security. When strategic industries depend on platforms headquartered abroad, sovereignty becomes conditional. A state that cannot guarantee its firms' access to cloud infrastructure or app marketplaces is no longer fully master of its economic destiny. Governance of platforms, then, ceases to be a commercial issue and becomes a geopolitical one.

Case sketches make this dynamic stark. A cloud provider once refused service to an overseas security start-up under pressure from domestic regulators, effectively crippling its product launch. An advertising platform quietly altered bidding rules that disadvantaged smaller regional players, consolidating the dominance of incumbents. A popular productivity app was removed from an app store during a diplomatic spat, its absence framed as a compliance issue though clearly aligned with state interests. Each case illustrates how policy toggles and operational discretion—legitimate tools of platform management—double as levers of geopolitical influence.

The philosophical tension is acute. Platforms justify their control by invoking trust, safety, and user protection—values that are hard to contest. Yet the more critical they become to global commerce, the less their decisions can be treated as private acts of governance. What begins as content moderation or technical enforcement shades into economic coercion and surveillance. Here lies the paradox: the very qualities that make platforms scalable—centralised rules, integrated telemetry, frictionless distribution—also make them uniquely vulnerable to abuse.

The challenge for policymakers and executives alike is to recognise that espionage in this new environment is less about illicit access than about legitimate vantage points. Abuse no longer requires breaking in; it requires only permissioned observation and discretionary control. A platform does not need to steal a trade secret when it can infer intent from telemetry, predict strategy from metadata, or throttle execution through policy toggles. The tools of administration have become the instruments of intelligence.

As firms and states grapple with this reality, the stakes sharpen. If platforms are infrastructures of sovereignty, who governs them, and under what principles? Can transparency mechanisms, audit trails, or international norms prevent the abuse of platform leverage, or will geopolitics render such safeguards cosmetic? And if governance fails, will states seek to build rival platforms, fragmenting global commerce into rivalled spheres?

The unresolved question, the one that shadows every case, is whether trust in platforms can ever be reconciled with the asymmetries they create. So long as policy toggles can erase companies and telemetry can map strategies, governance will be contested terrain. The contest is no longer over who holds the secrets, but over who holds the switches.

Insider risk and supply-chain ingress

In December 2020, security researchers uncovered what would become one of the most consequential cyber-espionage campaigns of the decade: the SolarWinds compromise. Attackers had slipped malicious code into an otherwise routine software update, piggybacking on the trust between vendor and customer. Thousands of firms and government agencies installed the backdoored update, effectively inviting adversaries into their networks. No firewall was breached, no password stolen—the compromise came pre-packaged, signed, and delivered through ordinary supply channels. It was a demonstration that in the age of interconnected systems, the softest target is not always at the perimeter but in the dependencies that organisations treat as safe by default.

The paradox is stark: the very practices designed to streamline modern business—outsourcing, contracting, modular software development—also multiply points of vulnerability. Every procurement decision, every third-party tool, every subcontractor creates a chain of implicit trust. A single weak link can unravel the whole. Unlike the romanticised spy who sneaks into an office to copy blueprints, today's insider may be a contractor with legitimate access or a supplier whose code update arrives invisibly poisoned. The risks are embedded, mundane, and scalable.

To grasp insider risk, one must first see it not as a matter of character alone but as a convergence of incentives. Debt is a powerful lever: an employee drowning in obligations may be susceptible to inducements that promise relief. Ideology adds another dimension—an insider convinced they are serving a higher cause can rationalise betrayal as loyalty to a different tribe. Grievance is perhaps the most corrosive of all. An employee who feels wronged, overlooked, or humiliated may strike back not with protest but with sabotage. In each case, the personal becomes geopolitical when the insider's access becomes a weapon in the hands of adversaries.

Supply chains extend these vulnerabilities beyond the walls of any single firm. Build servers, for instance, compile and package software before release; a compromised server can infect every downstream product without detection. The notorious case of the CCleaner utility, whose installer was laced with malware in 2017, illustrates this vividly: millions of users downloaded what they believed to be a trusted tool, unwittingly delivering access to their own systems. Poisoned updates exploit the trust organisations place in digital signatures and update mechanisms—trust that adversaries are increasingly adept at abusing.

Third-party software development kits (SDKs) represent another underappreciated vector. Mobile apps, desperate to monetise, often embed advertising or analytics SDKs from outside vendors. Those SDKs, in turn, may contain hidden capabilities to exfiltrate data or deliver payloads.

Developers may never review the code themselves, relying instead on contractual assurances. Yet once an SDK is embedded, it becomes a quiet insider, operating with the permissions granted to the host app, invisible to end users and often overlooked by regulators.

Procurement and contracting add still more layers of exposure. A contractor with temporary access to a corporate network can copy sensitive files, plant persistent malware, or simply observe workflows. Because they are often excluded from the tightest security vetting, contractors are paradoxically both essential and weakly defended. In some cases, entire procurement chains have been leveraged: counterfeit components with hidden backdoors inserted into hardware supply lines, or maintenance contractors persuaded to install "updates" on equipment that were anything but. The lesson is clear: dependencies are not just economic but also strategic liabilities.

Yet the response cannot simply be to retreat from interdependence. Modern commerce depends on modularity and specialisation. The challenge is instead to build habits of scrutiny that extend beyond vendors to their dependencies and sub-dependencies. A firm that vets its supplier but ignores the supplier's suppliers has only addressed the first step in a chain that may stretch across continents. Adversaries understand this better than many executives: the cheapest way to breach a fortified target is not to attack directly but to compromise the overlooked partner that holds the keys.

Comparative case studies reinforce this point. In one instance, a defence contractor's systems were breached not through direct assault but via a janitorial subcontractor whose network credentials were less protected. In another, attackers infiltrated a telecommunications firm through a widely used software library maintained by a single underfunded developer, whose GitHub repository became a staging ground for malicious code. These episodes reveal a sobering truth: the map of risk is not congruent with the organisational chart. Following dependencies, not just vendors, is the discipline required.

Philosophically, the phenomenon highlights an enduring human theme: trust as both enabler and weakness. Trust allows organisations to scale, to cooperate across borders, to innovate without reinventing every component. But that same trust is what espionage exploits. Debt, ideology, and grievance are not exotic motivators but everyday human realities, reminding us that the insider threat is rarely a matter of villainy alone. It is the ordinary turned dangerous, the trusted turned compromised.

The strategic question, then, is how societies and firms balance openness with resilience. Can supply chains be mapped and stress-tested with the same rigour as financial portfolios? Should insider risk be treated less as a rare betrayal and more as a systemic probability to be managed continuously? And if dependencies are the true terrain of espionage, what new norms or architectures might reduce the asymmetry between trust and exploitation?

What remains unresolved—and urgently pressing—is whether firms and governments can adapt fast enough. Dependencies proliferate faster than defences. Each new contractor, each new SDK, each new procurement decision redraws the map of risk. To follow those dependencies with vigilance requires resources, imagination, and above all humility. The question lingers: will organisations learn to see their insiders and suppliers not as footnotes but as frontline actors in the great contest over information and power?

Data brokerage and corporate reconnaissance

In the mid-2010s, a small hedge fund began consistently anticipating the quarterly earnings of major retailers with uncanny accuracy. It was not the result of insider leaks or lucky guesses, but of satellite imagery—counting cars in car parks to predict sales volumes. When regulators later examined the practice, they found nothing unlawful. The fund had merely stitched together publicly available and commercially purchasable data into a sharper picture than the companies themselves disclosed. It was a reminder that in the digital age, secrets do not need to be stolen; they can be inferred.

This paradox defines modern corporate reconnaissance: competitors are both more opaque and more transparent than ever before. Traditional espionage once meant sneaking into vaults or bribing insiders. Today it is often a matter of piecing together fragments—an online CV here, a procurement notice there, a leaked dataset from a third-party vendor. A single shard of data may tell little. But triangulated against dozens of others, patterns emerge: strategic priorities, launch timelines, even hidden vulnerabilities. The art lies not in possession of a single file but in the capacity to aggregate, correlate, and interpret.

The infrastructure of this practice is now industrialised. Commercial data brokers harvest and sell vast quantities of information: location trails from mobile apps, purchasing histories from loyalty schemes, scraped profiles from social networks. What was once ephemeral—where a person walked, what they bought, whom they connected with—becomes a permanent dataset, tagged, segmented, and monetised. For competitors with the means to buy, these markets provide reconnaissance of extraordinary granularity. A rival's hiring surge in one city may hint at a new project; its executives' travel patterns may forecast partnerships or acquisitions.

The rise of open-source intelligence, or OSINT, extends the field further. Tools designed for law enforcement or journalists are equally available to corporate analysts. Satellite imagery, customs records, maritime tracking, and financial disclosures—all ostensibly public—become potent when cross-referenced. When Tesla began shipping vehicles through obscure European ports, hobbyists tracking shipping manifests had evidence of expansion before official announcements. The democratisation of such techniques blurs lines between hobbyist curiosity, commercial strategy, and national intelligence gathering.

Yet reliance on single leaks remains a novice's game. A solitary document or dataset, out of context, can mislead as easily as it can illuminate. The true craft lies in triangulation. For instance, a leaked email about a company exploring new markets may mean little alone. But matched with hiring data from LinkedIn, procurement orders for region-specific materials, and a spike in advertising expenditure, it becomes confirmation of intent. This mosaic approach resembles intelligence analysis more than journalism: weighting sources, testing consistency, and resisting the temptation of premature certainty.

The ethical boundaries here are fraught. What counts as intelligence, and what counts as intrusion? Scraping a public-facing website for information available to anyone is widely accepted; phishing an employee to steal credentials is criminal. Buying data from a broker sits uncomfortably between: legal in many jurisdictions, but morally ambiguous when individuals never consented to the resale. For firms, the danger is reputational as much as legal. A company found purchasing sensitive data, even if lawfully available, may be judged as intrusive by customers or regulators. The competitive temptation is strong, but so are the risks of crossing invisible lines.

Examples abound of how these practices tilt markets. During the COVID-19 pandemic, demand for personal protective equipment was tracked not only through official tenders but also through shipping records and customs filings. Firms with access to such data were able to outbid competitors and secure supply. Similarly, pharmaceutical companies have monitored clinical trial hiring via public job boards to anticipate rivals' research focus.

None of this required breaking into labs; it required attentiveness to digital exhaust.

The philosophical tension is worth pausing on. Intelligence in its classical sense always lived in the shadows, in secrets stolen or guarded. But in the platform age, secrets often evaporate not through betrayal but through aggregation. Each of us leaks signals constantly, from location pings to metadata trails. Organisations are no different. The puzzle is whether we should treat inference from such data as fair competition, or whether there is something corrosive in a world where every trace is commodified and weaponised.

Taxonomy helps. We might distinguish between *surface data* (truly public and deliberately disclosed), *ambient data* (generated as a by-product of digital life, like metadata), and *latent data* (private but obtainable through purchase or breach). The more reconnaissance depends on surface or ambient data, the easier it is to defend as legitimate. The more it drifts into latent data, the closer it comes to espionage. For policymakers and executives, clarity on these categories is essential, both to guide practice and to set norms.

Ultimately, the problem is not that data exists, but that the brokerage system has transformed it into a liquid market. Competitors do not need spies if they can subscribe. What is being sold is not just information but *perspective*: the capacity to see connections that those inside the firm may miss. This inversion—outsiders sometimes knowing more than insiders—reshapes corporate strategy. It also challenges traditional regulatory frameworks, which still treat leaks and breaches as exceptional events rather than the baseline condition of doing business.

The unresolved question is whether firms and societies can adapt without descending into paranoia or overregulation. If everything leaves a trace, should the goal be to erase footprints, to flood the environment with noise, or to embrace transparency as a new normal? And as the brokerage of data continues to expand, will the line between intelligence and intrusion sharpen—or will it dissolve entirely, leaving competition governed not by what one knows but by how fast one can stitch the fragments together?

Litigation as discovery fishing

In 2012, a smartphone patent war unfolded between two of the world's largest technology companies. The headlines focused on touchscreen gestures and rounded-corner designs. But beneath the surface, the true contest was not simply about intellectual property. It was about access: each side sought, through discovery motions, to prise open the rival's product roadmaps, supplier contracts, and market strategies. The legal battle was a theatre, but the backstage drama was one of intelligence gathering, with subpoenas acting as fishing nets cast into corporate waters.

This paradox is worth dwelling on. Litigation is ostensibly about remedying wrongs—breach of contract, theft of trade secrets, patent infringement. Yet in practice, it often functions as an intelligence operation conducted under the shield of law. Discovery rules in many jurisdictions compel companies to hand over troves of internal documents, emails, and financial data. A lawsuit can thus expose more than a data breach. Unlike hacking, which is furtive and illegal, discovery operates under judicial blessing. Its weapon is not malware but procedural compulsion.

For firms engaged in high-stakes competition, this dynamic creates an incentive to litigate strategically. One lawsuit may be filed less to win damages than to trigger disclosure. Another may be designed to stall a rival's product launch, burdening them with injunctions and compliance obligations. The costs of litigation—both financial and reputational—become instruments of pressure. The courtroom doubles as a proxy battlefield where discovery requests can dig deeper than any corporate reconnaissance team could legally manage.

Cross-border litigation magnifies the effect. American courts, with their expansive discovery obligations, are particularly attractive to foreign litigants. Through subsidiaries or jurisdictional claims, firms can draw opponents into systems that demand disclosure far beyond what would be allowed at home. Conversely, companies often seek protective orders—judicial restrictions on how discovered information can be used—to prevent sensitive data from becoming a competitive weapon. The dance between expansive discovery and protective containment becomes a terrain of strategy, where legal craft shades into geopolitical positioning.

The mechanics are revealing. Imagine a start-up preparing to launch a disruptive product. A lawsuit by an incumbent competitor—perhaps over a minor licensing dispute—can force the start-up into months of document review, draining resources and delaying launch schedules. The very act of complying with discovery can consume more bandwidth than engineering the product itself. Even if the suit eventually fails, the delay may achieve the incumbent's goal. In this sense, litigation acts as a brake on innovation, wielded by those with the resources to fight slower than they compete.

There are also subtler manoeuvres. Discovery often uncovers information that, while irrelevant to the case at hand, is invaluable commercially. Internal projections, confidential partnerships, or notes from regulatory strategy sessions may slip into the open. Lawyers are bound to use such information within the confines of litigation, but in practice, knowledge once seen cannot easily be unseen. The very act of forcing competitors to catalogue and expose their inner workings produces intelligence that lingers long after the court case ends.

Examples abound. In pharmaceutical disputes, discovery has unearthed early-stage research data, giving rivals clues to scientific directions. In energy sector litigation, supply contracts revealed under subpoena have offered insights into pricing strategies across continents. Even when courts grant confidentiality, the mere revelation that a competitor is pursuing a particular avenue can shift market expectations and investor behaviour. Litigation thus spills from courtrooms to trading floors, influencing valuations and deal-making.

Philosophically, this raises troubling questions. The law is supposed to be a forum for justice, not espionage. Yet the structure of discovery makes it a uniquely legalised form of intrusion. What distinguishes it from outright spying is its procedural legitimacy and transparency: judges oversee, parties contest, and rules apply. But to the targeted company, the effect can feel indistinguishable from coercion. The very safeguards of the legal system—the compulsion to tell the truth, the penalties for withholding—make discovery fishing more effective than clandestine theft.

There is also a geopolitical dimension. Multinational corporations straddle legal systems with varying rules of disclosure. A clever litigator can use this asymmetry to compel revelations in one jurisdiction that would be guarded in another. Governments, too, are not blind to the intelligence value of litigation. Regulatory agencies often monitor high-profile cases, using evidence disclosed under discovery to inform investigations. In this way, private lawsuits feed into public policy, creating a feedback loop where corporate battles supply ammunition for state interventions.

Critics argue that this dynamic corrodes the legitimacy of the legal system. When lawsuits are filed primarily as discovery expeditions, justice becomes secondary to strategy. The courtroom becomes a stage, the pleadings a script, and the audience—investors, regulators, competitors—the true target. Yet defenders counter that the transparency of discovery serves a broader public good. By compelling disclosure, litigation can surface misconduct, expose anti-competitive practices, and level asymmetries of information. The line between manipulation and accountability is thin, and often subjective.

The practical lesson for firms is sobering. In an age where data is a strategic asset, every lawsuit must be treated as both a legal and an intelligence risk. Preparing for litigation means not only marshalling arguments but also auditing what hidden vulnerabilities may be dragged into the open. Asset inventories, document retention policies, and cross-border compliance regimes become part of counterintelligence. A company that treats litigation as mere legal nuisance is one that risks bleeding its secrets through the very system meant to protect them.

The unresolved tension lies in whether litigation can ever be disentangled from its espionage function. As long as discovery exists, it will tempt competitors to use lawsuits as nets to trawl for information. Attempts to limit abuse—narrowing discovery, expanding protective orders—run the risk of weakening accountability for genuine wrongs. Attempts to maintain transparency risk enabling intelligence harvesting under the cloak of justice. The question is whether societies will recalibrate this balance, or whether the courtroom will remain one of the most powerful and paradoxical tools of corporate spying.

Counterintelligence for firms

In 2014, one of the world's most innovative chipmakers discovered that its crown jewels—years of proprietary research on processor architecture—had been siphoned away not through a dramatic cyber intrusion, but through the quiet actions of an insider. The individual had access, the company lacked rotation of privileges, and there was no culture that encouraged colleagues to flag anomalies without fear of reprisal. By the time investigators pieced together what had happened, competitors abroad were already integrating similar designs into their own products. The episode was not merely a private loss; it reshaped a segment of the global semiconductor market.

The paradox is clear: firms can spend millions on cutting-edge cybersecurity solutions, but without counterintelligence practices rooted in organisation-wide vigilance, they remain vulnerable. Corporate espionage does not always arrive in the form of a malicious attachment or a shadowy hacker collective. It often hides in plain sight—within the access rights granted to engineers, the procurement processes managed by contractors, and the silences maintained by staff who fear that raising concerns will be seen as disloyalty. Counterintelligence, then, is not an exotic cloak-and-dagger discipline reserved for governments. It is a core function of corporate survival in a competitive and interconnected world.

The starting point is deceptively simple: know what you have. Many firms do not maintain comprehensive *asset inventories*, meaning they cannot reliably say which datasets, code repositories, or prototypes exist, who has access to them, or where they are stored. Without this map, defences are a patchwork of guesswork. Asset inventories are not bureaucratic chores; they are the cartography of security. Only by knowing the terrain can anomalies be spotted, whether in download patterns, data flows, or unexpected access requests.

From there, compartmentation becomes vital. The principle of "need to know" is often honoured in theory but neglected in practice. Engineers are granted broad permissions for convenience, senior staff retain access long after roles change, and third-party contractors are given entry to systems with few safeguards. Each of these is a doorway left ajar. Compartmentation requires firms to accept a measure of friction: rotating access, limiting permissions, and regularly auditing who can see what. The inconvenience is a cost of resilience, just as fire drills momentarily disrupt productivity but prevent catastrophe.

Anomaly hunting adds another layer. Counterintelligence is not only about reacting to leaks but cultivating habits of noticing. Unusual log-ins at odd hours, shifts in procurement patterns, or sudden interest in dormant projects are not always coincidences. Yet detection depends on both technology and culture. Automated monitoring can flag statistical deviations, but human intuition—someone noticing a colleague repeatedly photographing whiteboards, or raising questions unrelated to their role—remains irreplaceable. Encouraging employees to voice such concerns without stigma transforms an organisation from a collection of individuals into an alert system.

This is where culture becomes decisive. Shame-free reporting sounds like a soft ideal, but it is hard security. Too many firms, fearing internal friction or reputational damage, punish or marginalise those who raise alarms. The result is silence—and silence is the ally of espionage. By contrast, environments that treat anomaly reporting as a professional duty, akin to quality assurance or health and safety checks, convert small observations into strategic defences. Employees must know that raising a flag will not brand them paranoid or disloyal but recognised as guardians of shared assets.

Rotating access reinforces this ethos. No one should hold perpetual control over critical systems or sensitive datasets. Rotation reduces the risk of compromise, ensures fresh oversight, and prevents entrenchment of hidden vulnerabilities. In practice, it means scheduled privilege reviews, temporary credentials for specific projects, and institutional memory that is distributed rather than locked into individuals. The discipline resembles checks and balances in democratic systems: authority is effective when exercised, but corrosive when left unchecked.

Practical measures coalesce into what can be called a maturity model for corporate counterintelligence. At the lowest level, firms respond only after breaches, treating espionage as freak accidents rather than recurring risks. At the next, they adopt inventories, audits, and rotation protocols, embedding resilience into routine. At the highest level, counterintelligence becomes cultural: anomaly detection is second nature, reporting is stigma-free, and access is continuously rebalanced. The firm no longer thinks of security as a wall around its assets but as a living system of vigilance and adaptation.

The stakes extend beyond corporate balance sheets. In sectors such as semiconductors, pharmaceuticals, or renewable energy, the theft of intellectual property reverberates nationally. When firms neglect counterintelligence, they unwittingly weaken their country's competitive position, forfeiting years of taxpayer-supported research and development to adversaries. Conversely, firms that institutionalise counterintelligence become not only more secure but also more reliable contributors to national resilience. Economic security, in this sense, is inseparable from national security.

Yet the tension endures. Counterintelligence must be rigorous but not paralysing, vigilant but not distrustful, disciplined but not cynical. Too much suspicion corrodes collaboration; too little invites exploitation. The art lies in embedding practices so seamlessly that they become habits—quiet, continuous, and largely invisible. The open question is whether firms will make this investment before the next high-profile theft reminds them, at great cost, why counterintelligence is no longer optional but existential.

Chapter 6

Lawfare: Winning in Court to Win the World

In May 1998, a little-noticed filing in a Washington, D.C. court claimed damages against a foreign state-owned enterprise. The complaint was not front-page news, yet within weeks insurers began to reassess the risk of underwriting projects linked to that enterprise. Credit tightened, deals were delayed, and rival bidders suddenly had space to manoeuvre. What looked like a technical matter of jurisdiction was, in reality, a battlefield decision: the use of a legal claim not primarily to win damages, but to alter the balance of commercial power.

The paradox is that courts, designed as neutral arbiters of justice, have become arenas where strategy can eclipse verdict. A case does not have to be won outright to succeed. Sometimes the act of filing—producing headlines, raising doubts, forcing discovery—is the victory itself. The costs imposed are measured not only in legal fees but in altered reputations, frozen transactions, and recalibrated policies. To see courts as mere forums for dispute resolution is to miss their function as theatres where law becomes both weapon and performance.

The strategic exploitation of legal systems—what scholars and practitioners call *lawfare*—is neither a novelty nor a marginal tactic. It is a form of conflict that spans borders and sectors, binding together investor-state arbitration, NGO litigation, shareholder actions, and regulatory filings into one continuum. At stake is more than who prevails in a given case. What is contested is precedent, perception, and the allocation of compliance costs across the global economy. When a company sees its stock price fall after a well-timed lawsuit, or when a government rethinks its subsidy regime after an adverse arbitral award, we glimpse the wider field on which lawfare operates.

Jurisdiction, once thought a dry matter of technical law, emerges as a strategic lever. Forum shopping—the deliberate choice of one court over another for speed, sympathy, or reach—reshapes how global business is conducted. A single filing in London can ripple through a supply chain in Southeast Asia; a motion in New York can determine whether European subsidiaries freeze payments. This is law as logistics: timing dockets to coincide with sanction announcements, or aligning hearings with media cycles to maximise reputational impact. The courtroom is thus linked to the newsroom and the boardroom, each amplifying the other.

But the reach of lawfare extends beyond the bench. The rule-writing of standards bodies—mundane committee votes over technical specifications—often locks in geopolitical advantage more durably than a courtroom win. Standards determine which products are interoperable, which suppliers are certified, which markets open or close. Here the battlefield is procedural minutiae: who sits on committees, how votes are counted, and which interpretations prevail. A small procedural victory in a standards forum may silently redirect billions of dollars in trade, shaping industries for decades.

Reputation is the currency that ties these domains together. A lawsuit is rarely pursued in isolation; it is accompanied by press briefings, coalition letters, and orchestrated reports designed to amplify its symbolic weight. Naming and shaming are not afterthoughts but central tactics: the legal brief and the press release form a twin strike, raising the cost of capital for the target and forcing counterparties to reassess risk. Lawfare succeeds when the shadow of compliance looms larger than the substance of law.

For those on the receiving end, defence requires more than competent counsel. It demands a counter-strategy: pre-emptive audits to reduce vulnerabilities, literacy in treaty obligations, and rapid-response teams able to blunt reputational shocks. Non-disclosure agreements and settlements offer limited shelter, for the power of lawfare lies less in resolution than in process—the pressure applied in the interim, the uncertainty leveraged as a weapon. The asymmetry is profound: those with resources and sophistication can wield courts against smaller rivals, NGOs can use filings to shape corporate conduct, and states can leverage extraterritoriality to extend their reach.

The rise of lawfare forces a rethinking of sovereignty, competition, and security. In a world where software code and shipping contracts alike are subject to legal challenge in distant courts, the battlefield is no longer defined by territory but by jurisdiction. The question is not whether law will be used as a weapon—it already is—but who will learn to master its forms, anticipate its vectors, and defend against its excesses.

The chapters that follow open the curtain on this theatre: showing how legal filings create global consequences, how standards embed geopolitics in seemingly technical language, how reputational campaigns tie briefs to balance sheets, and how firms and states alike can adapt. For now, the essential insight is stark: to understand modern power, one must understand law not only as a rule but as an instrument. The court docket is a battlefield, and those who read it merely for precedent may already be losing the war.

Courts as a continuation of policy by other means

When Argentina defaulted on its sovereign debt in 2001, the crisis appeared to be primarily economic. Yet the defining battles of the following decade were not fought in Buenos Aires or at IMF headquarters, but in courtrooms in New York. Hedge funds that had refused to accept restructuring terms pursued Argentina through every legal avenue, seizing assets abroad and tying the country's hands in capital markets. Their legal manoeuvres forced a sovereign state to negotiate on their terms. It was an extraordinary demonstration that the courtroom could function as a battlefield, where financial leverage and legal ingenuity were deployed as weapons of war.

The paradox is stark: the law, imagined as neutral and universal, is now routinely wielded as a strategic instrument. Legal claims are not only about justice but about shaping political outcomes, setting precedent, and imposing costs on adversaries. Governments, corporations, NGOs, and even individuals have recognised that litigation can achieve what diplomacy, lobbying, or even sanctions cannot. A lawsuit may never reach a final judgment, but the act of filing—its timing, its framing, its headlines—can shift perceptions and policies. Courts, in this sense, are theatres where the performance often matters as much as the verdict.

Lawfare, as this mode of struggle is often called, is not limited to the disputes of sovereign debt. Investor–state arbitration has become a favoured venue for multinational corporations to push back against regulatory measures they deem hostile. When tobacco firms sued Australia and Uruguay over plain-packaging laws, the intent was not only to protect trademark rights but to send a chilling signal to other governments considering similar regulations. Even when the plaintiffs lost, the litigation succeeded in delaying policies, consuming public resources, and raising doubts in legislatures worldwide. The case illustrates how lawfare thrives on time: delay itself becomes a strategic victory.

NGOs have also mastered this terrain, using courts to press states and companies on human rights, environmental obligations, and transparency. The Dutch NGO Urgenda's lawsuit compelling the government to reduce greenhouse gas emissions showed how judicial rulings could force national policy shifts with global implications. These cases reveal that lawfare is not simply a tool of the powerful. It can also empower weaker actors who lack financial or military leverage, but who can craft compelling legal arguments and mobilise public opinion around them.

The effect is amplified because litigation is never confined to legal journals. Every major case generates headlines, tweets, and television segments. The language of pleadings becomes material for press releases; court filings are timed to coincide with policy debates. In the digital age, even a provisional injunction can circulate worldwide within hours, shaping investor sentiment, regulatory postures, and diplomatic exchanges. Lawfare exploits this dynamic: courts provide the stage, but the real audience is global opinion. The judgment may take years, but the narrative impact is instantaneous.

The use of courts as strategic instruments raises questions about legitimacy. Critics argue that lawfare risks politicising the judiciary, eroding trust in legal institutions. If lawsuits are filed not primarily for resolution but for leverage, does this hollow out the rule of law? Yet others contend that this tension is not a corruption of law but a recognition of its true nature: law has always been political, and courts have always mediated between power and principle. The difference today is the scale of global interconnection and the sophistication of actors who exploit it.

What makes lawfare distinctive is not only the diversity of cases but their cumulative effect on norms. Every ruling, even when narrowly decided, contributes to precedent. Arbitrations set expectations for how future investment treaties will be interpreted. Human rights cases expand or contract the boundaries of accountability. Environmental rulings can establish obligations that ripple across industries. These outcomes show that lawfare is not merely tactical but normative: it shapes the terrain on which future conflicts will be fought.

The rise of strategic litigation also blurs the line between public and private interest. Corporations sue states to defend market access, while activists use the same mechanisms to constrain corporate behaviour. States themselves launch or sponsor cases to advance foreign policy aims. China has challenged WTO rulings, the United States has used domestic courts to enforce extraterritorial sanctions, and European governments have faced a wave of climate litigation. Each case is framed as a matter of justice, yet each also advances strategic goals. Lawfare thrives in this ambiguity.

For the attentive observer, the key is to see courts not as endpoints but as nodes in wider campaigns. A lawsuit against a corporation may be paired with shareholder activism, NGO reports, and media exposure. Investor-state arbitration may coincide with lobbying for treaty renegotiation. Even minor procedural motions can be amplified as victories or provocations, fuelling public narratives. Litigation is thus integrated into a broader ecosystem of influence, where law functions as both lever and signal.

The implications are profound. To underestimate lawfare is to misread modern power. The armies and navies of the twenty-first century are often legal teams, whose victories are measured in headlines, precedents, and the costs imposed on adversaries long before a gavel falls. The courtroom has become a stage on which actors rehearse struggles that shape the distribution of capital, the scope of sovereignty, and the norms of international order. The unanswered question is whether legal systems can sustain their legitimacy under this strain—or whether they will become indistinguishable from the political contests they increasingly host.

Extraterritoriality and forum shopping

In 2018, a small courtroom in Texas became the setting for a drama that reverberated through Asia's semiconductor industry. A judge's decision to grant a preliminary injunction in a patent dispute forced a major smartphone manufacturer to halt distribution of several models in China—despite the case being filed in the United States. Investors panicked, supply chains scrambled, and competitors gained breathing space. The lesson was clear: jurisdiction is not a neutral container of law but a weapon in its own right, one whose reach extends far beyond the borders on the courtroom walls.

The paradox is difficult to ignore. Law is nominally territorial, rooted in the sovereignty of a state. Yet in practice, litigants move across jurisdictions like traders seeking favourable markets. This practice—forum shopping—has become a core tactic of corporate and geopolitical contest. Plaintiffs weigh not only the substance of law but also the tempo of proceedings, the sympathy of judges, and the scope of discovery. In an interconnected economy, the choice of forum can determine not just the outcome of a case, but the speed of a rival's product launch, the security of an entire supply chain, or the direction of regulatory reform in multiple countries.

One striking example lies in the realm of antitrust enforcement. American courts have long been favoured for their expansive discovery rules, allowing plaintiffs to compel vast disclosures of internal documents. European regulators, by contrast, may be slower but wield powerful remedies that can reshape entire industries. When Qualcomm was targeted in competition cases, its rivals and regulators coordinated across jurisdictions—U.S. lawsuits providing the discovery, Chinese regulators applying pressure in licensing negotiations, and European authorities imposing fines. The mosaic of forums created a pressure cooker in which legal outcomes and market outcomes became inseparable.

Jurisdictional arbitrage also thrives in cross-border bankruptcy. When the shipping giant Hanjin collapsed in 2016, creditors and ports scrambled to secure assets across dozens of countries. The company's filings in South Korea, the United States, and Singapore triggered a jurisdictional race, with each court asserting authority over different fragments of the company's fleet and finances. For a time, ships laden with goods were stranded offshore because no port was certain which jurisdiction's orders would prevail. This was law as logistics in its most literal sense: the docket determined whether Christmas goods reached shelves on time.

Extraterritoriality complicates matters further. The United States, in particular, has extended its legal reach across borders by tying jurisdiction to dollar transactions, internet traffic, or even the presence of a correspondent bank. European banks processing Iranian payments, Asian firms supplying sanctioned entities, and Latin American subsidiaries of U.S. companies have all found themselves pulled into American courtrooms. For Washington, this reach is strategic leverage; for others, it is an intrusion into sovereignty. The tension is not simply legal but geopolitical, as states bristle at the idea that a foreign court can dictate domestic business decisions.

Critics of forum shopping argue that it undermines fairness: justice becomes a contest of resources, with those able to afford global legal teams choosing favourable venues while weaker parties are dragged along. Yet defenders note that forum choice can also be a counterweight, allowing smaller actors to find sympathetic venues when their home courts are captured or constrained. NGOs suing corporations over environmental damage often choose European jurisdictions precisely because local courts are unreliable. In this light, forum shopping is less manipulation than adaptation—an effort to find procedural justice in a fragmented world.

The choreography of filings reveals a deeper truth: litigation is not an isolated act but a timed intervention. A lawsuit filed in London may be synchronised with sanctions announced in Washington, creating a one-two punch that cripples a company's financing. An injunction secured in Munich may arrive just as a competitor launches a marketing campaign, turning a legal ruling into a commercial ambush. Lawyers speak of "docket strategy," but its significance lies far beyond law firms—it shapes when factories reopen, when shipments resume, and when markets stabilise.

Consider also how courts become amplifiers of diplomatic messages. When the European Union lodged competition cases against American tech giants, the filings were not only about market structure but about signalling Europe's regulatory stance to the world. Similarly, Chinese courts granting anti-suit injunctions against Western companies conveyed not just legal authority but geopolitical defiance. These cases highlight how forum shopping is not merely opportunistic manoeuvring but part of broader contests over norms, sovereignty, and power.

For businesses, the implication is sobering. It is no longer sufficient to track vendors and customers; firms must map the jurisdictions in which their adversaries might file claims. The logistics of law run parallel to the logistics of trade. A single filing can reroute a global supply chain, tie up assets, or expose sensitive data through discovery. The most resilient organisations treat courts as part of the operating environment, alongside ports, tariffs, and currencies.

The strategic use of jurisdiction raises a profound question: if law can be bent to strategic advantage in this way, what becomes of the promise of equal justice? Perhaps fairness lies not in the neutrality of any single court but in the competition between them—a global marketplace of legal forums where outcomes reflect not only statutes but power. Yet this competition, like all markets, risks volatility. Who decides when extraterritorial reach is legitimate and when it is coercion? Where is the boundary between tactical filing and abuse?

These unresolved tensions are what give extraterritoriality and forum shopping their enduring significance. To study them is to glimpse the machinery beneath global order, where law is not a constraint upon politics but one of its primary tools. The challenge for the reader is not merely to follow the cases but to map how law travels—how filings, injunctions, and judgments move through the arteries of commerce and diplomacy, carrying consequences far beyond the courthouse door.

Standards bodies and rule-writing

In 1981, a technical committee meeting in Geneva quietly decided the future of video playback. Two formats—VHS and Betamax—were vying for dominance. The formal victory of VHS was not sealed by consumer preference alone but by the intricate politics of standards bodies, licensing arrangements, and the momentum created by early adoption clauses. The story reminds us that wars are often won not on battlefields or in courtrooms but in committee rooms, where what looks like a minor procedural vote can define markets and shape geopolitics for decades.

The paradox of standards is that they are invisible until contested. We rarely notice the protocols that make Wi-Fi work, the safety requirements that allow planes to fly, or the reporting rules that govern cross-border banking. Yet within those standards lie choices that benefit some actors and burden others. Compliance is not neutral: it creates winners and losers. To participate in the writing of rules is to influence the architecture of global trade, technology, and security. That is why countries and corporations invest heavily in placing delegates on committees and working groups that most of the public has never heard of.

Participation, however, is only the beginning. The structure of decision-making—how votes are weighted, how consensus is defined, how objections can be stalled—shapes outcomes as much as the technical arguments. In the International Telecommunication Union (ITU), for example, each member state has one vote, regardless of its technological capacity. This empowers coalitions of smaller countries to swing outcomes, provided they are coordinated. In contrast, industry-led organisations like the Internet Engineering Task Force (IETF) operate by "rough consensus," a procedural culture that rewards persistence and technical credibility but can also be exploited by orchestrated campaigns.

Case studies reveal the stakes. When Chinese companies pushed for elements of their 5G proposals at the ITU and 3GPP, they were not merely arguing over bandwidth efficiency but embedding architectures that would advantage domestic manufacturers and align with state surveillance models. Western firms, in turn, mobilised diplomatic resources, dispatching not only engineers but also government envoys to influence votes. The decisions were coded into technical specifications, yet the underlying contest was geopolitical. The result was a clash that shaped global infrastructure and revealed standards bodies as arenas of statecraft.

Quiet victories in such forums often outlast spectacular legal wins. A lawsuit may delay a competitor's product launch by months; a standards vote can define the product's technical requirements for a decade. For example, the decision to make certain encryption methods optional rather than mandatory in early internet protocols created a legacy of vulnerabilities that governments later exploited for surveillance. Similarly, the choice of emissions testing methodologies at the United Nations Economic Commission for Europe determined the automotive industry's trajectory long before "Dieselgate" scandals brought attention to the manipulation of standards.

The tactics employed in these bodies are subtle but potent. Drafting early and seeding language in technical documents allows one side to set the frame of debate. Building coalitions of sympathetic delegates creates procedural momentum, especially when meetings are long and technical fatigue sets in. Even the scheduling of votes—late on a Friday, or at sessions in far-off locations—can tilt outcomes, favouring well-resourced delegations that can endure the grind. Standards politics is less about rhetoric than about endurance, process mastery, and foresight.

Critics argue that technical standards should be insulated from politics, that code and compliance should reflect objective efficiency. But this view underestimates the inherently normative nature of standards. To decide whether data must be stored locally or can flow across borders is not just a technical matter but a question of sovereignty. To specify acceptable levels of facial recognition accuracy is not just a statistical choice but an ethical stance on bias and discrimination. Standards bodies may cloak themselves in neutrality, yet every rule encodes a worldview.

The philosophical tension lies in the invisibility of these decisions. Citizens rarely scrutinise standards meetings, yet they live inside their consequences. Businesses often comply without understanding who wrote the rules or why. Even policymakers can be caught off guard when they realise that a strategic technology has been shaped by technical committees rather than legislatures. In this sense, standards bodies are battlegrounds hidden in plain sight: democratic oversight is thin, yet the outcomes rival treaties in their importance.

For those navigating this terrain, the imperative is twofold. First, to recognise that abstention is not neutrality. When firms or governments decline to participate, they leave the field to rivals who will fill the vacuum. Second, to build capacity—not only technical expertise but also procedural literacy, so that engineers and diplomats can operate fluently in the slow, grinding negotiations that define standards. Quiet victories are cumulative; neglect is equally cumulative in its costs.

As the digital and physical infrastructures of the world converge, the stakes of standards politics will only deepen. Who controls the protocols of artificial intelligence safety, quantum encryption, or supply-chain traceability will effectively control the levers of future commerce and security. Yet unlike court battles, whose outcomes are public, or diplomatic summits, which attract media glare, the drama of standards often unfolds unnoticed.

The unresolved question is whether societies can afford such invisibility. Should technical standards be treated with the transparency and scrutiny of international treaties? Or does the efficiency of global commerce depend on keeping these processes insulated from overt political contest? The answer remains uncertain, but what is clear is that those who master the rule-writing forums are not just writing code; they are scripting the future balance of power.

Naming, shaming, and the reputational lever

In January 1996, Shell faced a double storm: Greenpeace activists boarding its Brent Spar oil storage platform in the North Sea and an intensifying media campaign accusing the company of planning to dump the structure in the ocean. The ensuing outcry triggered boycotts in Germany, led to petrol stations being vandalised, and forced Shell into an abrupt U-turn. What began as a technical decision about decommissioning infrastructure turned into a reputational crisis with material costs. The lesson was clear: in modern conflict, the courtroom is only one arena. The court of public opinion, mobilised through naming and shaming, can be equally decisive.

This interplay between legal filings and reputational campaigns has become a hallmark of contemporary lawfare. A lawsuit, even before its merits are tested, can serve as a vehicle for narrative framing. The mere act of filing is often enough to generate headlines. These headlines, in turn, fuel coalition letters, activist reports, and press strategies designed to paint counterparties as irresponsible, unethical, or even dangerous. The strategy is not just to win the case but to raise the adversary's cost of capital, tighten their regulatory leash, and alter the risk calculus of their investors and lenders.

Litigation provides the skeleton; public campaigns supply the flesh. Consider the wave of climate-related lawsuits filed against oil majors in the 2010s. The suits themselves rarely delivered quick courtroom victories. But they gave activists a focal point for press conferences, social media pushes, and shareholder resolutions. When pension funds in Scandinavia or university endowments in the United States announced divestments, the real battlefield was not strictly legal—it was reputational, translated into financial terms. The balance sheet became the scoreboard.

The mechanics of these campaigns are both artful and deliberate. Press strategies often prioritise timing: releasing allegations on the eve of shareholder meetings, or coinciding with quarterly earnings calls, to maximise pressure. Coalition letters allow diverse groups—NGOs, unions, academics, faith leaders—to converge around a single narrative, lending it moral weight and breadth. Proxy reports, produced by seemingly independent research outfits, provide the evidentiary backbone that investors and journalists can cite. Each piece alone might be insufficient, but together they form an ecosystem of pressure designed to make the counterparty radioactive.

Corporations are acutely sensitive to this dynamic. A lawsuit may appear manageable when assessed only in terms of potential damages or legal fees. Yet once reputational risk is factored in—boycotts, regulatory scrutiny, investor unease—the cost multiplies. This is why many firms settle early, not out of legal weakness but to halt the narrative spiral. In some cases, the reputational blow is more damaging than the eventual legal outcome, especially in sectors dependent on consumer trust or regulatory goodwill.

The philosophical tension lies in the legitimacy of these tactics. On one hand, naming and shaming can serve the public good, exposing harmful practices that might otherwise remain hidden. It gives citizens, NGOs, and smaller states tools to challenge powerful actors in ways that traditional legal channels alone might not permit. On the other hand, the reputational lever can be wielded opportunistically, weaponising perception rather than fact. The danger is that guilt is presumed once headlines circulate, long before courts adjudicate.

Case sketches illustrate this duality. In mining, litigation over environmental damage in Latin America often overlaps with activist campaigns in Europe, where investors and regulators are more receptive to reputational arguments. In pharmaceuticals, lawsuits over opioid distribution were accompanied by meticulously orchestrated press exposés, turning courtroom evidence into a broader narrative about corporate negligence. And in technology, antitrust suits have been synchronised with campaigns that portray firms as monopolistic threats to democracy. In each instance, the legal and reputational tracks are braided together, inseparable and mutually reinforcing.

Yet the practice is not confined to NGOs or grassroots movements. States themselves deploy reputational levers through strategic litigation. Investor–state disputes are sometimes publicised not merely to recover damages but to stigmatise host governments as unreliable partners. Conversely, governments may highlight corporate litigation to signal to foreign investors that certain practices are unwelcome. The theatre of law, amplified by media choreography, becomes part of statecraft.

For those on the receiving end, the defensive challenge is profound. It is no longer enough to retain top-tier legal counsel; firms must also prepare communication strategies, investor briefings, and stakeholder outreach to blunt reputational fallout. The skill set required blends law, public relations, finance, and geopolitics. A courtroom victory is hollow if the reputational damage lingers, reshaping capital flows and regulatory attention.

The unresolved tension is whether reputational campaigns enhance justice or distort it. Does raising the cost of capital for a polluter, for instance, accelerate accountability where courts are too slow? Or does the intertwining of legal briefs and media narratives risk creating a system where perception eclipses fact, where headlines, not judgments, deliver the decisive blow? The answers are not fixed, and the consequences ripple far beyond any single case. For in the age of invisible wars, it is not only tanks or treaties that matter, but also the fragile currency of trust—and how quickly it can be devalued.

Defending against legal overmatch

When Chevron faced a multi-billion-dollar judgment in Ecuador over environmental damage, its lawyers did not simply prepare appeals. They launched a global counter-litigation campaign, challenging enforcement efforts across multiple jurisdictions, discrediting opposing counsel, and leveraging international treaties to limit exposure. The case illustrates a sobering reality: in legal contests, the party with deeper resources and sharper preparation often dictates the battlefield. For smaller firms, NGOs, or states, this imbalance can feel like facing an opponent armed not only with better lawyers but also with time, patience, and political reach. The paradox of lawfare is that the law, intended as a leveller, becomes another domain where asymmetry thrives.

The concept of *legal overmatch* arises when one side enjoys structural advantages: vast in-house legal teams, budgets that allow endless motions and appeals, or treaties whose clauses favour incumbents. The danger is not merely losing a case but being worn down by process itself—through delay, discovery burdens, or reputational attrition. To defend effectively, organisations must treat legal preparedness as a strategic discipline, not a reactive cost centre.

Pre-emptive audits form the first line of defence. Too often, vulnerabilities emerge not from malice but from neglect: inconsistent record-keeping, poorly drafted contracts, or ambiguous compliance practices. A proactive review—of supply-chain agreements, intellectual property filings, and employment policies—functions like a stress test. By simulating potential disputes before they occur, firms can identify points of leverage an adversary might exploit. These exercises are not glamorous, but they dramatically reduce the element of surprise when litigation arrives.

Equally critical is **treaty literacy**. Multinationals and even states have discovered too late that bilateral investment treaties or free trade agreements include investor–state dispute settlement mechanisms that allow counterparties to escalate grievances to international arbitration. A government regulation aimed at protecting public health, for instance, can be challenged as an expropriation of corporate assets. Firms that understand these instruments in advance can tailor policies or contractual structures to minimise exposure. Conversely, NGOs and states can identify treaty provisions that might bolster their defensive stance, ensuring they are not blindsided by clauses drafted decades earlier under very different assumptions.

Then comes the necessity of **rapid-response counsel**. In reputationally sensitive disputes, the first 72 hours after a filing can determine whether the narrative solidifies against a defendant. Swift engagement—both in court and in the public sphere—prevents an adversary from framing the story unopposed. This does not mean rushing arguments, but rather having pre-agreed protocols: who authorises statements, which law firms are on standby, and how evidence is marshalled at speed. Litigation today unfolds as much in headlines and social media feeds as in hearing rooms; delay is tantamount to concession.

Yet even with preparation, there are limits to classic defensive tools. **Non-disclosure agreements (NDAs)** and settlements, for example, can no longer be relied upon as blanket shields. Courts and regulators have grown sceptical of NDAs used to silence whistle-blowers or conceal systemic issues. Confidential settlements may halt one lawsuit but invite scrutiny elsewhere, as counterparties or journalists interpret secrecy as an admission of guilt. The defensive calculus must weigh not just the immediate legal relief but the long-term reputational trajectory. In some contexts, transparency—acknowledging weaknesses and outlining reforms—may blunt more attacks than secrecy ever could.

The deeper challenge is cultural. A firm can have watertight policies and elite lawyers, yet still falter if employees fear reporting anomalies. Counterintelligence lessons apply here: shame-free reporting mechanisms and rotating access privileges are essential for spotting early signs of legal risk, from compliance shortcuts to contract mismanagement. By cultivating a culture where raising concerns is rewarded rather than punished, organisations build the internal radar that prevents small missteps from escalating into existential threats.

Defending against legal overmatch also demands philosophical clarity. It requires asking: what is the boundary between legitimate legal defence and aggressive obstruction? Resource-rich actors can bury adversaries in motions or discovery requests, yet in doing so they risk public condemnation for abusing process. Conversely, under-resourced actors may resort to publicity campaigns that shift the fight from courtrooms to newsrooms. Navigating this terrain demands not only tactical skill but also a principled understanding of legitimacy, lest defence itself becomes another form of reputational liability.

National competitiveness is bound up in these dynamics. A country whose firms are repeatedly blindsided by cross-border litigation will see investment chilled and innovation stifled. By contrast, firms with maturity models that institutionalise legal hygiene—audits, treaty awareness, rapid response, cultural resilience—become less vulnerable to surprise, more agile in adaptation, and more credible partners internationally. Legal preparedness is not simply a defensive measure; it is part of strategic capacity in a world where courts are theatres of geopolitical competition.

The unresolved tension remains: can smaller players ever truly defend against adversaries who can outspend and outlast them? Preparation narrows the gap, but does not erase it. The ethical dilemma of asymmetry lingers—whether justice is served when victory depends less on right and wrong than on resources deployed. Yet it is precisely by confronting this uncomfortable truth that firms, governments, and civil society can craft practices that restore some balance, however imperfect. The alternative—resignation to surprise and defeat—is no defence at all.

Chapter 7

Cyber Operations Without Cyber Hysteria

When a major city briefly lost power in the dead of winter, headlines screamed of "cyber Pearl Harbor" and "digital 9/11". Commentators spoke in absolutes: civilisation itself perched on the brink of collapse. Yet the truth, later revealed, was more prosaic. A limited intrusion, quietly contained, had disrupted control systems long enough to spark fear, not catastrophe. The gap between what actually occurred and how it was framed is the heart of the cyber problem: not what systems can do, but what people believe they might do.

For two decades, cyber has been a word that stirs more panic than precision. Military planners invoke it as the invisible fifth domain of warfare. Journalists attach it to every breach, hack, or malfunction. Corporations and governments alike inflate threats, sometimes sincerely, sometimes strategically, to justify budgets or legal powers. Lost in the noise is a sober truth: cyber operations are potent, but not limitless. They are tools of espionage, sabotage, and signalling, each with distinct logics and limitations. Confusing them has fuelled both hype and misallocation, leaving societies simultaneously over-fearful and under-prepared.

This chapter sets out to reclaim perspective. It does not deny that code can topple centrifuges or black out neighbourhoods. But it resists the theatrical imagination that equates every phishing email with Armageddon. Cyber operations, like all instruments of statecraft and commerce, are constrained by physics, economics, and human behaviour. Attackers rely on patience, persistence, and careful pre-positioning; defenders succeed not by eliminating risk but by raising the cost of intrusion and shrinking the window of opportunity. The drama lies not in spectacular explosions but in the slow grind of infiltration, discovery, and adaptation.

We begin by separating sabotage, espionage, and signalling—three categories too often collapsed into the catch-all of "cyberattack". Sabotage seeks disruption of infrastructure or services, but it is risky and rarely sustained. Espionage, by contrast, thrives on invisibility, siphoning information in ways that can shape negotiation tables and boardrooms for years. Signalling operates in the theatre of perception, where states leak proof of compromise not to damage, but to warn or deter. Understanding these distinctions clears the fog of magical thinking and replaces it with operational clarity.

From there, we trace how successful campaigns privilege persistence over spectacle. The most dangerous adversaries are not those who launch noisy assaults but those who live quietly inside systems—exploiting trusted tools, abusing legitimate processes, and shaping data without detection. The stories of long dwell times and poisoned updates reveal that patience, not payload, is the true measure of cyber power. This insight demands a reframing of priorities: budgets should tilt towards detection, response, and resilience rather than cinematic attribution hunts.

We then move outward, to the infrastructures that stitch the digital world together. Domains, routing protocols, content distribution networks, and cloud control planes are not just technical curiosities; they are coercive choke points. Whoever controls them holds levers of economic and diplomatic influence, able to tilt negotiations or pressure rivals without firing a shot. The seams between public and private custodianship are where both vulnerability and leverage accumulate. To understand cyber is to understand these seams.

Attribution introduces another paradox. States sometimes rush to publish evidence of adversary campaigns, while at other times they cloak incidents in silence. The decisions are not purely technical—they are policy acts. A glossy intelligence report, carefully redacted, is as much a message as an analysis. The ambiguity surrounding attribution is not a flaw of the system; it is part of the system, enabling deniability for some and deterrence for others. Readers must learn to read these revelations not as neutral disclosures but as deliberate instruments in a wider strategy.

Finally, the chapter closes by returning to the mundane, where resilience is built. Asset clarity, immutable backups, and disciplined drills matter far more than grandiose visions of cyber doomsday. The real ethic of cyber defence lies in seeing resilience as a civic duty—an obligation not only of corporations and governments but of citizens who depend daily on digital lifelines. Measuring dwell times, constraining lateral movement, and shrinking recovery windows may not capture headlines, but they decide whether societies weather storms or spiral into panic.

What emerges is a chapter that neither dismisses nor dramatises. Cyber is serious, but it is not sorcery. It is a field where power accrues not through spectacle but through structure, patience, and design. The reader is invited to step beyond hype into clarity, to see both the menace and the limits, and to carry forward an ethic of measured vigilance. The hysteria is unnecessary; the risks are real; and the wisdom lies in knowing the difference.

What cyber can and cannot do

When a piece of malicious code known as Stuxnet was discovered in 2010, analysts quickly grasped its significance: here was software engineered not to steal data but to spin Iranian centrifuges into self-destruction. For many observers, it confirmed the long-feared arrival of digital weapons that could leap from the screen into the physical world. The headlines came thick with metaphors of apocalypse. Yet a quieter truth emerged beneath the hysteria: Stuxnet was neither universal nor unstoppable. It was targeted, labour-intensive, and contingent on deep intelligence about a very particular industrial system. It was proof of possibility, not inevitability.

The paradox of cyber power lies here. It is simultaneously overestimated and underestimated. Overestimated when it is cast as an all-purpose doomsday switch, capable of collapsing entire societies at the push of a button. Underestimated when its true strengths—stealth, persistence, and access—are dismissed as minor nuisances compared to conventional weapons. The real measure of cyber lies not in Hollywood scenarios but in its distinct logics: sabotage, espionage, and signalling. Each operates differently, with different constraints, risks, and strategic payoffs.

Sabotage sits at the most visible end of the spectrum. It captures attention precisely because it is rare. Knocking out Ukraine's power grids in 2015 and 2016 or tampering with water utilities in the United States show what disruption looks like. But the very visibility of sabotage makes it costly. Once detected, systems can be patched, defenders harden their posture, and political blowback may exceed any short-term disruption. Sabotage demonstrates capability, but its strategic shelf-life is short. It is the spectacular act that makes headlines but seldom rewrites balance sheets or treaties.

By contrast, **espionage** is the quiet workhorse of cyber operations. It is not designed to make lights flicker but to siphon information. Corporate R&D pipelines, diplomatic cables, military logistics, and health records are all targets for those who understand that knowledge can shift negotiations or shape markets more effectively than destruction ever could. Consider the breach of the US Office of Personnel Management in 2015, which exposed security clearance files of millions of officials. No system was brought down, but the long-term intelligence value—insight into backgrounds, habits, and vulnerabilities—was enormous. Espionage thrives on patience: months or even years of undetected presence. Its power lies in accumulation rather than spectacle.

Then there is **signalling**, the most misunderstood category. Here the purpose is neither to destroy nor to collect, but to send a message. When governments reveal a cyber intrusion, they are not simply exposing the adversary—they are choosing to communicate. A carefully timed press release or threat intelligence report may be intended to deter further action, rally allies, or justify new regulations. Ambiguity is the point. By leaving just enough proof on the table, states project capability while preserving deniability. The announcement becomes part of diplomacy, a tool in negotiations, and a way of shaping perceptions both at home and abroad.

Seen together, these categories show why apocalypse scenarios are misleading. Cyber is not a magic button that collapses economies overnight. Its greatest influence comes from the interplay of patience and perception. The most effective campaigns are those that slowly entrench access, map systems, and exfiltrate data—what professionals call pre-positioning. Malware discovered on critical infrastructure is often less about triggering chaos now and more about leaving options for leverage later. The danger is not always in what happens today but in the latent capability for tomorrow.

This has profound implications for policy and enterprise practice. Governments that prepare only for cinematic sabotage miss the slow erosion of advantage through espionage. Companies that focus solely on perimeter defence risk overlooking insider compromise or long-term surveillance. Conversely, overhyping existential threats can lead to wasteful spending and distorted priorities, where money flows to theatrical deterrents rather than resilient baselines. Sobriety, not hysteria, is the foundation of effective strategy.

The temptation to imagine cyber as omnipotent is understandable. It plays on ancient fears of invisible enemies and unseen sabotage. Yet the logic of cyber is neither mystical nor limitless. It is bounded by the need for access, by the fragility of tools once exposed, and by the calculus of retaliation. Just as Stuxnet required intimate engineering knowledge, every operation depends on context. A tool built for one plant, one router, or one application does not automatically scale to others.

But to downplay cyber is equally dangerous. The theft of trade secrets worth billions, the manipulation of political discourse through strategic leaks, the quiet shaping of supply chains—all demonstrate that digital operations can tilt global balances without firing a shot. The challenge is not to decide whether cyber is decisive or trivial, but to understand what it can and cannot do.

The lines separating sabotage, espionage, and signalling are not neat. A single intrusion may contain elements of all three: pre-positioning for sabotage, harvesting intelligence, and leaving breadcrumbs for deterrence. Untangling these threads is the task of policymakers, executives, and citizens alike. Each must learn to read beyond the headlines, to see the difference between noise and signal, panic and precision.

What cyber can do is reshape incentives, unsettle assumptions, and provide levers of influence that are often invisible until they matter most. What it cannot do is suspend the rules of strategy, erase the constraints of politics, or replace the fundamentals of resilience. The theatre of cyber is real, but its scripts are subtler than catastrophe. The question, then, is whether societies can discipline themselves to focus less on imagined apocalypses and more on the slow, cumulative pressures that truly shift the world.

Campaign design: persistence over spectacle

In 2020, when the SolarWinds breach was disclosed, the shock was not about fireworks. No critical infrastructure had collapsed, no airports shut down, no public displays of chaos. What unsettled investigators was the opposite: the extraordinary quietness of it all. Malicious code had slipped into a widely trusted software update, and for months, adversaries sat inside networks across governments and corporations without announcing themselves. The campaign was not designed for a cinematic climax. It was built for persistence. It was about remaining unnoticed long enough to extract, map, and prepare. The most powerful cyber operations are rarely the loudest.

The paradox is stark. In public imagination, cyber conflict resembles a Hollywood script—lights going dark, missiles misfiring, chaos unfolding in seconds. In reality, the currency of success is not shock but dwell time. An adversary that lurks silently inside an organisation for six months gains more strategic value than one who detonates a payload in six minutes. The longer the residence, the greater the opportunity to steal, influence, and shape. Cyber power is not an explosion; it is an occupation.

Living off the land exemplifies this philosophy. Rather than dropping conspicuous malware, intruders exploit the tools already embedded in a system: administrative consoles, scripting languages, and cloud-native functions. These are legitimate instruments, used daily by staff. Their dual-use nature blurs the line between normal and malicious, allowing attackers to blend into the background noise of IT operations. By hiding in plain sight, adversaries extend their tenure, ensuring they can extract more than any destructive strike would ever yield.

The craft extends further into **quiet data shaping**. Adversaries do not merely copy information; they may alter logs, adjust configurations, or subtly skew datasets. These shifts are rarely dramatic enough to trigger alarms. Instead, they warp decision-making over time, planting small distortions that accumulate into strategic advantage. A supply chain's timelines may appear consistently longer than they are. A financial model may quietly undervalue risk. These operations reveal why persistence matters more than payload: the true power lies not in a crash, but in a drift.

For defenders, this demands a reframing of priorities. Too often, boards and policymakers invest in dramatic capabilities designed to stop spectacular attacks. Attribution reports—who did it, from where, and with what tool—become the public climax of a breach narrative. Yet attribution is often secondary. The crucial task is *detection* and *ejection*: finding the intruder earlier, disrupting their dwell time, and limiting what they can achieve. Spending that prioritises rapid anomaly detection, lateral movement monitoring, and response drills does more to protect value than chasing after geopolitical theatre.

This recalibration forces a cultural shift. Executives accustomed to demanding instant answers about "who" must learn to ask about "how long" and "how deeply." Security teams need the latitude to treat intrusions not as failures of defence but as inevitable frictions to be managed. Just as every lock can be picked, every digital barrier can be tested. What matters is not the absence of breach but the speed of recognition and the efficiency of expulsion.

The strategic patience of adversaries also invites philosophical reflection. In human affairs, endurance has always outlasted spectacle. Empires crumble not through a single dramatic defeat but through years of incremental erosion. Cyber mirrors this pattern. To obsess over the spectacular is to mistake theatre for substance. The enduring contest is fought in the shadows, through repetition and persistence, through the mundane grind of occupying rather than obliterating.

Consider how this perspective reframes national strategy. A government confronted with frequent, low-level intrusions must decide whether to expend political capital on public accusation or to quietly strengthen detection capacities. Too much emphasis on spectacle risks exhausting credibility. Too little attention to persistence risks ceding the field. Balance is found not in dramatic retaliation but in resilience, in raising the baseline so that long-term occupation becomes costly and unsustainable.

For companies, the lesson is equally stark. Cybersecurity spending skewed towards visible deterrents or brand protection may impress shareholders, but it leaves the core unguarded. Investment in log analysis, behavioural monitoring, and staff drills may be less glamorous, but it is these capabilities that decide whether an adversary dwells for days or for years. The quietest line items in a budget often carry the greatest weight.

What makes this discussion unsettling is the asymmetry it reveals. Spectacle is easy to narrate and politicise. Persistence is difficult to detect, harder to explain, and costly to address. The incentive structures of media, politics, and corporate governance naturally privilege the visible. Yet the strategic contest unfolds beneath the visible line, in the long stretches of silence where adversaries entrench themselves.

The unresolved question is whether societies can discipline themselves to privilege patience over drama, substance over theatre. Will boards and governments learn to reward investments in the invisible, or will budgets continue to chase headlines? In cyber conflict, the campaigns that matter most are not those that erupt in noise but those that whisper and endure. The real contest is whether defenders can learn to hear the whispers before the walls give way.

Infrastructure as leverage

When Pakistan sought to block access to YouTube in 2008, it did not censor content locally. Instead, a misconfiguration—or, as some argued, a deliberate redirection—on its domestic internet routers propagated through the Border Gateway Protocol (BGP), the digital signpost system that directs global traffic. Within hours, much of the world could not reach the platform. A national censorship order had spilled into a global outage, not through malice or malware, but through a tweak in infrastructure rules. The incident revealed a truth few outside the technical community had grasped: whoever controls the choke points of the internet can shape what billions see, trade, and communicate.

This paradox defines modern cyber operations. We often imagine power online as residing in code—malware, exploits, firewalls. Yet the deepest levers are infrastructural. Domain Name System (DNS) servers, BGP routes, content delivery networks (CDNs), and cloud control planes are the bones and arteries of the digital realm. Whoever commands them can disrupt adversaries, coerce compliance, or quietly tilt markets. These levers are less visible than bombs or sanctions, but no less potent. The geopolitics of the 21st century runs not only through oil pipelines and shipping lanes, but through protocols and data centres.

Take DNS, often described as the internet's "phonebook." By deciding how domain names resolve into addresses, authorities can make a site disappear as effectively as demolishing its physical headquarters. DNS blocking has been wielded as a sanctions tool, from cutting off pirate streaming hubs to limiting access to sanctioned financial institutions. Yet the power runs deeper: control over root servers, managed by a small set of organisations and overseen in part by U.S. and allied entities, embeds strategic advantage into technical plumbing. For all the talk of decentralisation, the internet still rests on concentrated points of authority.

BGP carries its own vulnerabilities. The protocol assumes good faith announcements about which networks control which addresses. That assumption has been abused repeatedly, sometimes for espionage, sometimes by accident. In 2018, traffic to Google services was briefly routed through China and Russia, a reminder that redirection can be orchestrated with little notice. Such events reveal that global commerce—payments, logistics, cloud applications—can be slowed, intercepted, or disrupted by infrastructure manipulation. The capacity to hijack flows without firing a shot places BGP in the arsenal of coercive tools, even if it is rarely acknowledged in formal doctrine.

Content delivery networks add another layer of leverage. By caching content close to users, CDNs accelerate speed and reduce strain. But they also act as gatekeepers. During political crises, governments have leaned on CDN providers to restrict or throttle content, knowing that control of a handful of providers translates into control of global distribution. More subtly, CDNs shape the economic terrain: a provider's decision to prioritise or deprioritise certain traffic can influence which businesses thrive and which languish. In disputes over censorship or licensing, the infrastructure itself becomes the bargaining chip.

Cloud control planes extend this logic into the corporate heart of modern life. A few global providers host critical data and workloads for governments, banks, and firms. The authority to suspend accounts, adjust service levels, or limit access functions as an invisible sanction mechanism. When Russia invaded Ukraine, Western cloud providers curtailed services for Russian institutions. The move was not simply technical housekeeping; it was a strategic gesture, demonstrating how private actors now exercise coercive influence once reserved for states. In effect, infrastructure has become both battlefield and diplomatic theatre.

These examples reveal a crucial seam: the fusion of public and private control. States do not own the internet's arteries outright. Instead, they regulate, coerce, or partner with the firms that do. This creates ambiguity. Who is responsible for defending global routing tables against hijacks—national cyber commands, or private carriers? When cloud providers act to suspend adversary accounts, are they enacting state policy, or pre-empting it? The blurred line between private infrastructure and public strategy complicates governance and forces us to rethink where national security truly resides.

The diplomatic implications are profound. Traditional coercion—sanctions, tariffs, military posturing—operates in visible arenas. Infrastructure leverage works in the shadows. A routing table adjustment can accomplish what years of negotiations might not. A cloud suspension can impose costs faster than a tribunal. Yet because these moves appear technical, they often evade scrutiny or democratic debate. The language of "network maintenance" or "terms of service" masks decisions with geopolitical weight. This opacity serves both states and companies, but it leaves publics uncertain about who truly governs the networks they depend upon.

Philosophically, the infrastructure-as-leverage paradigm challenges our understanding of sovereignty. The notion of territorial borders fades when disruption can be routed through cables and protocols controlled across jurisdictions. Power flows less from who holds territory than from who administers the technical rules of interconnection. It is sovereignty reimagined as configuration file and service agreement. For policymakers trained in the vocabulary of borders and treaties, this is disorienting terrain. Yet for adversaries who grasp it, the terrain is ripe for exploitation.

Defensively, the challenge is to build resilience not only in endpoints and applications but in the connective tissue itself. Efforts to secure DNS with DNSSEC, to monitor BGP anomalies, to diversify CDN reliance, and to negotiate cloud contracts with contingency planning are all attempts to mitigate this dependence. But each measure encounters political resistance: firms resist transparency that could reveal business practices; states hesitate to cede authority to multilateral governance. The very distribution of power across public and private spheres makes systemic resilience hard to achieve.

The unresolved tension is whether societies will continue to treat infrastructure as a neutral utility or acknowledge it as a battlefield. If the latter, we must grapple with new ethical and strategic dilemmas. Should cloud providers act as instruments of foreign policy? Should BGP misconfigurations be treated as accidents or as acts of war? Should infrastructure governance be internationalised to reduce coercion, or would that simply create new arenas of competition?

What is clear is that control of the internet's plumbing is no longer merely technical. It is coercive, strategic, and contested. The question is whether we will learn to see these choke points as levers of power before they are pulled in ways that leave us with no choice but to notice.

Attribution, signalling, and plausible deniability

In April 2021, a joint statement from the United States, the United Kingdom, and the European Union attributed a sprawling cyber-espionage campaign—known as Hafnium—to China. The press release was notable not for its technical detail, but for what it chose not to include. The forensic evidence remained classified, the narrative of compromise was partial, and the sanctions announced were modest. Yet the point was not proof; it was theatre. By naming China publicly, the states involved were less concerned with persuading experts than with broadcasting a message to multiple audiences: adversaries, allies, markets, and domestic publics. Attribution was policy, not prosecution.

This moment captures the paradox of cyber attributions. They are both declarations of fact and tools of strategy. The evidence may be technical—IP addresses, malware families, time zones of compilation—but the act of attribution is political. States decide *when* to reveal, *how much* to reveal, and *why*. In some cases, silence speaks louder than exposure. When intrusions are quietly monitored rather than publicly condemned, it signals tolerance or a desire to learn. When a breach is loudly denounced, it often means the strategic calculus favours deterrence over secrecy.

The ambiguity is not a flaw; it is the feature. In traditional warfare, clarity of authorship is assumed—an artillery shell lands, and its trajectory can be traced. In cyber operations, the chain of custody is inherently murky. False flags, proxy actors, and shared tools blur responsibility. Into that fog, attribution statements inject selective light. The goal is rarely to resolve doubt completely; it is to steer perception in directions that suit national interests.

The theatre of threat intelligence reports illustrates this dynamic. Commercial firms and state agencies release analyses of campaigns, often accompanied by catchy operation names and maps of global infections. These reports are read by policymakers, journalists, and corporate boards, not just technical audiences. What is shown is carefully curated: enough indicators to demonstrate credibility, but rarely the crown-jewel intelligence that could compromise sources. What is withheld is equally important: specific access methods, operational tradecraft, or links that reveal ongoing surveillance. Reports are thus less forensic artefacts than crafted performances, designed to shape norms, reassure stakeholders, and intimidate rivals.

Consider Russia's position. The Kremlin has consistently denied involvement in cyber operations even when confronted with detailed accusations—from the 2016 U.S. election interference to the NotPetya attack of 2017. The denials are implausible, but they serve a purpose. Plausible deniability sustains strategic ambiguity, complicating proportional response. By denying, Russia forces adversaries to either escalate without incontrovertible proof or swallow the cost in silence. This dynamic keeps the playing field advantageous to the actor who thrives in the grey zone.

China adopts a more measured variation. It often frames accusations as Western smear campaigns, while simultaneously investing heavily in domestic cyber capacity. By not accepting responsibility, Beijing avoids legal culpability, while signalling to domestic audiences that it resists external pressure. Meanwhile, careful observers note that Chinese cyber tactics align with broader strategic objectives: industrial policy, Belt and Road expansion, and geopolitical positioning. The attribution debate becomes less about whether China did it—most assume it did—and more about what the *accusation* is meant to achieve.

There are contrasting philosophies among democratic states as well. Some favour radical transparency, publishing detailed indictments and unsealing court documents, as the U.S. Department of Justice has done in charging named officers of foreign militaries. Others prefer quiet diplomacy, raising issues bilaterally without public exposure. Each approach has costs. Public attribution can burn intelligence sources and invite counter-disclosures. Silence can embolden adversaries or undermine allied trust. Balancing secrecy with deterrence is therefore less about finding a formula than about adjusting to the moment.

Philosophically, attribution raises questions about truth and performance. When states curate evidence and time disclosures for maximum effect, do they erode trust in the very concept of fact? Or do they simply acknowledge that facts are always filtered through strategy? For citizens and institutions navigating this terrain, scepticism must be disciplined rather than cynical: to ask not only *what happened* but *why are we being told this now, in this way?* Learning to read attribution as policy instrument rather than pure revelation is a civic skill in the digital age.

Practically, attribution also interacts with markets. Public announcements of breaches can tank share prices, trigger regulatory scrutiny, and reshape corporate strategy overnight. A company named as the victim of state-linked intrusion may face reputational damage even if it was targeted precisely because of its strategic importance, not its negligence. Conversely, threat intelligence firms gain visibility and credibility through public attributions, feeding a cycle where commercial incentives shape the narrative of national security.

For adversaries, ambiguity provides cover to probe, persist, and experiment. For defenders, the ambiguity complicates response but also creates space for signalling restraint. The dance of disclosure, denial, and deterrence becomes a dialogue, conducted through press releases, technical blogs, and diplomatic communiqués. The stage is crowded, the lines rehearsed, but the outcome remains unpredictable.

The unresolved question is whether this strategic ambiguity stabilises or destabilises. Does plausible deniability prevent escalation by giving states off-ramps, or does it normalise a culture of impunity where intrusions proliferate unchecked? The answer is not clear, and perhaps cannot be. What is certain is that attribution in cyberspace will remain a contest of narratives as much as a contest of code. To understand it is to see the world not in binaries of true or false, guilty or innocent, but in the subtler shades of signal and silence.

Building resilient baselines

In March 2021, the city of Oldsmar, Florida, made headlines when its water treatment system was almost sabotaged by a remote intrusion. The attacker attempted to raise the sodium hydroxide levels to toxic concentrations. What saved the town was not an advanced cyber shield, nor an intelligence tip-off. It was a baseline: an alert operator who noticed the anomaly and reverted the change before it spread harm. The drama captured global attention, but the lesson was quieter—resilience is often less about spectacular defences than about *preparedness*, *clarity*, and *habits*.

Resilience begins with the floor, not the ceiling. It is tempting for firms and governments to chase the latest detection technologies, hire expensive response teams, or invest in artificial intelligence to predict threats. Yet without a clear map of what assets exist, how they connect, and who is responsible, the most sophisticated detection system is like a smoke alarm installed in a building whose exits are bricked up. Asset clarity—knowing not just the devices but also the dependencies, the legacy systems, and the shadow IT—is the first practice of a resilient baseline. You cannot defend what you cannot see, and you cannot recover what you never inventoried.

Beyond visibility lies durability. Immutable backups—copies of critical data stored in a manner that cannot be altered by an attacker once written—represent the quiet strength of modern resilience. Ransomware syndicates thrive on exploiting the panic of organisations that lack safe, untouchable copies of their systems. Immutable storage flips the script: recovery becomes a matter of time and logistics, not ransom payments. The simplicity is deceptive; immutability is not a magic shield, but when combined with disciplined testing and separation of storage locations, it transforms what could be an existential crisis into a recoverable disruption.

Tabletop drills add the human dimension. Scenarios played out around a conference table may appear modest compared to technical simulations, yet they achieve something vital: they force decision-makers to *live* through uncertainty before the real event arrives. Who declares an incident? Who talks to regulators, to customers, to the press? How are trade-offs made between disclosure and containment? Practised in advance, these conversations strip away hesitation when time is most precious. A drill does not prevent a breach, but it reduces the chaos of response—turning panic into procedure.

Metrics anchor these practices in reality. Dwell time—the length an adversary remains undetected—is perhaps the most telling measure of resilience. Attackers rarely strike at once; they linger, probe, escalate. Shrinking dwell time requires not omniscience, but layers of monitoring, anomaly detection, and healthy scepticism. Similarly, measuring the cost of lateral movement—how difficult it is for an intruder to pivot from one compromised system to another—reveals whether an organisation has true segmentation or merely decorative firewalls. Finally, recovery windows—how quickly core services can be restored—speak to the lived resilience of a system, where the gap between technical theory and operational reality is most often exposed.

The discipline of baselines is not only technical but cultural. Shame-free reporting matters as much as firewalls. If employees fear reprisal for clicking a malicious link or misconfiguring a system, small incidents will fester into systemic breaches. Cultures that encourage immediate reporting, paired with constructive response, outpace those that punish. Likewise, rotating access—ensuring no single insider holds unchecked, long-term control—reduces both malicious risk and the fatigue that leads to negligence. These cultural practices often cost less than advanced tooling, yet they yield more durable security.

The deeper insight is that resilience is cumulative. Micro-habits, from patching schedules to credential hygiene, aggregate into macro-resilience: the ability of a society to withstand shocks without collapse. This is why resilience is not only a corporate or governmental task but a civic one. Just as public health depends on individual hygiene and collective norms, so too does digital resilience rest on the ordinary decisions of organisations, employees, and citizens. Resilience is not the absence of breach, but the capacity to absorb and adapt without surrendering function or trust.

Yet an unresolved tension remains. By raising baselines, societies reduce the likelihood of catastrophic failure. But they may also normalise a condition of constant low-level intrusion, where adversaries continue to probe without triggering alarm. Does resilience, in this sense, become complicity—acceptance of a world where adversaries are always inside, just managed rather than repelled? Or does it represent maturity: the recognition that in the age of persistent cyber operations, strength lies not in perfect defence but in the refusal to be destabilised? The answer lies not in the abstract but in practice, in how each organisation and citizen chooses to treat resilience—as a box-ticking exercise, or as a duty to one another.

Chapter 8

PsyOps at Civilian Scale

On the eve of the Second World War, British officials wrestled with a fear greater than bombs: panic. The memory of the First World War's shell shock and mutinies lingered, and policymakers dreaded that morale on the home front might collapse under air raids. What they discovered, to their surprise, was the opposite. Even as bombs fell on London, communities adapted with a kind of stubborn defiance. People lit cigarettes in shattered buildings, went dancing among rubble, and coined jokes in the shelters. The state learned something that remains true today: civilian morale is not merely a backdrop to conflict—it is an instrument of power, one that can be fostered, fractured, and redirected.

Now that same insight is playing out on digital platforms, in advertising exchanges, and across political campaigns. Psychological operations, once the preserve of military units targeting foreign soldiers, now reach into the lives of ordinary citizens through memes, hashtags, tailored videos, and targeted ads. These campaigns may not carry the shock of artillery, but they alter something more enduring: how people think, feel, and trust. When civic trust is raised or lowered by design, when identity salience is pressed like a button, then the battlefield is no longer a front line—it is the everyday mind.

The paradox is stark. Democratic societies pride themselves on open debate, yet that very openness provides fertile ground for manipulation. Segmentation tools designed for consumer choice are repurposed for shaping political identities. Priming techniques borrowed from behavioural science are weaponised to amplify grievances or soothe dissent. The effect is cumulative. When repeated at scale, small nudges ripple outward into voter turnout, compliance with public health measures, or willingness to support sanctions. What looks like noise on a feed is, in reality, the steady recalibration of collective mood.

This chapter treats emotions not as ephemera but as infrastructure. Fear can harden borders, pride can mobilise sacrifice, disgust can fracture cooperation. States and non-state actors alike have begun to treat these levers with the same seriousness as pipelines or shipping routes. Marketing science has long known how to link feeling with action; now statecraft absorbs those lessons with unnerving fluency. The ethical stakes are high. When governments normalise emotional manipulation within their own societies, they risk corroding the very trust that sustains democracy. Yet ignoring the phenomenon is equally perilous: adversaries are unlikely to share such scruples.

Compact stories—memes, rituals, slogans—prove more resilient than dense reports or nuanced truths. Energy debates are often captured not by climate data but by the symbolic force of a photograph of a coal worker's hands. Migration arguments rarely hinge on demographic analysis but on the emotional tug of a single anecdote. Rituals, whether flag ceremonies or viral challenges, work because they encode belonging and repetition. Whoever writes the stickiest stories governs the perception of reality. That is why counter-rituals and narrative inoculation matter: they provide cultural hygiene without collapsing into censorship.

Oversight is perhaps the hardest frontier. Microtargeting thrives in the opacity of digital advertising and private datasets. Regulators struggle to see what messages were served, to whom, and with what effect. The ad auction, optimised for revenue, was never designed for democratic accountability. Yet there are paths forward. Privacy-preserving audits, comparative regulatory experiments, and public repositories of political ads provide beginnings. The problem is not insoluble, but it demands creativity rather than resignation.

And yet, resilience cannot be legislated alone. Civic rituals provide the social equivalent of fire drills: practices that embed resistance in habit rather than decree. Town-wide fact-checks, designated slow-news days, or public explanation duties for leaders may seem quaint. But repetition builds norms, and norms build durability. Just as a national anthem sustains identity beyond words, these rituals scaffold collective scepticism and patience—qualities essential in a world of engineered outrage.

What follows is not a manual of manipulation, but a field guide to recognition and resistance. The reader will see how morale, emotion, narrative, data, and ritual can be tuned like instruments, sometimes to stabilise, often to destabilise. The challenge is double-edged: to confront how fragile civic trust can be, while also realising how deliberately it can be strengthened. The stakes are not abstract. They shape whether societies fracture under pressure or cohere in defiance. And if the twentieth century taught us that bombs alone cannot break a people, the twenty-first is teaching us something equally unsettling: minds, not armies, may prove the most decisive terrain.

Targeting minds, not armies

In 2014, as fighting erupted in eastern Ukraine, the conflict was not confined to trenches and artillery lines. On social media feeds in Kyiv, Moscow, and far beyond, a parallel struggle unfolded: targeted posts sought to erode confidence in government, heighten ethnic division, and sow suspicion between neighbours. The battles were not measured in territory gained but in doubts planted. This was not propaganda in its blunt, twentieth-century form, but precision-guided psychological operations at civilian scale. The target was not the soldier at the front—it was the citizen scrolling at home.

Such moments reveal a disquieting truth: in the twenty-first century, national resilience is as much a function of collective morale as of military hardware. Armies still clash, but the strategic calculus increasingly turns on whether publics trust their institutions, maintain cohesion, or fracture under manipulation. Civilian minds have become the decisive terrain. When they are shaped with skill, governments can mobilise compliance, tolerance for sacrifice, and resistance against external pressure. When they are fractured, states bleed legitimacy faster than any army can defend it.

At the heart of this shift lies the machinery of segmentation. Marketing professionals have long known that audiences are not monoliths. A message that motivates a student may alienate a retiree; what inspires loyalty in one region may spark resentment in another. Tools built for commerce—psychographic profiling, behavioural tracking, microtargeting—now enable operatives to calibrate political and psychological appeals with extraordinary granularity. A campaign can be orchestrated not only to reach millions but to whisper tailored suggestions to each fragment of that mass. This is not scattershot propaganda. It is rifle-shot persuasion, distributed at scale.

Segmentation becomes potent when coupled with priming—the subtle activation of associations that steer perception before conscious deliberation. A well-timed reminder of past humiliation, a fleeting image of disorder, or a slogan that ties civic duty to identity can tilt how an audience interprets new events. Behavioural psychologists have shown how primed stimuli nudge choices in consumer contexts; geopolitical actors adapt the same logics for strategic effect. When populations are primed to distrust, even neutral policies appear sinister. When primed for pride, sacrifice can be embraced as virtue.

The most powerful lever, however, is identity salience. Humans are plural beings: parents, professionals, patriots, believers. Which identity rises to the surface at a given moment determines how events are read and decisions made. A government facing external pressure may seek to elevate national identity over partisan affiliation, while an adversary may try to fracture along ethnic, religious, or regional lines. By nudging which self is foregrounded, psychological operations convert the complexity of human identity into a battlefield of alignments. The aim is not to persuade everyone of a single narrative but to rearrange the salience of identities so that collective behaviour shifts.

Consider how civic trust itself becomes a dial. In societies where trust in institutions is high, compliance with emergency measures can be swift and voluntary; disinformation struggles to take root. Where trust is low, the same measures are met with suspicion, resistance, or conspiratorial reinterpretation. Foreign actors exploit this asymmetry, amplifying grievances in fragile contexts and attempting to depress trust where it is robust. But governments, too, engage in the calibration. They stage national rituals, elevate trusted messengers, and saturate communications with reassurances designed to lift the trust dial upward in moments of crisis. In both directions, the manipulation of trust proves more decisive than the manipulation of facts.

Examples abound. During the COVID-19 pandemic, states and activist networks deployed segmentation and priming to influence compliance with health measures. Some governments emphasised collective solidarity, framing mask-wearing as an expression of civic pride. Others, less successfully, framed it in technical or punitive terms, which in some contexts hardened resistance. In energy transitions, identity salience has been key: framing renewable adoption as a patriotic duty produces different outcomes than presenting it as a bureaucratic regulation. What emerges is a lesson in strategic psychology: the framing of identity and trust often matters more than the underlying policy.

This reality introduces tension. Democracies depend on persuasion, but where does persuasion end and manipulation begin? Marketing techniques imported into political life may erode the very autonomy that democratic choice presupposes. Yet abstaining from such tools may leave a society vulnerable to adversaries willing to use them without restraint. The ethical terrain is as fraught as the strategic one. To treat morale purely as an asset risks instrumentalising citizens as means rather than ends. To ignore its strategic value risks national weakness.

The reframing of psychological operations from the battlefield to the civic sphere compels us to think differently about defence. Firewalls and interceptors guard borders; what guards the collective psyche? If morale is a national asset, should it be cultivated like infrastructure—maintained, audited, and stress-tested? Or is such cultivation inherently paternalistic, a step too far into managing minds? These unresolved questions will shape not only the future of security but the texture of civic life itself.

What is clear is that the centre of gravity has shifted. The wars of our time are not won solely by tanks or treaties but by the steadiness of civilian trust under pressure. In a world where the mind has become both battlefield and resource, the challenge is stark: how to defend democratic resilience without hollowing its foundations in the process. The answer remains unfinished, and that uncertainty ensures the stakes remain high.

Emotions as infrastructure

In 2008, the world watched as financial markets convulsed, yet it was not balance sheets alone that determined the severity of the crisis. Fear spread faster than contagion in mortgage-backed securities. Households curtailed spending, firms froze investment, and politicians scrambled to reassure a public whose confidence had evaporated almost overnight. The infrastructure that collapsed was not only financial—it was emotional. Confidence, trust, and fear proved to be the hidden plumbing that carried flows of capital and compliance.

This is not an isolated truth of economics. In politics and national security, emotions function not merely as private experiences but as collective levers. Leaders invoke pride to mobilise sacrifice, disgust to stigmatise out-groups, and fear to accelerate compliance with emergency decrees. These are not side effects of communication; they are central instruments. Just as roads channel commerce and power grids sustain industry, emotions channel political behaviour and sustain legitimacy. To understand them as infrastructure is to see that they can be engineered, disrupted, and weaponised.

Fear is perhaps the most obvious lever. It shortens decision horizons, narrows the range of acceptable debate, and makes populations more willing to trade liberty for security. After the terrorist attacks of 11 September 2001, fear was deliberately cultivated to enable sweeping counterterrorism policies and foreign interventions. Polling showed that fear of a follow-on attack remained high years after, sustaining public tolerance for surveillance and military campaigns. Fear can also be manufactured more subtly: amplified crime statistics, images of disorder, or warnings of external enemies all raise the cost of dissent. Yet reliance on fear corrodes over time, leaving brittle societies that mistake vigilance for resilience.

If fear constrains, pride expands. It generates willingness to endure cost in the service of something larger. States appeal to national pride when mobilising for war or austerity. The Marshall Plan's success was not only in delivering aid but in framing reconstruction as a shared victory narrative for Europeans. Pride makes burdens feel chosen rather than imposed. Yet, like fear, pride is double-edged: when manipulated for exclusionary ends, it veers into chauvinism and fuels confrontation. Still, without some calibrated pride, societies drift towards apathy. It is the emotional engine that convinces individuals their small acts of compliance—paying taxes, serving in civil defence, adopting new technologies—participate in a grander story.

Disgust operates in quieter, more insidious ways. It draws the boundary between the pure and the polluted, the acceptable and the taboo. Political actors deploy it when casting opponents as corrupt, migrants as contaminating, or ideas as toxic. Disgust primes populations to exclude rather than engage, hardening lines of identity. At its most dangerous, it enables dehumanisation, preparing ground for policies that would otherwise be unconscionable. Yet disgust also has constructive uses: anti-smoking campaigns or environmental movements have drawn upon it to stigmatise harmful practices. Unlike fear or pride, disgust often works below conscious awareness, bypassing rational debate altogether.

What makes these levers so powerful is that they are measurable and predictable. Marketing science has demonstrated how emotional priming shapes purchasing behaviour; statecraft adapts the same techniques to shape political choices. Political strategists test which images of threat most reliably trigger fear, which symbols stir pride, which phrases spark disgust. Algorithms optimise delivery, ensuring each segment of the population receives the stimulus most likely to shift its behaviour. In this sense, emotional infrastructure is not metaphorical: it is designed, monitored, and maintained with the same precision as any physical system.

But here lies a dangerous tension. To govern is necessarily to communicate, and to communicate is inevitably to evoke emotion. Yet when the management of fear, pride, and disgust becomes normalised as a deliberate technique of domestic politics, the line between persuasion and manipulation erodes. Citizens become less participants than instruments. The very emotions that bind communities are retooled as control surfaces. Over time, this corrodes the trust that makes democratic societies resilient.

The challenge, then, is not to banish emotion from politics—it is to recognise when emotional engineering crosses into exploitation. Citizens must be trained, as consumers of information, to notice when their affect is being manipulated. Is fear being invoked proportionately to risk? Is pride being appealed to in inclusive or exclusionary ways? Is disgust being triggered to stigmatise genuine harm or to delegitimise dissent? These are questions that belong not only in seminar rooms but in living rooms, newsrooms, and parliaments.

There is an irony worth holding onto. The infrastructure of emotion cannot be fully centralised. Attempts to over-engineer it often backfire. Manufactured fear can provoke defiance; overplayed pride can look hollow; weaponised disgust can discredit those who wield it. Emotions remain stubbornly human, filtered through context and culture. This unpredictability is a safeguard of sorts, but only if citizens remain conscious of their own role in the feedback loop.

The stakes are clear. If we continue to treat emotions as tools to be exploited without restraint, we risk hollowing the very democratic norms that depend upon authentic trust and voluntary compliance. If, instead, we treat emotions as civic infrastructure to be stewarded carefully, we can sustain societies resilient enough to withstand manipulation from both within and without.

But stewardship requires vigilance. Who decides when fear is justified, pride appropriate, disgust warranted? Can democratic institutions referee such judgments without sliding into paternalism? Or will emotional governance always remain a contested frontier, where power cloaks itself in the language of feeling? The answers are unsettled, and perhaps unresolvable—but the recognition that emotions are infrastructure is the first step in ensuring they are not quietly rewired beyond repair.

Memes, rituals, and the stickiness of simple stories

When complex truths stumble, simple stories sprint. The paradox is familiar: scholars, policymakers, and scientists labour to explain intricate realities, while a three-word slogan or a viral image can decide elections, alter investment flows, or ignite social unrest. It is not that people are incapable of understanding complexity—history is filled with moments when publics grappled with nuance—but that in contested spaces, where attention is scarce and trust fragile, the compact narrative nearly always outcompetes the complicated one.

Consider the energy transition. Scientists and economists present detailed roadmaps involving carbon pricing, grid integration, and storage technologies. Yet one meme—"drill, baby, drill"—or a ritualised chant about "green tyranny" can collapse the conversation into something immediately graspable and emotionally resonant. The complexity of how renewables scale is no match for the stickiness of a story about jobs being stolen or freedom curtailed. In public debate, compression beats explanation.

The same dynamic is evident in migration politics. Data-rich reports outline demographic shifts, labour market complementarities, and fiscal impacts. But against this stands the ritualised image of a caravan or a crowded boat, which functions less as fact than as symbol. It lodges in memory, repeated and reinforced through rallies, headlines, and shareable graphics. The story is simple: threat or rescue, invasion or hospitality. Once such frames harden, detailed analysis struggles to dislodge them, not because the evidence is weak but because the narrative architecture has already been set.

Why do compact narratives outperform? Cognitive science suggests several reasons. Simplicity reduces cognitive load, making stories easier to recall and share. Repetition through ritual—whether in political rallies, hashtags, or talk-show refrains—cements familiarity, which audiences subconsciously equate with truth. Identity salience adds further adhesive: when a story aligns with how people see themselves, it becomes less a claim to be assessed and more a badge to be worn. Memes are not merely bits of content; they are portable rituals, binding individuals into imagined communities.

This raises a strategic dilemma for open societies. If the most effective narratives are compact and sticky, does this condemn truth-tellers to permanent disadvantage? Not necessarily. The answer lies not in censorship, which tends to backfire by fuelling martyrdom narratives, but in cultivating counter-rituals and narrative inoculation. Just as vaccines expose the body to weakened pathogens, so can societies expose citizens to common manipulative tropes in advance. Teaching people to recognise the skeleton of a false dichotomy or a scapegoating meme arms them with antibodies against future iterations.

Counter-rituals matter as well. Shared practices—fact-checking sessions in classrooms, slow-news Fridays in workplaces, or public explanation duties where leaders must justify decisions in plain language—create collective moments that privilege reflection over reflex. They may not eradicate the appeal of simple stories, but they can dilute their monopoly over the public imagination. Rituals are not only tools of those who seek to mislead; they can also anchor cultures of resilience.

Still, there is no escaping the asymmetry. A viral image can circulate globally in hours; a peer-reviewed report may take years to produce and days to read. But rather than despairing, one might see this asymmetry as an invitation to rethink how truth is communicated. Compact narratives need not always be false. The abolitionist slogan "Am I not a man and a brother?" condensed moral truth into a phrase more powerful than any treatise. The challenge for our time is to craft simple stories that clarify rather than distort, that dignify complexity rather than erase it.

And yet the tension remains. If societies learn to arm themselves against manipulative memes, will they also blunt the power of inspiring ones? Can narrative inoculation protect without rendering publics cynical or fatigued? Rituals can sustain civic health, but they can also ossify into empty gestures. The balance between hygiene and vitality is delicate.

What is certain is that memes and rituals are not cultural trivia. They are battlegrounds where norms, policies, and futures are decided. Simple stories will always be sticky; the question is whether societies can learn to make that stickiness serve truth rather than undermine it. The answer will not be found in laboratories or courts alone, but in the everyday habits of attention, repetition, and narrative we choose to endorse—or resist.

Microtargeting and the audit problem

In 2016, a political consultancy most voters had never heard of claimed it could sway elections by combining harvested Facebook data with psychometric profiling. Whether Cambridge Analytica truly possessed the power it boasted is less important than the revelation it triggered: campaigns were no longer broadcast spectacles but finely calibrated conversations, often invisible to all but their recipients. One voter was told their pension was safe; another, that it was under threat. Both messages came from the same candidate. The paradox was glaring—democracy depends on a shared public square, yet digital platforms were enabling private stages where persuasion could be tailored, tested, and tweaked without scrutiny.

The problem has only deepened since. Opaque ad systems now handle billions of micro-impressions daily, drawing on private datasets amassed from browsing histories, consumer purchases, geolocation trails, and even inferred personality traits. These systems operate with a precision far beyond traditional polling or focus groups, yet oversight is crippled by their very design. Regulators, researchers, and even political opponents often cannot see what messages are being served, to whom, or with what effect. The advertising platforms, for their part, cite commercial confidentiality and user privacy as reasons for withholding detail—creating an accountability vacuum in which manipulation can flourish.

This opacity is not a side effect; it is a feature. Personalisation is the product being sold, whether to brands or political operatives. In such an environment, classic democratic safeguards—press scrutiny, open debates, public rebuttals—are weakened, because much of the persuasion occurs in the shadows. If oversight mechanisms cannot pierce these shadows, societies are left with anecdote and suspicion rather than evidence. That uncertainty alone corrodes trust: when voters suspect their neighbours are being told different "truths," cohesion fractures, even if the messages themselves are mundane.

The question, then, is whether audits of these systems are possible without violating individual privacy or compromising legitimate commercial interests. The answer is yes—if oversight is reimagined. Several experiments point the way. In the European Union, researchers have proposed requiring platforms to maintain real-time "ad libraries" that record targeting parameters and spending levels. The United States Federal Trade Commission has explored rules obliging disclosure of algorithmic decision-making criteria. In the United Kingdom, independent initiatives have built browser plug-ins to collect the political ads users receive, pooling them into databases for public analysis. Each approach offers partial visibility: none yet provides the comprehensive picture societies need.

One promising idea is differential auditing. Rather than examining raw user-level data, auditors can analyse statistical aggregates that reveal patterns without exposing identities. For instance, instead of showing which specific citizens saw which ad, platforms could be compelled to release anonymised counts of how many people in given regions or demographic groups received certain categories of messaging. This allows investigators to detect whether pensioners are disproportionately targeted with fear-based appeals, or whether certain neighbourhoods are being saturated with disinformation. The technical tools for such audits already exist; what is lacking is the political will to mandate them.

Comparative regulatory experiments offer additional lessons. Germany's NetzDG law, designed to curb online hate speech, has forced platforms into publishing transparency reports—imperfect but precedent-setting. Canada has piloted frameworks for political ad registries, while Taiwan has pioneered rapid-response teams to identify and publicise disinformation campaigns in real time. Each jurisdiction grapples with trade-offs: between free expression and accountability, between corporate secrecy and public interest. No single model is transferable wholesale, but the diversity of approaches underscores that oversight is not impossible.

Still, the audit problem is more than a technical puzzle; it is a philosophical one. Surveillance capitalism and democratic transparency pull in opposite directions. The same data systems that allow microtargeting also allow auditing; yet granting regulators access to them risks entrenching state overreach. The challenge is to design oversight that is powerful enough to reveal manipulation but restrained enough to respect privacy. This requires careful attention to proportionality, independent governance, and procedural safeguards—less the blunt hammer of total transparency than the scalpel of targeted accountability.

The stakes are high. Without credible oversight, suspicion metastasises. Citizens cannot know whether the messages they see are typical or exceptional, whether their communities are being courted or segmented, whether rivals are playing by the rules or bending them. Oversight is not only about catching bad actors; it is about restoring confidence in the fairness of the communicative environment itself. Democracy depends as much on shared perception as on shared institutions.

Yet an unresolved tension lingers. The more effective oversight becomes, the more sophisticated microtargeting techniques will grow—shifting from overt ad buys to subtler forms of influence like influencer marketing, sponsored content, or algorithmic amplification that leave fewer traces. Audits may chase the last generation of tactics while the next quietly takes shape. The question is not whether oversight can be designed, but whether it can keep pace. Can democratic societies construct audit systems agile enough to evolve alongside the platforms they monitor? Or will microtargeting always remain one step ahead, exploiting opacity as both shield and weapon? The answer will shape not only the integrity of elections but the texture of civic trust itself.

Civic rituals for resilience

Every society relies on rituals, whether it admits it or not. Some are formal—parliamentary openings, judicial oaths, and national holidays. Others are improvised—weekly football fixtures, the queue at the post office, or the shared silence after a tragedy. They matter not because they change facts directly, but because they bind people to each other and to common expectations. In an age where disinformation spreads faster than correction, and outrage outpaces reflection, the question is not whether we have rituals but whether we have the right ones. Can communities design civic routines that reinforce resilience instead of eroding it?

Consider the early months of the COVID-19 pandemic. In Italy, balcony singing emerged spontaneously: neighbours leaning out of windows to affirm life and solidarity, day after day. It was modest, improvised, even a little awkward. Yet it restored a sense of connection during confinement and reminded people that they were part of something larger than their individual anxieties. That is the quiet power of ritual: it scales a norm by repetition, embedding expectations through practice rather than decree. If a balcony song can encourage endurance under quarantine, then surely societies can craft similarly simple, repeatable gestures to fortify truth, trust, and democratic durability.

The starting point is recognising morale as a civic asset, not merely an incidental by-product of politics. Just as armies drill to condition discipline, citizens can drill to condition resilience. Town fact-checks—regular gatherings, digital or physical, where contested claims are examined together—sound almost quaint. Yet their effect could be profound. By shifting verification from an individual burden to a collective habit, they transform accuracy into a shared expectation rather than a lonely chore. When neighbours convene to assess whether a viral story is credible, they are not only clarifying facts; they are rehearsing a democratic ethic of mutual responsibility.

The same logic applies to what might be called *slow-news Fridays*. In practice, this could mean schools, offices, or civic groups committing once a week to pause the reflex of endless scrolling and instead discuss a limited set of curated stories. The act is not about silencing information but about resisting the velocity of content that disorients more than it informs. Ritualised slowness, in this sense, becomes a counterweight to algorithmic acceleration. The repetition of restraint—knowing that every Friday the pace will be checked—conditions a habit of reflection that seeps into the rest of the week.

Leaders, too, need rituals that tether authority to explanation. Imagine a norm where elected officials, once a month, were obliged to hold what might be termed a *public explanation duty*: not campaign-style rallies, but sessions explicitly dedicated to clarifying decisions, assumptions, and trade-offs. Such events would not eliminate spin, but they would routinise a form of accountability that is proactive rather than reactive. The act of explanation, repeated over time, reorients leadership from crisis firefighting to expectation-setting. Citizens, in turn, learn to demand clarity as a normal part of governance rather than an exceptional concession.

Sceptics will note that rituals can be hollow. Indeed, many existing civic observances—national anthems before sporting events, rote recitations in classrooms—are endured rather than embraced. The difference lies in whether rituals are tethered to lived realities. Town fact-checks only matter if they address the claims circulating in that community, not abstract debates chosen by distant elites. Slow-news Fridays only matter if they foster conversations about issues people actually face. Rituals fail when they drift into symbolism without substance; they succeed when they embed practice into daily life in ways people can feel and measure.

Anthropologists remind us that rituals often outlast the institutions that birthed them. Consider the handshake, a once-practical demonstration of unarmed intent that endures as a social contract centuries after swords vanished from belts. Designing civic rituals for resilience means aiming not for immediate spectacle but for gradual accretion: practices that, repeated enough, become invisible but indispensable. Their quiet endurance is their strength.

There is also a moral dimension. Rituals can be manipulative, as propagandists have long understood. Marches, chants, and ceremonies can entrench conformity as easily as solidarity. The task, therefore, is not to abandon ritual but to design it with safeguards: transparency, voluntariness, plurality. Fact-check sessions must welcome dissent; slow-news days must resist becoming sanctioned narratives. The goal is not uniformity of thought but resilience of discourse. A democracy's health lies not in suppressing difference but in equipping citizens to manage it without tearing apart.

The most promising rituals will be those that travel lightly across cultures. One community may prefer town hall discussions, another might lean on religious congregations, and another on school assemblies. What matters is the repeatable rhythm that reinforces shared habits: questioning claims together, slowing down to reflect, demanding explanation from those in power. These rituals create a civic muscle memory, preparing citizens to withstand waves of manipulation or crisis not with panic but with practised composure.

Yet a lingering tension remains. Rituals take time and collective attention, both of which are scarce in modern life. Can communities commit to them without them devolving into token gestures? Or will the very speed and distraction these rituals aim to counteract also prevent their adoption? The answer is not obvious. But the choice is unavoidable: either societies consciously cultivate rituals that sustain resilience, or they drift into habits that corrode it. The question that hangs is stark—will our future civic routines be balcony songs of solidarity, or endless scrolls of fragmentation? The answer will shape not just how democracies endure crises, but whether they endure at all.

Chapter 9

Supply Chains as Frontiers

In the spring of 2021, a container ship wedged diagonally across the Suez Canal halted nearly 12 per cent of global trade for six days. The images of the stranded Ever Given, dwarfed by the desert and a handful of bulldozers, were almost comical in their absurdity. Yet beneath the memes and headlines lay a sharper lesson: the modern economy, with all its digital sophistication and global reach, could still be brought to its knees by a single blocked waterway. A chokepoint, long known to naval strategists, had reminded the world that leverage lies not only in the vastness of networks but in the geometry of their narrowest passages.

This was not a novelty. Centuries earlier, the Portuguese empire secured wealth and influence not by conquering continents but by fortifying straits and harbours. Whoever commanded Malacca, Hormuz, or the Cape of Good Hope could dictate the flows of goods far beyond their immediate horizons. Maritime empires were built on recognising that power radiates outward from constriction points, where the many must pass through the few. Today's supply chains, with their semiconductor foundries, rare earth processing facilities, and cloud control planes, are governed by the same principle. The names and technologies differ, but the geometry of dependence remains stubbornly familiar.

What distinguishes the present moment is scale and intimacy. The oil shock of the 1970s left motorists queuing for petrol; today, a shortage of microchips leaves entire industries paralysed, from cars to washing machines. The chokepoints are less visible to the public eye yet more deeply embedded in daily life. The logic of maritime straits has migrated into server farms, logistics software, and standards bodies. To understand geopolitics now requires understanding procurement contracts, warehouse inventories, and the fragility of shipping schedules. The frontier of contest is not a distant battlefield but the circulation of the ordinary.

This chapter begins by charting those chokepoints and showing how control of a few nodes shapes the options available to many nations. From semiconductor fabs that take years to replicate, to the rare earth refineries clustered in a handful of provinces, to the straits where naval patrols and insurance premiums decide the price of global energy—these points reveal the map of leverage more starkly than any alliance communiqué or military parade. History clarifies the logic: maritime empires knew what modern policymakers sometimes forget—that economic power concentrates wherever traffic converges.

From this geometry, we turn to the economics of resilience. Much has been made of "friend-shoring" and "de-risking," slogans meant to reduce reliance on fragile or hostile partners. Yet resilience is not free. Redundancy and relocation impose costs, and only in some cases does the insurance premium of duplicated supply chains pay off. We will examine how to distinguish policy theatre from genuine strategic autonomy, tracing the numbers that show when a diversified supply line buys leverage and when it merely buys headlines. Procurement choices, often treated as mundane, are in fact strategic decisions that shape national freedom of manoeuvre.

Controls and restrictions, too, become instruments of design. Export controls on semiconductors, biotech materials, and advanced machinery do more than deny access; they alter the trajectory of learning curves and innovation pathways. Raising the cost of imitation or delaying the time to mastery is itself a form of power. The United States, the European Union, and China all understand that what is denied today shapes what is possible tomorrow. We will explore the dynamics of these measures—not as blunt obstacles but as tools of engineering, shaping capability landscapes in ways that outlast press statements.

Beyond the visible drama of controls lies a quieter battlefield: standards and certifications. To the untrained eye, they appear bureaucratic—labels, audits, compliance checks. Yet these are often the means by which rivals are excluded without ever being named. Private compliance morphs into public power when access to markets hinges on certification regimes designed in one capital but binding in many others. The audit state, as we will see, can rival the gunboat in determining who trades and who stalls. Detecting these disguised trade barriers is a craft in itself, requiring attentiveness to the paperwork that masks strategy.

Even the humdrum matter of inventory conceals leverage. Days of cover—the number of days a country or company can operate from stockpiles—

can change bargaining positions as surely as tank divisions once did. From strategic petroleum reserves to rare earth buffers, from grain silos to vaccine doses, inventory is a form of policy instrument. It allows states to ride out shocks, to negotiate without panic, and to deter coercion by showing preparedness. The world of clipboards and stock counts thus intersects with the theatre of diplomacy.

What unites these themes is a reframing: supply chains are not neutral backdrops against which politics plays out, but arenas of politics themselves. They are frontiers where power is exercised, contested, and reconfigured. To trace a supply chain is to map the contours of sovereignty and dependence, not simply to log shipments. The flows of goods and components are, in effect, the flows of influence.

The stakes are profound. Do societies see their supply chains as conveniences to be outsourced until trouble strikes, or as frontiers to be managed with foresight and care? Are chokepoints vulnerabilities to be feared, or levers to be wielded responsibly? As we move through the chapter, the answers will become clearer—but the enduring lesson is already in view: resilience and leverage are two sides of the same coin, and the geometry of dependence defines the shape of tomorrow's power. The page ahead will not just describe supply chains; it will reveal why they have become the nervous system of modern strategy.

Chokepoints and the geometry of dependence

In March 2021, a container ship lodged itself diagonally in the Suez Canal. For six days the Ever Given blocked one of the world's most vital arteries, freezing twelve per cent of global trade. The surreal image of a skyscraper-sized vessel jammed in a desert ditch—mocked online with cartoons of tiny diggers against a hulking hull—was more than a shipping accident. It was a vivid reminder that the vast complexity of global commerce rests on surprisingly few points of passage. For all the talk of globalisation as diffuse and borderless, it remains vulnerable to the physics of bottlenecks.

This paradox—that an economy of staggering scale can be halted by a single blockage—runs through the story of supply chains. The geography of dependence is not evenly spread but concentrated in nodes, where control of the few can dictate outcomes for the many. The same logic that once empowered maritime empires to project dominance through control of straits and harbours is alive today in semiconductor fabrication plants, rare earth processing facilities, and even the software that orchestrates container logistics. The map of power is less about borders than about intersections.

Historical analogies sharpen the point. The Portuguese in the sixteenth century did not attempt to conquer entire continents; they instead fortified and taxed the Malacca Strait, Hormuz, and the Cape of Good Hope. With these three points, a modest fleet could govern the terms of trade between Asia, Africa, and Europe. The Dutch East India Company refined the model, using control of spice islands and shipping lanes to magnify influence far beyond its size. The principle was always the same: command the choke and you command the flow.

The modern equivalents are no less decisive. Taiwan's leading semiconductor fabrication plants, concentrated in a handful of facilities, account for a vast share of the world's advanced chips. This makes them not only economic assets but geopolitical fulcrums, as essential to global manufacturing as oil fields once were to energy security. A disruption in Hsinchu can stall automotive production in Detroit, telecommunications rollouts in Berlin, and consumer electronics launches in São Paulo. The interdependence is not abstract; it is immediate, measurable, and deeply asymmetric.

Rare earth processing offers another case. Mining of these minerals is dispersed, yet the bottleneck lies in the refining stage, which is overwhelmingly dominated by Chinese facilities. It is not the presence of raw material in the ground but the capacity to turn ore into usable components that determines leverage. When Beijing hinted at restricting exports during disputes with Japan in 2010, it exposed the fragility of supply chains underpinning everything from wind turbines to missile guidance systems. Control at a single stage radiates influence across industries and continents.

Maritime chokepoints remain as consequential as ever. The Strait of Hormuz, through which a significant portion of the world's oil supply passes, is monitored as a barometer of global stability. The Bab el-Mandeb, narrower still, connects the Red Sea to the Gulf of Aden and thus the Suez Canal. Naval patrols, insurance premiums, and even pirate activity there reverberate in energy prices worldwide. These straits remind us that the geometry of dependence is not confined to high technology but persists in the ancient logic of narrow waterways.

Less visible, but equally vital, are the digital chokepoints embedded in software. Modern logistics depends on a handful of platforms that manage shipping schedules, customs clearance, and container tracking. When a cyberattack paralysed Maersk's IT systems in 2017, the world's largest shipping company had to reinstall thousands of servers and computers, halting operations at ports and warehouses across multiple continents. The incident showed that code, like canals, can function as a constriction point, where failure cascades into systemic paralysis.

The geometry of dependence can be visualised as a series of funnels. Inputs from diverse sources converge on narrow passages—be they straits, refineries, fabs, or data centres—before fanning out again to serve global demand. The narrower the funnel, the greater the leverage of whoever controls it. Unlike conventional military superiority, which demands large-scale resources, chokepoint power often hinges on precision: the ability to dominate a small but decisive node. It is a geometry that rewards subtlety as much as scale.

But dependence also generates dilemmas. For those who control a chokepoint, the temptation to wield it coercively is counterbalanced by the risk of spurring diversification or technological substitution. OPEC learnt this lesson in the wake of the 1973 oil embargo, which prompted consumer states to build reserves, diversify suppliers, and invest in alternatives. Similarly, threats to semiconductor supply chains have accelerated investments in fabrication plants across the United States, Europe, and East Asia. The power of the choke is real, but so too is the incentive it creates for bypass.

There is also a philosophical question here about visibility. Chokepoints often operate in the shadows of public awareness until a crisis makes them headline news. Most citizens had never heard of the Malacca Strait until piracy flared in the 2000s, nor thought about the Suez Canal until the Ever Given wedged itself across it. Yet these points shape their daily lives, dictating the prices of fuel, electronics, and food. The geometry of dependence is thus not only strategic but civic: it binds populations to places they may never see but on which they nonetheless rely.

The lesson is sobering. Networks promise resilience through redundancy, yet in practice they often consolidate through efficiency. The pursuit of lowest cost, fastest delivery, and just-in-time inventories magnifies dependence on narrow nodes. Efficiency breeds fragility. The chokepoint becomes both the enabler of global abundance and the Achilles' heel of its security.

To think strategically about the twenty-first century is therefore to think geometrically. Where are the funnels? Who commands them? What substitutes exist—or could exist—with sufficient investment? These questions matter as much as counting armies or fleets. Indeed, they may matter more, because in a world of dense interconnection, the geometry of dependence often defines the contours of choice itself.

The paradox remains unresolved. Chokepoints are at once the lifelines and vulnerabilities of global order. They concentrate power but also catalyse resistance. They simplify strategy even as they complicate politics. And so the map of dependence is never finished; it shifts with technology, with investment, with the ingenuity of those who seek to circumvent constraint. To study it is not merely to analyse logistics, but to glimpse the architecture of modern power—and to ask, uneasily, what happens when the next blockage appears.

Friend-shoring, de-risking, and the cost curve

When governments promise to "bring production home" or "only trade with trusted partners", the rhetoric resonates with voters and boardrooms alike. In the aftermath of the COVID-19 pandemic, with container ships queued at ports and masks rationed by ministries, the appeal of supply chain sovereignty was undeniable. Yet behind the political slogans lies a stubborn arithmetic: resilience is expensive, and not all redundancy is worth its cost. The gap between announcement and execution often reveals whether friend-shoring and de-risking are genuine strategic investments or simply theatre staged for reassurance.

Consider the case of semiconductors. The United States has pledged tens of billions of dollars to subsidise fabrication plants in Arizona, seeking to reduce reliance on Taiwanese and South Korean giants. At the same time, the European Union has advanced its own "Chips Act", aspiring to double its global share of production by 2030. On paper, these initiatives are framed as insurance policies against geopolitical disruption. Yet the fabrication of leading-edge chips requires capital outlays in the tens of billions, multi-year lead times, and deeply embedded supplier networks spanning photolithography, chemicals, and design software. Relocating production does not simply mean moving machines; it requires recreating an entire ecosystem. The cost curve is steep, and the payback period uncertain.

By contrast, certain sectors reveal that redundancy can be surprisingly affordable. Japan's efforts after the 2011 Fukushima disaster illustrate this. Faced with vulnerability in rare earth supplies—where China then processed more than 90 per cent of global output—Tokyo financed stockpiles and encouraged alternative suppliers in Australia and Vietnam. The programme cost a fraction of a single semiconductor fab but yielded meaningful leverage, reducing China's ability to apply unilateral pressure. Not all resilience projects require gold-plated redundancy; some depend on targeted buffers and political imagination.

Friend-shoring, meanwhile, raises its own contradictions. The idea—prioritising trade and investment among "trusted" nations—emerged as a middle path between globalisation and outright autarky. It is an attempt to reconcile economic efficiency with geopolitical reliability. Yet defining a "friend" in economic terms can be slippery. Mexico and Canada may be secure partners for U.S. supply chains, but what of India, whose strategic choices remain independent? Or Vietnam, which trades heavily with both Washington and Beijing? Aligning procurement with alliances often runs into the messy reality that firms source where costs are lowest and capacities deepest. Geopolitical neatness rarely maps onto economic geography.

The cost curve exposes another tension: resilience at the national level does not always align with efficiency at the firm level. A company deciding whether to dual-source components must weigh increased costs against the low probability—but potentially catastrophic—impact of disruption. Governments, however, may value insurance differently, willing to subsidise redundancy as a public good. This divergence creates friction: firms resist mandates that cut margins, while policymakers see strategic autonomy as priceless. Bridging this gap requires new financing models, from tax incentives to shared stockpiles, to make resilience economically rational for private actors.

Historical parallels show the trade-offs vividly. During the Cold War, the United States and its allies invested in redundant shipping and aviation capacity to guarantee military mobility. Much of it sat idle in peacetime, a drag on budgets, yet it proved indispensable in crises. The same logic applies today to pharmaceuticals or energy transition minerals. Strategic autonomy is rarely free, but the absence of redundancy can exact costs measured not only in currency but in sovereignty.

Yet not every policy labelled "de-risking" delivers substance. Some initiatives are better understood as signalling devices, intended to reassure domestic audiences rather than restructure supply chains. A government may announce the creation of a "strategic stockpile" without defining inventory levels or rotation policies. Companies may declare their commitment to "friend-shoring" while quietly maintaining dependencies in less publicised tiers of their supply networks. Such gestures matter symbolically, but they do not change the underlying geometry of dependence. The theatre of resilience can lull societies into complacency, creating the illusion of safety without its substance.

A more subtle danger lies in over-correcting. Excessive duplication of production can waste resources, inflate consumer prices, and fragment global research and development. If every region insists on producing its own semiconductors, biopharmaceuticals, and batteries independently, the world risks losing the benefits of scale that fuel innovation. Strategic autonomy becomes a cover for protectionism, reducing efficiency without meaningfully enhancing resilience. The cost curve here is not just steep but negative, leading to higher expenses with little added security.

Philosophically, the debate over friend-shoring and de-risking reflects a deeper dilemma: how much uncertainty can a society tolerate? Total security is unattainable, yet societies differ in their willingness to live with exposure. Some prize efficiency and accept the risks of occasional shocks. Others view resilience as a civic duty, even if it entails paying more for goods or slowing growth. Neither stance is inherently irrational; both depend on cultural attitudes toward risk, trust, and the role of the state.

The question, then, is not whether resilience pays, but when—and for whom. For a firm, the value may lie in preserving reputation and continuity through a crisis. For a nation, it may rest in the ability to make strategic decisions without coercion. Procurement choices, from sourcing contracts to subsidies, thus carry implications that reach beyond balance sheets. They shape the latitude of future policy, the autonomy of diplomacy, and even the tenor of domestic politics.

What emerges is a paradox. The more loudly leaders declare their commitment to friend-shoring and de-risking, the more sceptical one should be. The real work is quiet, technical, and often invisible: redesigning procurement contracts, aligning incentives, and quantifying trade-offs. Resilience is not achieved by rhetoric but by painstaking adjustments along the cost curve. It is here, in the arithmetic of redundancy, that sovereignty is either secured or squandered.

Yet the dilemma remains unresolved. How far should societies go in paying for resilience when efficiency beckons with cheaper goods and faster growth? How much redundancy is insurance, and how much is excess? These questions will not vanish; they are the structural condition of an interconnected world. And they press us to ask: when the next disruption comes—whether a pandemic, a blockade, or a political rupture—will the promises of resilience prove durable, or will they collapse as theatre exposed?

Export controls as design tools

In October 2022, Washington announced sweeping restrictions on the export of advanced semiconductors and the tools required to make them. To many, it seemed like a bureaucratic footnote—a new set of licensing requirements, technical thresholds, and compliance forms. Yet within weeks, the reverberations were felt from Shanghai to Eindhoven. Entire supply chains were disrupted, firms scrambled to reconfigure operations, and governments from Tokyo to Brussels were drawn into hurried consultations. What appeared as paperwork was in fact an act of engineering: a deliberate attempt to reshape the technological trajectory of a rival nation.

Export controls have long been associated with denial—blocking access to sensitive technologies so adversaries cannot develop weapons or critical systems. But in today's interdependent economy, controls function less as blunt embargoes and more as *design tools*. They do not merely prevent; they sculpt. By raising costs, slowing learning curves, and dictating which paths are accessible, export restrictions subtly but powerfully alter the evolution of entire industries. In this sense, they operate less like walls and more like dams—redirecting flows rather than halting them outright.

Semiconductors provide the clearest illustration. At the leading edge of chipmaking, every process node—measured in nanometres—represents years of accumulated expertise and billions of dollars in investment. Learning is cumulative: access to cutting-edge equipment accelerates mastery, while exclusion compounds disadvantage. By restricting sales of extreme ultraviolet (EUV) lithography machines—manufactured almost exclusively by a single Dutch company—the United States and its allies have not only slowed China's progress towards sub-7nm chips but have also increased the costs of any indigenous workaround. The result is not an absolute halt but a deliberate stretching of time, a shift in slope on the learning curve. The objective is to preserve a lead long enough to retain strategic leverage.

Biotechnology offers another example. Restrictions on certain gene synthesis equipment and reagents, particularly those with dual-use potential, are framed as safeguards against biological weapons. Yet they also shape the wider research environment. Laboratories denied easy access to automated synthesis tools face slower iteration cycles, reduced collaboration opportunities, and higher costs. This is not accidental: controls serve both as guardrails against malicious use and as design features that dictate the pace and scope of legitimate progress. The tension is stark: how to encourage beneficial science while constraining capabilities that might, under different circumstances, destabilise security.

Export controls as design instruments generate spillovers that extend far beyond their intended targets. For allies, the demands of harmonisation can be burdensome. Japanese and Dutch firms caught between Chinese customers and American restrictions must reconcile economic incentives with strategic obligations. For developing economies, being excluded from key technologies risks entrenching dependency and limiting participation in high-value industries. Thus, the controls designed to secure one nation's autonomy can inadvertently reduce the autonomy of others. Power radiates outward not only through coercion but through the architecture of constraint.

Critics argue that such measures are self-defeating. By denying access to Western tools, controls incentivise rivals to invest more heavily in indigenous capabilities. China's drive to cultivate its own semiconductor equipment industry accelerated precisely in response to U.S. restrictions. History offers echoes: Cold War embargoes spurred Soviet advances in aerospace, albeit at higher costs and longer timelines. Controls, therefore, do not erase ambition; they recalibrate it. The question is whether the delay they impose is strategically valuable enough to outweigh the spur they provide.

Proponents counter that *time itself is a strategic resource.* In fast-moving fields, even a two- or three-year lead can translate into disproportionate military and economic advantages. By slowing a competitor's progress, controls allow the initiator to consolidate its own position, scale production, and embed standards that become global defaults. The contest is not simply over who can build, but over who can build *first* and set the tempo. Export restrictions, from this perspective, are less about exclusion than about choreography.

Philosophically, the use of export controls raises deeper questions about the boundary between security and openness. Science and technology thrive on diffusion, cross-pollination, and shared infrastructure. Every barrier erected in the name of national interest narrows the channels through which ideas and innovations circulate. Yet complete openness carries its own risks, enabling adversaries to leapfrog developmental stages. The tension is not new—Renaissance Venice restricted the emigration of glassmakers to protect its secrets—but the stakes are higher in an era where a handful of technologies underpin not only economic competitiveness but also military primacy and societal resilience.

The design metaphor illuminates both the promise and peril of export controls. Like any engineering tool, their effectiveness depends on calibration. Too loose, and the rival adapts quickly, eroding the intended advantage. Too tight, and the restrictions create perverse incentives, encourage circumvention through third countries, or undermine the very industries meant to be protected by cutting them off from profitable markets. The art lies in balancing denial with diffusion, ensuring that allies and partners remain aligned while adversaries face compounding hurdles.

A subtler dimension lies in the narrative power of controls. Announcements of sweeping export bans serve not only practical purposes but also symbolic ones: they signal resolve, rally domestic constituencies, and shape expectations about future technological landscapes. Yet symbolism can cut both ways. If the controls prove porous or ineffective, credibility suffers. The difference between engineering and posturing lies in execution—whether the restrictions actually bend trajectories or merely decorate speeches.

Export controls, then, are not the end of the story but the scaffolding upon which the future is built. They are instruments of *design politics*, reshaping the possibilities available to others while preserving space for one's own innovations. They reveal that in the invisible wars of the twenty-first century, power lies not only in possession but in prevention, not only in invention but in obstruction.

Still, the enduring question remains: can these tools be wielded with enough precision to protect security without suffocating the very openness that fuels progress? The answer will decide whether export controls emerge as instruments of sustainable strategy or as blunt artefacts of anxiety. And until that answer becomes clear, every licensing decision and embargo line will be more than an administrative detail—it will be a sketch in the blueprint of global order.

Standards, certifications, and the audit state

When Japan banned imports of American apples in the late 1990s, the stated reason was phytosanitary: a concern about fire blight. Scientific consensus suggested the risk of transmission was negligible, yet the inspections demanded by Tokyo were so onerous, and the certification hurdles so exacting, that exporters withdrew. It was a trade restriction by other means—delivered not through tariffs or quotas, but through the language of safety and compliance. The lesson endures: in an interconnected economy, the true barriers are often disguised as neutral procedures.

The paradox of the modern trading system is that its openness depends on a thick lattice of rules, labels, and audits. These instruments are supposed to create trust, to assure buyers that food is safe, toys are non-toxic, and aircraft components are reliable. Yet the same tools can be wielded strategically. Standards are rarely just technical checklists. They embody choices about measurement, thresholds, and authority—choices that tilt markets and determine who can participate. To be outside a standard is to be outside the market.

Nowhere is this clearer than in the realm of digital infrastructure. Consider the European Union's General Data Protection Regulation (GDPR). Officially a privacy regime, it also became a de facto trade instrument. Companies worldwide seeking access to the European market had to reconfigure their data practices to comply, incurring costs that favoured incumbents with large compliance departments. What looked like a human rights measure was simultaneously a mechanism for asserting regulatory gravity. In effect, private compliance became public power, with Brussels shaping global norms far beyond its borders.

Certification regimes in emerging technologies show the same double-edged edge. The safety audits imposed on drones, for instance, have differentiated markets in subtle ways. Requirements for data localisation or certified encryption algorithms exclude some foreign suppliers, particularly when those suppliers originate from geopolitical rivals. The test is not always about technical merit; it is about trust—codified in paperwork, enforced through audits, and legitimised under the guise of consumer or national protection.

This bureaucratic face of strategy is easily overlooked because it lacks spectacle. There are no warships patrolling standards bodies, no dramatic headlines when a certification is tightened. Yet the economic consequences are profound. An automotive manufacturer whose battery technology fails to meet new "sustainability audits" may lose entire markets overnight. A logistics firm unable to satisfy cybersecurity certifications can be excluded from government contracts. Power is exercised not by visible coercion but by shaping the thresholds of entry.

Detecting when such measures function as disguised barriers requires attention to the asymmetries they produce. One cue is *specificity*: standards that map neatly onto the production strengths of one country while disadvantaging others. Another is *opacity*: audit requirements so complex that only domestic firms with insider knowledge can realistically comply. A third is *plasticity*: the sudden tightening of criteria coinciding with political tensions. These signals reveal the strategic undercurrent in regimes that otherwise appear technocratic.

Historical parallels help illuminate this logic. The British Empire's maritime dominance in the eighteenth century was sustained not only by naval power but by control of shipping registries, insurance practices, and port inspections. Vessels that failed to meet British standards found themselves unable to dock or to secure financing. The form has changed, but the function is similar: embedding strategic advantage in the bureaucracy of exchange.

What complicates today's picture is the fusion of public and private authority. Governments may set overarching frameworks, but it is often corporations or industry consortia that operationalise standards. Cloud providers dictate compliance protocols that become mandatory for their clients. Payment networks impose fraud-detection regimes that reshape entire retail sectors. Audits are nominally private, but their geopolitical consequences are public. This blurring of lines makes it harder to locate accountability and easier to deploy power without visibility.

The philosophical question is whether such practices can ever be disentangled from protectionism. Proponents argue that standards advance legitimate goals—safer products, more resilient systems, higher ethical baselines. Critics counter that the very act of setting thresholds is political, privileging certain values, suppliers, and knowledge systems over others. Both views contain truth. Standards are indispensable for coordination in complex markets, yet they are never value-neutral. Recognising their strategic character is not to delegitimise them, but to strip away the pretence of impartiality.

For policymakers and enterprises alike, the challenge is to navigate this audit state without succumbing to cynicism or complacency. Simply dismissing all standards as barriers misses the genuine benefits they confer. Yet accepting them at face value is naïve. The task is interpretive: to read certifications as instruments of power, to map whose interests they serve, and to prepare adaptive strategies accordingly. This means investing not only in compliance departments but in geopolitical literacy.

The rise of the audit state signals a shift in how influence is projected. Instead of tariffs or blockades, control manifests through conformity assessments and labelling rules. Instead of open confrontation, exclusion is achieved through technicalities that few citizens will ever notice. The battlefield is the form, the checklist, the certificate. The stakes are markets worth billions, and the outcome is strategic alignment disguised as paperwork.

Yet a lingering tension remains. Can international cooperation on standards be sustained when their strategic uses become obvious? Will nations accept shared frameworks if they suspect that the hidden purpose is exclusion? Or will the proliferation of incompatible regimes fragment global markets into spheres of regulatory influence? The answers are unsettled—but one thing is certain: to understand power today, one must look not only at armies and sanctions, but at the fine print of the audit.

Inventory as strategy

In the spring of 2020, as the world reeled from the first wave of the pandemic, the United States discovered that its national stockpile of N95 masks had been left to dwindle after years of neglect. Hospitals were reduced to reusing equipment meant for single use, improvising protection out of household materials. The shortage was not just a logistical failure; it was a strategic humiliation. The richest country on earth found itself bidding against its own states, allies, and rivals for basic protective gear. A nation that had long spoken of air superiority and cyber supremacy learned the hard way that power can falter over the absence of a box in a warehouse.

The episode underscored a paradox. Inventory—those dusty pallets of commodities or components that accountants often treat as liabilities—can decide the tempo of crises. For firms, it buffers supply shocks; for states, it shapes bargaining positions. A country with ninety days of oil reserves can afford to withstand pressure in a way that one with nine cannot. A manufacturer with diversified component stock can negotiate terms; one with bare shelves must capitulate. Inventory, in other words, is not a footnote to strategy. It *is* strategy, in material form.

This recognition is not new. The Second World War was as much a contest of logistics as of battles. The Allied decision to prioritise convoys of fuel and food across the Atlantic kept armies moving and civilian morale intact. Japan's decision to attack Pearl Harbor was itself driven by America's embargo of oil and metals, which threatened to immobilise the Japanese fleet within months. Inventory here was not a passive stockpile but a coercive instrument—an enabler for one side, a chokehold on the other.

Modern economies, however, have spent decades chasing "just-in-time" efficiencies, treating inventory as waste. Lean supply chains deliver cost savings in calm seas, but they magnify vulnerability in storms. The 2011 earthquake and tsunami in Japan, for example, wiped out production of a few key automotive parts. Plants as far away as Detroit and Stuttgart stalled within days, revealing that the absence of a small stock of microcontrollers could halt entire industries. The geometry of dependence, normally invisible, suddenly became painfully clear.

Strategists have begun to revisit the mathematics of buffers. Consider oil: the International Energy Agency requires its members to hold reserves equivalent to at least ninety days of net imports. That number is not arbitrary; it reflects an estimate of how long alternative supplies can be mobilised in a crisis. In semiconductors, by contrast, most states entered the 2020s with mere days or weeks of cover. When COVID-19 disruptions met surging demand for electronics, queues stretched across industries from automotive to consumer goods. Governments rushed belatedly to fund domestic fabs, but chips cannot be conjured in months. A shelf of silicon wafers would have been a strategic asset worth billions.

The same logic applies beyond commodities. Vaccine production during the pandemic hinged on precursors like lipid nanoparticles, whose scarcity limited output. Some countries hedged by funding multiple candidates and reserving manufacturing slots—*inventory by option*. Others waited, trusting markets to deliver, and found themselves at the back of the queue. The difference was not scientific but strategic: whether policymakers treated stockpiles and contractual options as serious levers of national security.

There is also a philosophical dimension to inventory. To hold excess is to accept inefficiency in the name of resilience. Accountants mark it as cost; strategists see it as freedom of manoeuvre. The trade-off is not simply economic. It is temporal. Stockpiles buy time—days or weeks in which leaders can deliberate, alternatives can be mobilised, or adversaries can be deterred. Inventory is a time machine, shifting the balance between urgency and patience.

Yet not all buffers are equal. Hoarded commodities can decay, expire, or distort markets. Strategic petroleum reserves, for example, require rotation and maintenance; poorly managed, they can become stale or unusable. Stockpiles can also generate false confidence. The Soviet Union maintained massive grain reserves, yet chronic mismanagement meant that release often came too late to prevent shortages. The lesson is that inventory must be governed by rigorous metrics: dwell times, replenishment cycles, and recovery windows. It is not enough to possess; one must manage.

Private firms face similar dilemmas. The global shipping giant Maersk, paralysed by the NotPetya cyberattack in 2017, learned the value of *digital inventory*: offline backups of operational software that allowed recovery. In this sense, inventory extends beyond physical goods to include data, spare capacity, and even institutional memory. To lose them is to forfeit resilience; to maintain them is to preserve the ability to act under pressure.

Policymakers increasingly turn to stockpiles as instruments of influence. China's dominance in rare earth processing has been reinforced by its ability to restrict exports during diplomatic disputes. By signalling willingness to use inventory leverage, Beijing has shaped foreign companies' investment strategies and governments' industrial policies. Likewise, the United States' release of oil from its reserves in 2022 was not only about calming fuel prices but about demonstrating capacity to manage markets in the face of geopolitical shocks. The message travels as much through the existence of reserves as through their use.

For all their power, inventories raise tensions between transparency and secrecy. Publicly declaring days of cover can reassure markets and deter coercion, but it can also signal vulnerability. Quietly building reserves may reduce exposure, yet secrecy risks leaving allies uncertain and adversaries unimpressed. States must therefore choreograph disclosure: revealing enough to reassure, withholding enough to keep options open.

The broader lesson is that the mundane matters. Pallets, tanks, and warehouses may lack the drama of aircraft carriers or cyber arsenals, yet they can decide bargaining outcomes and national trajectories. A well-maintained buffer can spell the difference between resilience and panic, between autonomy and dependence. Inventory is not glamorous, but it is geometry in practice: a tangible expression of how resources, time, and leverage intersect.

The unresolved question is how far societies are willing to carry this insight. Will electorates accept higher costs today in exchange for buffers that may never be used? Will leaders frame inventory not as dead weight but as insurance, as freedom preserved in advance? Or will the pursuit of efficiency continue to hollow out resilience, leaving nations once again surprised when empty shelves translate into strategic defeat? The shelves themselves, silent and unassuming, will bear witness to which path is chosen.

Chapter 10

The Metrics of Invisible Power

In 1944, a British statistician named Patrick Blackett persuaded commanders to move the gun turrets on merchant ships not by rhetoric but by numbers. He had shown, through painstaking analysis of hit rates, that the guns were placed in the wrong positions. Once repositioned, survival odds improved. It was a reminder, in the thick of a kinetic war, that measurement, not bravado, determines outcomes. The lesson applies no less today, when the weapons are sanctions, narratives, and malware rather than shells and torpedoes.

Invisible power—whether economic, informational, or digital—relies for its effectiveness not only on what is projected but on what is counted. A speech that shifts no attitudes, a sanction that starves no revenue, or a cyber intrusion that never disrupts is wasted effort. Yet governments and corporations alike often celebrate gestures over outcomes, mistaking the noise of activity for the signal of effect. It is tempting to tally press releases, budget allocations, or the number of adversaries "called out" in public statements. Such metrics soothe bureaucracies but mislead strategies. What matters is behaviour change—has an adversary adjusted trade routes, altered propaganda lines, or modified network configurations in response? That is the real currency of power.

The difficulty, of course, is that behaviour is subtle and contested. The Iranian rial may collapse under sanctions pressure, but was it the embargo, corruption, or oil prices that drove the fall? Russian disinformation campaigns may flood social media, but does virality equal persuasion? The risk of false proxies is constant: counting tweets instead of minds changed, ships interdicted rather than strategies redirected. The history of warfare is littered with armies who measured the wrong thing—body counts in Vietnam, bomb tonnage in Korea—mistaking visible effort for strategic progress. Invisible wars risk repeating the same error at scale unless better dashboards are built.

That is why the discipline of measurement deserves its own chapter. Here we treat metrics not as dry appendices but as instruments of power in themselves. They guide what is resourced, what is rewarded, and ultimately what is fought. Sanctions without monitoring are theatre. Cyber campaigns without dwell-time analysis are noise. Narrative pushes without sentiment tracking are guesswork. In domains where outcomes are opaque, it is the metrics that anchor accountability. Without them, leaders can claim victory while losing ground.

The stakes are high. Consider sanctions: policymakers often cite the number of entities blacklisted or the breadth of export bans. Yet the question is not "how many lists were compiled?" but "did the targeted regime alter its calculus?" Measuring anomalies in trade flows or tracing evasive routing of commodities tells more about efficacy than press conferences ever will. Likewise, in cyber, the median time intruders spend undetected in networks—the dwell time—is a sharper indicator of resilience than headline-grabbing announcements of attribution. Each number chosen, each dashboard designed, reflects a philosophy of power: whether one prizes image or influence, ritual or reality.

Metrics also shape ethics. Poorly designed measures invite surveillance excess, as states grope for precision in messy human domains. Counting every click risks crossing into manipulation; tracking every transfer can collapse financial privacy. A culture of measurement can either deepen legitimacy—if guided by restraint and transparency—or erode it by normalising panoptic oversight. Thus the question of *what* to count bleeds into *how* to count, and whether citizens consent to the gaze.

This chapter proposes a recalibration. Instead of clinging to easy but empty numbers, it urges decision-centred metrics tied directly to adversary behaviour. It imagines dashboards that integrate sanctions, narratives, and cyber not as siloed pursuits but as interlocking campaigns. It offers methods—quasi-experiments, causal graphs—that instil humility rather than false certainty. It highlights the rise of the citizen-analyst, empowered by open data to audit statecraft and contribute to collective situational awareness. And it argues that ethics must be designed into measurement from the outset, not bolted on as decoration.

Invisible wars will be won not by the loudest claims but by the quiet discipline of counting the right things. The reader will leave this chapter equipped not only with sharper tools but with a different sensibility: an instinct to ask, when confronted with sweeping announcements or glossy dashboards, "what exactly is being measured, and does it matter?" That habit—more than any single statistic—is the foundation of strategic literacy in a world where power hides in numbers.

What gets measured guides what gets fought

In 1967, American officials reported that the war in Vietnam was being won. The evidence seemed solid: body counts, sorties flown, villages "secured." Yet while the tallies looked impressive, the war itself was being lost. Numbers were abundant, but they measured effort rather than effect, outputs rather than outcomes. The enemy adapted, morale eroded, and political will collapsed. The story is not just about Vietnam—it is about the perennial danger of bad proxies, where flawed measurement not only misleads but actively steers strategy in the wrong direction.

The paradox is simple yet devastating: what is easiest to count is often least important, and what truly matters resists tidy quantification. Governments prefer metrics that can be updated weekly and fit neatly on a chart. Corporations lean toward numbers that satisfy shareholders or soothe regulators. Yet wars without bullets—sanctions campaigns, disinformation contests, cyber intrusions—demand sharper yardsticks. Counting tweets or blacklisted entities may create the appearance of progress but tells little about whether adversary behaviour is changing. Numbers can conceal as much as they reveal, and when strategy follows the numbers, campaigns risk fighting shadows.

The temptation to embrace bad proxies runs deep. In sanctions regimes, policymakers often highlight how many individuals or firms have been added to watchlists. But a longer list does not necessarily mean greater leverage. The real question is whether targeted elites face rising costs or change decisions. In information operations, volume is frequently mistaken for persuasion. Ten thousand retweets do not prove minds were shifted; they may simply reflect outrage or bots amplifying noise. Cyber defence too has its misplaced metrics: the tally of blocked phishing emails may impress executives, yet it is the *dwell time*—the period attackers remain undetected inside networks—that determines vulnerability. When the wrong indicators dominate dashboards, resources flow toward appearances rather than substance.

Decision-centred metrics offer a corrective. Instead of counting what is convenient, they focus on adversary adaptations. Has a sanctioned state shifted its trade routes through secondary markets? Have propaganda lines altered following platform bans? Did malware operators change their infrastructure after defenders hardened controls? Each of these requires more careful observation, but each ties measurement directly to strategy. The most telling indicators are often indirect—shifts in commodity prices, anomalies in logistics flows, subtle adjustments in state rhetoric. They demand patience, interpretive skill, and humility. But they anchor campaigns in reality rather than ritual.

Consider the case of Iran's nuclear negotiations. The efficacy of sanctions was not ultimately measured by the number of accounts frozen or companies listed, but by Iran's decision to enter talks when currency reserves dwindled and oil revenues collapsed. That behavioural shift—not the sanction tallies—demonstrated impact. Or take Russian disinformation in Europe: while social media managers fixated on post volumes, careful survey work revealed that public attitudes often remained stable. The campaigns succeeded less in changing beliefs than in deepening cynicism and disengagement. Measuring disengagement—declining voter turnout, reduced institutional trust—proved a truer gauge of harm than counting hashtags.

Measurement shapes accountability. When governments present misleading numbers, they shield themselves from scrutiny, claiming success where failure festers. When organisations adopt poor proxies, they waste money and erode trust. Accountability requires metrics that resist political theatre. That means tracking *consequences*, not inputs. In cyber defence, this may involve reporting recovery windows after intrusions rather than the number of alerts flagged. In narrative contests, it means assessing shifts in trust in institutions rather than the virality of campaign slogans. In sanctions, it is about identifying specific industries or elites whose behaviour changes, not the sheer size of sanctions lists.

Yet better measurement is not just technical; it is philosophical. It requires deciding what truly matters. Is the aim to deter aggression, constrain capacity, or alter long-term trajectories? Metrics follow from objectives. When objectives are vague, metrics drift. This explains why many campaigns default to bad proxies: they are measurable precisely because they sidestep hard questions about goals. A sanctions list can always be expanded, a tweet count always updated. Behavioural change, by contrast, is harder to capture, more ambiguous, and sometimes unflattering. But it is also the only measure that counts.

The deeper insight is that metrics are not neutral—they guide what is fought. If body counts dominate, wars chase kills. If sanction tallies dominate, diplomacy becomes a list-building exercise. If cyber campaigns fixate on attribution, resources flow toward naming culprits rather than ejecting them from networks. Measurement becomes destiny. The discipline of invisible wars therefore demands a discipline of counting. By choosing better metrics, policymakers can change incentives, refine tactics, and align strategies with reality. By clinging to poor ones, they risk fighting mirages while adversaries quietly advance.

The unresolved challenge is how to design metrics that are rigorous yet usable, honest yet politically sustainable. Too much precision invites paralysis, too little invites theatre. The path lies between: decision-centred measures tied to adversary behaviour, carefully interpreted and modestly presented. The future of non-kinetic campaigns may depend less on dazzling rhetoric than on the quiet craft of measuring what matters. And so the pressing question lingers: when the next "invisible war" unfolds, will leaders have the courage to count the right things—or will they once again mistake tallies for triumph?

A dashboard for sanctions, narratives, and cyber

On the morning after Russia's invasion of Ukraine, policymakers in Washington, Brussels, and Tokyo scrambled to impose sanctions, disrupt propaganda, and harden digital networks. Yet the question hung in the air: how would they know if any of it was working? The instinct was to count—how many banks cut off, how many posts deleted, how many servers patched. But such tallies told little about whether Moscow's calculus had shifted, whether publics were persuaded, or whether hackers had truly been deterred. What was missing was a dashboard: a disciplined way of combining disparate signals into a picture of strategic effect.

The paradox of invisible power is that it produces effects that are neither immediate nor easily measured. A missile strike leaves wreckage. A narrative strike leaves doubt. Sanctions corrode economies in silence, and cyber intrusions may remain undetected for months. Yet decisions still must be made—should sanctions be tightened, campaigns amplified, defences retooled? Without metrics that capture movement beneath the surface, policymakers are left navigating by feel. That is where dashboards, thoughtfully designed, can offer more than comfort: they can impose structure on the fog.

Building such dashboards requires distinguishing between *leading* and *lagging* indicators. A lagging indicator confirms impact after the fact—GDP contraction months after sanctions, public trust erosion long after disinformation spreads, network compromise discovered in an audit. A leading indicator, by contrast, provides an early signal—an unusual shift in cross-border payments, a sudden change in the tone of online discourse, a spike in the time hackers need to gain persistence inside a network. Both matter. The craft lies in linking the two so that early movements can be validated by later outcomes, creating feedback loops rather than static snapshots.

Take sanctions. A conventional dashboard might display the number of designated entities or the nominal value of frozen assets. But more revealing are anomalies in trade flows: sudden rerouting of exports through unlikely partners, unexplained spikes in shadow markets, or currency pressures emerging before official data registers. These deltas—small shifts in the geometry of commerce—can indicate whether sanctions are biting, being circumvented, or pushing adversaries toward alternative alignments. Without tracking these patterns, governments risk confusing administrative activity with strategic leverage.

Narratives present a different measurement puzzle. Here, volume is a seductive but misleading metric: the sheer number of posts or articles says little about persuasion. More telling is *sentiment delta*—the change in attitudes among targeted populations over time. Surveys, focus groups, and sentiment analysis of organic discourse can reveal whether messages are being absorbed, rejected, or producing fatigue. Even negative responses matter: if hostile narratives provoke defensive solidarity, they may backfire. A dashboard that overlays sentiment data with political behaviour—turnout rates, trust in institutions, voting patterns—moves beyond counting noise to measuring resonance.

Cyber operations demand another set of indicators. Traditional reporting often highlights intrusion attempts blocked, yet the more meaningful statistic is *dwell time*: how long attackers remain inside systems before detection and expulsion. A median dwell time shrinking from months to days signals genuine resilience. Combined with data on repeat incursions, patch adoption, and cross-sector coordination, such indicators tell a story not of effort but of effectiveness. A dashboard integrating these measures provides a dynamic portrait of digital health—one that moves beyond the illusion of safety toward tangible resilience.

Dashboards also offer a framework for testing attribution hypotheses. Suppose an economy shows anomalies in commodity flows following sanctions. Is this the result of sanctions themselves, or a separate market shock? Suppose online sentiment dips after a campaign of hostile messaging. Was it driven by the campaign, or by domestic political events? By juxtaposing leading and lagging indicators across domains—financial, informational, digital—analysts can test causal hypotheses, ruling out coincidence and reinforcing inference. It is not certainty, but it is structured doubt, which is often the most honest stance in contested spaces.

There is, however, a danger in dashboards: they can seduce by appearing comprehensive. A wall of charts creates the impression of control. But if the wrong indicators are chosen, or if context is stripped away, the dashboard becomes a theatre of numbers. The challenge is philosophical as well as technical: deciding which outcomes matter, which behaviours count as change, and which signals are trustworthy. A dashboard cannot replace judgement, but it can discipline it. It forces policymakers to specify assumptions, track trends over time, and confront disconfirming evidence.

Examples of composite dashboards already exist in fragments. Central banks monitor leading and lagging indicators to assess inflationary pressure. Cybersecurity agencies compile dwell times and patch rates to benchmark resilience. Public health officials overlay testing rates, hospitalisations, and excess mortality to capture the trajectory of epidemics. In each case, the value lies not in a single metric but in a mosaic that reveals patterns invisible to any one measure. Applying this mindset to sanctions, narratives, and cyber is less a technical leap than a cultural one: it requires treating invisible campaigns with the same analytic discipline as visible wars.

The broader lesson is that dashboards are more than tools; they are commitments. They commit institutions to transparency about what is being measured, humility about what remains uncertain, and discipline in aligning action to evidence. They also democratise oversight: a well-designed public dashboard allows citizens, journalists, and allies to scrutinise claims and hold leaders accountable. In contested spaces where rhetoric is cheap and data scarce, such openness can itself be a form of strategic strength.

The unanswered question is whether leaders are willing to adopt dashboards that may reveal discomforting truths. A sanctions campaign may show negligible behavioural change despite years of effort. A narrative offensive may register fatigue or backlash rather than persuasion. A cyber defence programme may expose persistent weaknesses. To measure honestly is to risk embarrassment. Yet to measure poorly is to risk defeat. The test of invisible power is not whether we can act, but whether we can see. The future of statecraft may hinge less on bold declarations than on the quiet discipline of dashboards—those unglamorous panels of numbers that, if chosen well, can reveal whether we are shaping the world or merely congratulating ourselves.

Causality under uncertainty

When the British blockade strangled German imports during the First World War, some observers credited the strategy with forcing Berlin to the negotiating table. Others argued the blockade had only a peripheral influence, pointing instead to battlefield losses and political turmoil. Even with hindsight, the causal chain remains contested: was the blockade decisive, contributory, or merely coincidental? This problem of attribution is not unique to historians. It confronts policymakers, analysts, and strategists every time they ask whether a sanction, a narrative campaign, or a cyber operation *worked*. The paradox is that action often feels most urgent precisely when evidence of cause and effect is murkiest.

The human mind craves certainty. We prefer clean stories: A causes B, which produces C. Yet in complex environments—economies, societies, networks—causality rarely presents itself in neat lines. What appears as cause may be correlation, and what looks like failure may simply be a delay in effect. When an online influence campaign coincides with falling trust in institutions, is the link causal, partial, or illusory? To admit uncertainty feels like weakness. But to ignore it risks hubris and miscalculation. The discipline of causal reasoning is, in essence, the craft of intellectual humility.

At the heart of this craft are tools that help us navigate without demanding impossible clarity. *Quasi-experimental designs*—such as difference-in-differences, synthetic controls, and natural experiments—allow practitioners to approximate the conditions of laboratory science in the wild mess of geopolitics. They exploit accidents of history: a new law implemented in one jurisdiction but not another, a sudden disruption of supply chains in one region but not its neighbour. By comparing outcomes across these "as if random" variations, analysts can tease out causal signals without pretending to command full experimental control.

Consider the sanctions imposed on Iran's oil exports in the early 2010s. Simply observing a drop in revenue proved little—global oil prices fluctuated, domestic mismanagement compounded difficulties, and black-market circumventions muddied the water. But by comparing Iran's export volumes to those of similar producers not targeted by sanctions, researchers constructed a synthetic control that clarified the unique impact of the restrictions. The insight was not absolute, but it was disciplined: the sanctions had a measurable effect, though not as great as rhetoric suggested. This kind of measured inference is far more useful for policymakers than sweeping claims of success or failure.

Causal graphs extend this discipline by making assumptions explicit. Instead of vague arrows in briefing slides, they force analysts to map the variables at play: propaganda campaigns, media coverage, public sentiment, election outcomes. They demand clarity about which links are hypothesised and which are merely observed. By doing so, they highlight where confounding variables—hidden drivers like economic shocks or institutional scandals—may be distorting the picture. Even if the graph cannot be populated with perfect data, it compels honesty about the structure of belief. Strategy, after all, rests not only on action but on models of how action is supposed to work.

Yet the most powerful tool in the causal kit may be the counterfactual. To ask "what would have happened otherwise?" is to confront the shadow world where the policy was never enacted, the campaign never launched, the embargo never imposed. Counterfactual reasoning disciplines both triumphalism and despair. If an adversary collapses after sanctions, but would likely have collapsed under the weight of its own internal contradictions, then sanctions may be less decisive than they appear. If a narrative campaign seems ineffective, but without it disinformation would have spread unchecked, then the intervention's value may be hidden in prevention. The counterfactual is a reminder that we measure not against perfection, but against plausible alternatives.

False certainty is the perennial temptation. Analysts often reach for easy proxies—media mentions, GDP figures, the number of cyberattacks blocked—as shorthand for causal impact. But such proxies can be dangerously misleading. Counting blocked attacks says little about whether adversaries adapted; tracking GDP ignores distributional effects that shift political stability. A poor metric can seduce leaders into believing they are winning when they are, in fact, bleeding. Simplicity is a virtue only when it clarifies, not when it obscures. The measure of a metric is whether it guides better decisions, not whether it is easy to present on a slide.

Case sketches from practice illustrate both pitfalls and promise. After the Arab Spring, some governments attempted to measure "stability" by monitoring protest frequency. When protests subsided, they inferred resilience. Yet deeper analysis showed that grievances had not disappeared;

repression had simply silenced visible dissent. When instability returned, leaders were blindsided. By contrast, in the global fight against ransomware, analysts began measuring *dwell time* and ransom payment patterns rather than raw attack numbers. This shift captured not just activity but adversary adaptation, allowing for interventions that tightened the noose around criminal business models. The difference was not technological but conceptual: measuring what mattered rather than what was easiest.

The broader philosophical lesson is that causality is never a fixed object waiting to be discovered. It is a set of hypotheses tested under conditions of uncertainty. To embrace this is not to resign oneself to ignorance but to cultivate a posture of disciplined doubt. This humility is not paralysis. It is what allows practitioners to act while acknowledging uncertainty, to adjust as evidence accumulates, and to resist the seduction of false clarity. In the long run, such intellectual honesty is not only a methodological choice but a strategic one. Adversaries often overstate their effectiveness; democracies that resist the same temptation preserve credibility both at home and abroad.

Still, the unresolved tension lingers: how much uncertainty can policymakers tolerate before action becomes politically impossible? Citizens demand verdicts, allies expect assurance, and leaders crave success narratives. The analyst, by contrast, often sees ambiguity, partial causation, and countervailing forces. Bridging this divide is one of the hardest tasks of modern statecraft. The future may belong not to those who claim certainty, but to those who can navigate its absence without losing direction. The question remains whether institutions, and the publics they serve, are ready to embrace the humility that causality under uncertainty demands.

Open data and the citizen-analyst

On the eve of Russia's invasion of Ukraine in 2022, some of the most accurate predictions of troop movements did not come from classified satellites or secret government briefings. They came from open platforms: TikTok clips of tanks moving along snowy roads, satellite images from commercial providers, and customs data showing unusual surges in fuel shipments. Amateur sleuths, journalists, and volunteers stitched together a mosaic of insight that rivalled the assessments of professional intelligence services. The paradox was striking: in an age of hyper-secrecy, the public sphere became a powerful site of foresight.

This was not an isolated episode. When the Panama Papers were released, it was the collaboration of journalists, analysts, and civic technologists who transformed a dense mass of corporate filings into a map of global corruption. During the COVID-19 pandemic, citizen-driven trackers offered faster, more transparent data than some state health agencies. These moments illustrate a shift: the monopoly on strategic knowledge has weakened, and motivated citizens, armed with open data, can now illuminate power's blind spots.

The term "citizen-analyst" captures this new role. Unlike the traditional researcher within government or academia, the citizen-analyst works outside formal institutions, often with minimal resources but maximal creativity. Their raw material is open data: customs records revealing anomalous trade flows, court dockets exposing hidden litigation, corporate filings tracing ownership chains. Such data, once obscure and inaccessible, is increasingly digitised, searchable, and sharable. What was once the preserve of insiders now sits a few clicks away.

The power of this lies not only in access but in aggregation. A customs entry showing unusual shipments of dual-use chemicals might seem trivial in isolation. Combined with corporate filings tying the exporter to a sanctioned entity, and with shipping logs indicating irregular routes, the pattern sharpens. Crowdsourced platforms make such aggregation possible at scale. The outcome is a distributed form of oversight: a thousand eyes catching what a single agency might miss.

Some of the most striking examples of this practice have emerged in financial transparency. Bellingcat's investigators famously pieced together the identities of Russian operatives implicated in the Salisbury poisonings by cross-referencing leaked passport data, online phone directories, and obscure corporate registrations. In doing so, they not only exposed state deception but demonstrated that open data, when harnessed rigorously, can challenge narratives crafted at the highest levels of government. Their work raised an uncomfortable question: if citizens can unmask covert operations with public data, what excuse remains for governments that claim ignorance?

Yet the citizen-analyst is not merely an adversarial figure. Their work also strengthens democratic oversight by making policy debates more evidence-driven. Take the case of export controls. Governments may announce sweeping restrictions on sensitive technologies, but open trade statistics allow citizen groups to test whether flows actually diminish. When anomalies persist—such as advanced chips still entering sanctioned economies through intermediaries—citizen-analysts can call attention to gaps that policymakers prefer to downplay. This is not cynicism; it is a form of accountability.

There is, however, a tension at the heart of open data. Its abundance can overwhelm as easily as it can enlighten. The citizen-analyst faces the risk of false positives—seeing intent where randomness suffices, attributing causality where coincidence rules. Crowdsourced audits, for all their promise, are vulnerable to bias, noise, and manipulation. False narratives dressed up as data visualisations can spread faster than careful analysis. The very openness that empowers vigilance can also enable disinformation.

That is why methodology matters as much as access. The most effective citizen-analysts combine transparency of method with humility of claim. They publish not only their findings but their sources, assumptions, and uncertainties. They invite replication and critique. In this sense, the citizen-analyst embodies democratic values not just in content but in form: knowledge as a shared, contestable enterprise rather than as decree. This ethic distinguishes genuine oversight from conspiracy-mongering.

Public dashboards are one of the most promising formats for this ethos. By curating leading indicators—such as sentiment shifts in online discourse, trade anomalies in sensitive goods, or unusual patterns in financial disclosures—citizen groups can make complex data legible to wider audiences. These dashboards are not replacements for official intelligence but complements: open, accountable, and interpretable. They offer a different kind of legitimacy, one rooted in transparency rather than secrecy.

Governments are not passive in this story. Some states now recognise the strategic value of open-source intelligence and actively court citizen-analyst contributions. NATO, for instance, has experimented with partnerships that integrate civilian-generated insights into military planning. Others take the opposite stance, seeking to restrict access to public records in the name of "security" but in practice shielding incompetence or corruption. The battle over open data is thus also a battle over democratic resilience: whether oversight is widened or narrowed, empowered or curtailed.

Philosophically, the rise of the citizen-analyst challenges long-standing hierarchies of knowledge. For centuries, statecraft assumed a vertical model: information flows upward to officials, decisions flow downward to citizens. Open data inverts this, enabling lateral flows where citizens can hold power to account in near real time. It redefines competence: no longer the monopoly of institutions but the product of networked communities. This diffusion is messy, but it may also be essential. In a world where manipulation and secrecy are rampant, only a distributed vigilance can balance concentrated power.

Yet the unresolved question remains: can citizen analysis scale without succumbing to chaos? Transparency without quality control risks an ecosystem flooded by noise. Institutional gatekeeping without openness risks ossification and mistrust. Between these poles lies a fragile middle ground: networks of civic trust, methodological rigour, and shared norms that allow open data to serve as infrastructure for democratic competence. Whether societies can cultivate this balance will determine whether the citizen-analyst becomes a pillar of resilience or a casualty of information overload. The answer is not given. It is a collective choice still in the making.

Ethics of measurement

In the wake of the September 11 attacks, the United States passed the Patriot Act, granting sweeping surveillance powers to agencies in the name of national security. For years, these powers expanded quietly, largely unexamined by the public, until the Snowden revelations in 2013 peeled back the curtain. What stunned many was not only the scale of data collection but the ease with which governments had normalised continuous observation of citizens. The lesson was stark: when measurement becomes indistinguishable from surveillance, the very tools meant to safeguard democracy begin to corrode it from within.

The paradox lies here: effective statecraft requires measurement, but every act of measurement touches human lives. To measure is to define, to categorise, to strip complexity into indicators. Yet when people are reduced to datapoints, their dignity can be lost in translation. The tension between precision and privacy, between oversight and overreach, cannot be resolved by technology alone. It is an ethical design problem at its core.

Consider the lure of comprehensive monitoring in cyber defence. Faced with the threat of foreign intrusions, some argue for logging every keystroke, storing every packet, retaining every trace. The technical instinct is to collect first and reason later. But this logic, left unchecked, drifts towards total surveillance. What begins as exceptional can become routine. The danger is not only to privacy but to legitimacy: a state that treats its citizens as permanent suspects undermines the very trust it seeks to defend.

Minimal-snoop principles offer a counterweight. Rather than hoarding information indiscriminately, these principles ask: what is the least intrusive measurement that still enables effective decision-making? If the goal is to detect systemic risk in financial flows, aggregate patterns may suffice without exposing every individual transaction. If the aim is to evaluate cyber resilience, anonymised dwell-time metrics can guide policy without tracking each employee's digital footprint. Restraint in data collection is not a concession to weakness; it is a discipline that preserves both efficacy and trust.

Sunset reviews provide a second safeguard. Extraordinary powers of measurement should never be indefinite. History shows that once data is collected, the temptation to repurpose it is nearly irresistible. A surveillance system built for counterterrorism may be used for immigration enforcement, then for monitoring political dissent. By mandating periodic reviews—where powers must be re-justified, recalibrated, or allowed to expire—societies impose friction against the slow creep of normalisation. Sunset clauses are less about bureaucracy than about memory: they remind institutions that urgency must always be balanced by accountability.

The ethical stakes are heightened in the global context. Export controls, sanctions enforcement, and cross-border cyber operations often require intrusive monitoring of transactions, communications, and infrastructure. Here, measurement intersects with sovereignty and cultural difference. A tool justified in one jurisdiction may appear illegitimate in another. States that claim to champion openness risk hypocrisy if their own citizens are shielded while others are monitored without constraint. In this sense, ethical measurement is not merely a domestic concern; it is part of the soft power equation, shaping how a nation is perceived abroad.

Marketing science provides a cautionary mirror. The same psychological profiling that allows firms to micro-target consumers is increasingly available to governments. Fear, pride, and disgust can be quantified and exploited, tracked through clicks and sentiment analysis. Yet here the line between measurement and manipulation blurs. A policy informed by such data may look effective in the short term, but if citizens feel nudged, herded, or gamed, the long-term consequence is cynicism. The metric becomes poison.

To treat ethics as decoration—a checklist at the end of design—is to misunderstand its function. Ethics in measurement must be architectural. It should shape the categories chosen, the granularity permitted, the uses allowed, and the reviews enforced. To design ethically is to encode respect for dignity into the system itself, making it harder for future operators to drift into excess. In this way, ethics is not a brake but a stabiliser: it prevents the very excesses that would undermine legitimacy and effectiveness alike.

The temptation is always towards more: more indicators, more granularity, more certainty. Yet wisdom often lies in subtraction. The challenge for states, firms, and citizens alike is to recognise that the legitimacy of power depends less on the reach of measurement than on the integrity with which it is wielded. To measure without demeaning, to collect without coercing, to count without erasing the human—these are not technical feats but civic ones.

And so the unresolved question lingers: in a world where data is abundant and tools of surveillance grow ever sharper, will societies learn to build measurement systems that preserve dignity as fiercely as they pursue security? The answer will decide not only how well states fight invisible wars but whether they deserve to win them.

Chapter 11

Deterrence Without Detonations

When the United States froze $300 billion of Russian central bank reserves in February 2022, it demonstrated something extraordinary: immense coercive power deployed without a single soldier crossing a border or a missile leaving a silo. In one stroke, the world saw that deterrence could be financial, silent, and instantaneous—yet no less consequential than tanks massed on a frontier. The episode revealed a paradox: the most forceful modern weapons are often invisible, operating not through firepower but through expectations, credibility, and the manipulation of systems on which nations depend.

For most of the twentieth century, deterrence was pictured in nuclear silhouettes and missile silos, its logic rooted in the threat of annihilation. Today, the terrain has shifted. Markets, networks, courts, and clouds have become the new battlegrounds. The challenge is no longer how to threaten overwhelming destruction but how to signal resolve with instruments designed for pressure, not for explosion. Sanctions, lawfare, and cyber tools all share this quality: they must be displayed with enough clarity to alter adversary behaviour, but withheld from such excess that they trigger uncontrollable escalation. The choreography is delicate, the stakes immense.

This new theatre of deterrence raises sharper questions. How does a state show that it has the capability to disrupt an opponent's banking system or paralyse logistics software without actually pulling the trigger? How can it prove credibility without triggering panic in markets or backlash among allies? These are not abstract puzzles; they are questions of survival, influence, and stability in a world where non-kinetic power is ascendant.

The logic of deterrence remains: clarity, capability, credibility. Yet each has been reinterpreted. Clarity lies not in broadcast threats but in calibrated exposure of tools—leaks of malware families, previews of sanction packages, rehearsals of cross-border audits. Capability is demonstrated through joint exercises in finance and cyber, not just military drills. Credibility is signalled by tripwires embedded in trade agreements or automated tariff escalations that remove human hesitation. The new logic depends less on spectacle and more on design.

Economic commitments illustrate the point. A tariff that automatically snaps into place when trade volumes cross a threshold is not a mere policy; it is a pre-set tripwire. Its very automation reduces the risk of misperception. Adversaries know the rulebook in advance. The deterrent force lies in its predictability, not its mystery. In this sense, law and economics are becoming arenas of engineering as much as strategy—systems must be built to convey reliability, not just to inflict cost.

Alliances, too, must evolve. NATO exercises once centred on tank manoeuvres and air defence; their modern equivalents may be joint sanctions rehearsals, coordinated cyber audits, or shared financial monitoring protocols. The deterrent effect comes from the pooling of credibility: an adversary knows it will not face one regulatory regime or financial jurisdiction but a coalition acting in synchrony. This is deterrence by interoperability, in which spreadsheets, legal briefs, and certification standards carry the weight once borne by armoured divisions.

But non-kinetic deterrence has its own traps. Pressure without off-ramps can harden resolve instead of shifting it. A cyber sanction or export control that cannot be reversed risks becoming permanent punishment, losing its signalling value and locking both sides into escalation. Designing ladders down—reversible penalties, temporary licensing, face-saving narratives—is as vital as building ladders up. Measurement plays a role here: knowing when deterrence has succeeded, when behaviour has shifted, and when pressure should be released requires credible dashboards of evidence. Without these, policymakers risk mistaking inertia for compliance.

Finally, deterrence in democratic societies cannot hide in shadows. Citizens must understand the doctrine, not only because transparency builds legitimacy but because panic is the enemy of stability. A public informed of the thresholds, tools, and limits of non-kinetic deterrence is less likely to interpret every sanction as a slide into war or every cyber clash as a prelude to collapse. Secrecy erodes trust; clarity sustains it. In this sense, deterrence is not only a strategic art but a civic project.

The paradox of our age is stark: the gravest threats to peace may be contained not by missiles that explode but by systems that constrain. To deter without detonations is to learn how to wield power that is silent yet palpable, hidden yet visible enough to shape choices. The choreography is unfinished, the doctrine still emerging. The question that looms over the chapter—and over our era—is whether states can refine this subtle art quickly enough to prevent the visible wars that deterrence was always meant to avoid.

How to signal resolve without escalation

In April 2021, the United States quietly released a cybersecurity advisory describing a new strain of malware—suspected to originate from Russian actors—that could burrow into industrial control systems. The advisory was accompanied by technical details so precise that the message was unmistakable: Washington not only knew of the tool, it had mapped its architecture and could neutralise it if necessary. No missile was launched, no formal ultimatum issued. Yet the exposure itself was a signal—a calibrated disclosure designed to deter without igniting open confrontation. It was resolved, packaged in the language of digital diagnostics.

This episode illustrates the paradox of modern deterrence. To convince an adversary that one is both willing and able to impose costs, a state must reveal just enough of its hand—without playing the card outright. In the nuclear age, signalling resolve meant visible missile deployments, publicised war games, or dramatic speeches about red lines. In today's world of sanctions, lawfare, and cyber operations, the signals are subtler: a leak of impending export controls, a legal filing timed for maximum visibility, or a sanctions list drafted with conspicuous specificity. Deterrence now operates less through spectacle than through suggestion, more through choreography than through confrontation.

Classic deterrence theory rested on three pillars: clarity, capability, and credibility. Each remains vital, but each has acquired new guises. Clarity, once embodied in presidential speeches or doctrinal manuals, now depends on transparency about rules of economic engagement or thresholds in digital space. Capability, formerly displayed through parades of hardware, must now be demonstrated by regulatory capacity, forensic skill, or economic reach. Credibility, the most elusive of the three, requires pre-commitments and mechanised responses—automatic tariff escalators, licensing snap-backs, or cyber sanctions that activate by algorithm rather than by whim. The art is not in raw capacity alone but in the design of signals that leave little room for misperception.

Take sanctions. A sprawling embargo announced with sweeping rhetoric often lacks deterrent effect, precisely because it appears blunt and politically driven. By contrast, a sanction package published with surgical detail—naming not just banks but the clearing mechanisms through which they operate—signals a mastery of the adversary's system. It conveys capability and resolve in one stroke. Similarly, in lawfare, a government might highlight a single court ruling on asset seizure, not for its immediate effect but to show a precedent ready to be multiplied if provoked. The disclosure is strategic theatre: a glimpse of the tools in reserve, sufficient to shape expectations.

Cyber deterrence raises sharper dilemmas. Revealing too much about an intrusion tool risks burning an intelligence asset; revealing too little fails to convey credibility. States have adapted by offering fragments—showing adversaries enough of the skeleton to hint at the full anatomy. This is choreography at its most delicate: hinting at destructive power while keeping the performance reversible. The message is not "we will strike you" but "we can, if you cross this line." In a world where attribution itself is contested, carefully timed exposures become the currency of deterrence.

Philosophically, signalling without escalation forces policymakers to inhabit contradiction. They must be both transparent and ambiguous, both firm and flexible. Too much opacity invites miscalculation; too much exposure invites escalation. The balance resembles a conversation more than a confrontation—a conversation where silence, pauses, and inflections carry as much weight as words. States communicate in footnotes, in regulatory drafts, in the selective leaking of cyber tools. The dialogue is legible to insiders yet invisible to most citizens.

But this invisibility is not without risk. If deterrence signals are too subtle, adversaries may ignore or misinterpret them. If they are too theatrical, they may corner an opponent into proving defiance. The Cuban missile crisis demonstrated the peril of ambiguous signals in the kinetic age; in the non-kinetic age, ambiguity proliferates in quieter forms. A half-announced sanction, a vaguely attributed cyberattack, a conditional legal threat—each can be read as bluff or as warning. The choreography of deterrence, therefore, is not only about sending signals but about shaping the interpretive environment in which those signals are received.

To craft deterrence without escalation requires recognising that power is increasingly performative. Resolve is demonstrated not in the detonation of weapons but in the controlled revelation of tools. The challenge is to make adversaries believe in capacities they hope never to witness, while keeping the instruments sheathed. In this dance of shadows and disclosures, credibility hangs on timing, proportion, and restraint.

The unresolved question is whether states can maintain this balance indefinitely. As adversaries probe for weakness, and as publics demand transparency, how long can signals remain calibrated rather than excessive? The risk is ever-present: that the choreography slips, the curtain falls, and what was meant as deterrence becomes provocation. The theatre of non-kinetic deterrence continues—but the ending of the performance is still unwritten.

Tripwires and commitments in economic space

In the Cold War, NATO's forward deployment of troops in West Germany functioned as a tripwire. The presence of allied soldiers meant that any Soviet advance, however limited, would trigger automatic involvement of the United States and Britain. The credibility of deterrence lies not in the size of the force but in the certainty of response. Today, in the domain of trade, finance, and digital infrastructure, nations are experimenting with analogous devices: pre-programmed tariffs, automatic licence withdrawals, and narrative red lines that commit them to response without deliberation. These are not men with rifles, but levers in code, law, and policy—tripwires embedded in the fabric of commerce.

The paradox is striking. Flexibility is often seen as a strength in statecraft, yet too much discretion invites miscalculation. When adversaries doubt whether a government will respond to provocation, deterrence weakens. The appeal of mechanised commitments is that they bind states to act predictably, not emotionally. A tariff that rises by fixed increments if imports exceed a quota is not a threat whispered across negotiating tables; it is a certainty, legible to counterparties and publics alike. In volatile environments, predictability itself becomes a stabiliser.

Consider the World Trade Organization's safeguard mechanisms. They allow countries to impose temporary tariffs automatically when imports surge beyond an agreed threshold. In theory, these rules transform what might otherwise be a political crisis into an administrative procedure. Instead of leaders scrambling to appease domestic industries under pressure, the system generates a known response, reducing accusations of arbitrariness. The deterrent effect is not just on exporters who might otherwise flood a market, but on political actors tempted to test the resilience of trade partners.

The same logic underpins "snap-back" provisions in export licensing. A company authorised to sell sensitive components abroad may do so under strict conditions. Breach those conditions—say, by diverting goods to a prohibited third party—and the licence is revoked automatically, without the need for political theatre. For adversaries, the message is clear: there is no grey zone to exploit. For regulators, the advantage is consistency. The tripwire transforms compliance into an engineering problem rather than a lobbying contest.

Narrative red lines function differently, but with similar aims. When governments declare, for example, that disinformation targeting election infrastructure will trigger economic retaliation, they create an expectation in advance. Such red lines shift the debate from *whether* to respond to *when* and *how*. The very act of articulation hardens the credibility of deterrence. Yet narrative commitments require careful calibration: if drawn too broadly, they risk entrapment; if drawn too narrowly, they invite probing just outside the boundary. The craft lies in making red lines precise enough to constrain but flexible enough to adapt.

Critics worry that mechanised responses strip away diplomatic discretion and remove the possibility of de-escalation. But here lies the tension at the heart of deterrence: the more discretion leaders preserve for themselves, the less certain adversaries are of their resolve. Tripwires tilt the balance toward stability by reducing ambiguity, though at the cost of some flexibility. The design challenge is to set thresholds that are neither trivial nor catastrophic, ensuring that responses escalate proportionately rather than spiralling into overreaction.

History offers illuminating parallels. The naval treaties of the interwar period included explicit tonnage limits that functioned as automatic triggers for suspicion and countermeasures if exceeded. During the oil shocks of the 1970s, the International Energy Agency created mandatory sharing rules—tripwires that committed members to release stockpiles if supplies fell below certain levels. In both cases, credibility flowed from predictability. The very existence of a mechanised rule reduced the likelihood that crises would metastasise into disorderly scrambles.

In contemporary practice, tripwires in economic space also serve domestic functions. Automaticity reassures publics that governments will not fold under pressure. It disciplines political leaders who might otherwise hesitate in the face of costs. And it signals to allies that commitments are not contingent on personalities or shifting moods. In a multipolar system, such predictability is an asset in coalition-building: partners are more willing to align when they know responses will be rule-bound rather than ad hoc.

Yet the danger remains that rigidity can outpace reason. A tariff escalator might activate in response to statistical noise rather than genuine manipulation. A narrative red line might compel action in a marginal case, leading to disproportionate costs. Mechanised commitments are not a substitute for strategy; they are instruments within it. The art lies in designing triggers that align with underlying interests and can be recalibrated as circumstances evolve. Sunset clauses, periodic reviews, and built-in escape hatches can temper rigidity without sacrificing credibility.

The larger insight is that deterrence in the economic domain cannot rest on improvisation alone. Credibility grows from systems that adversaries can model, anticipate, and respect. Tripwires and commitments create such systems, embedding deterrence into the machinery of commerce and regulation. They are less dramatic than tanks on borders, but no less consequential. The question that lingers is whether states will have the discipline to live with the constraints they build for themselves—or whether, in the heat of crisis, the temptation to override the tripwire will undo the very credibility they sought to create.

Alliances that actually deter

When NATO was founded in 1949, its deterrent force was not simply the aggregate of American nuclear weapons and European armies. It was the infrastructure of interoperability—common procedures, shared command structures, and the reassurance that an attack on one would draw in all. The message was as much bureaucratic as military: aggression would trigger not just a battlefield response but a cascade of pre-agreed actions, too tightly woven to unpick. Today, as the frontiers of contest shift to finance, law, and information systems, the same principle applies. Deterrence requires more than promises; it requires rehearsed, interlocking capacities that leave no daylight for adversaries to exploit.

Consider financial sanctions. The United States can freeze assets on its own, but the effect is magnified when allies act in unison. What makes coordination credible is not rhetoric but plumbing: interoperable payment-blocking systems, synchronised watchlists, and harmonised compliance protocols across jurisdictions. When Western governments moved to exclude Russian banks from SWIFT in 2022, the true signal lay not in the headlines but in the seamless technical execution across dozens of regulators and institutions. The deterrent lesson is plain: alliances that actually deter are those that function like operating systems, not debating clubs.

Legal instruments illustrate the same logic. Extraterritorial prosecutions of corruption or cybercrime gain weight when multiple jurisdictions share evidence standards, extradition pathways, and reciprocal recognition of judgements. For adversaries contemplating economic coercion or lawfare, the knowledge that courts in London, Brussels, and Washington will move in concert alters the risk calculus. Here, deterrence stems from institutional choreography: if rules are aligned, the costs of hostile acts escalate geometrically, not additively.

Exercises and joint audits, once the preserve of navies and armies, are emerging in these invisible domains. Multinational stress tests of banks, coordinated cyber incident drills, or joint audits of supply chain resilience are the non-kinetic equivalents of military war games. Their purpose is not only to reveal vulnerabilities but to demonstrate preparedness to adversaries watching closely. A successful drill communicates that allied systems can withstand shocks and retaliate through coordinated levers—be they sanctions, asset seizures, or narrative countermeasures. In the absence of such rehearsals, commitments risk sounding like wishful thinking.

Pooling capabilities across finance, law, and information systems also raises the entry costs for aggressors. A lone country imposing sanctions risks evasion; a bloc covering most global clearing houses makes circumvention far harder. A single nation publishing disinformation rebuttals may be ignored; a coordinated narrative backed by credible data from multiple allies is harder to dismiss. Just as interoperability in military supply chains once made alliances more than symbolic, interoperability in data standards, audit regimes, and compliance systems makes twenty-first century alliances operationally formidable.

There is, however, a philosophical tension. The more alliances bind themselves through interoperable rules and automated triggers, the less freedom each member retains to adjust responses unilaterally. The very rigidity that creates deterrent credibility can constrain discretion. Yet history suggests this trade-off is necessary: deterrence works when adversaries know that allies cannot wriggle out of commitments. For democracies, the challenge is to design alliances whose automaticity strengthens resolve without eroding sovereignty.

Case studies underscore the point. The European Union's General Data Protection Regulation (GDPR), though often viewed through the lens of privacy, functions strategically by setting global compliance benchmarks. Firms worldwide align with it to preserve market access, effectively outsourcing their standards to Brussels. This is deterrence through bureaucracy: the cost of non-compliance is exclusion from one of the world's largest markets. In cyber defence, the Tallinn Manual and NATO's Cooperative Cyber Defence Centre represent embryonic attempts to pool legal doctrine and operational drills, signalling that aggression in cyberspace will encounter harmonised responses.

The implications extend beyond governments. Private firms—banks, insurers, logistics operators—become instruments of collective deterrence when they adopt interoperable standards. The closer these systems are knitted together, the harder it is for adversaries to pry them apart. But reliance on private actors also introduces fragility: who ensures consistency across jurisdictions? Who pays for rehearsals that resemble military exercises in scale but lack the same political prestige?

What emerges is a reframing of alliances for the invisible front. Deterrence is no longer just about tanks parked in readiness; it is about dashboards aligned, audits rehearsed, and sanctions primed to fire in unison. It is about demonstrating that aggression will activate not only military clauses but financial, legal, and informational circuits, each already tested for resilience. The adversary must face the prospect of systemic, synchronised pushback—consequences too broad to calculate or evade.

The open question is whether states and their partners can build this level of interoperability before crises force their hand. It is easier to declare solidarity than to harmonise data schemas or legal doctrines. Yet without that hard work, alliances risk being ornamental, inviting challenges rather than deterring them. The silent drills of finance and law may lack the drama of marching troops, but they are fast becoming the frontline test of credibility. The measure of alliances that actually deter will be found not in communiqués but in the quiet precision of systems that leave no room for doubt.

Escalation ladders you can climb down

In October 1962, when the world teetered on the edge of nuclear war, the most remarkable achievement of Kennedy and Khrushchev was not merely that they avoided escalation. It was that they engineered a way back. The removal of Soviet missiles from Cuba was paired with a quiet withdrawal of American Jupiter missiles from Turkey, allowing both sides to claim victory while stepping away from catastrophe. The lesson is enduring: deterrence is not simply about climbing higher on a ladder of threats; it is about designing rungs that allow descent without humiliation.

Yet in the economic, legal, and digital contests of today, the habit of escalation without exit has hardened. Sanctions are imposed but rarely lifted. Trade restrictions linger long after their original rationale fades. Cyber retaliations accumulate in tit-for-tat spirals, with neither side clear how to restore equilibrium. The paradox is stark: by removing off-ramps, states increase the risk of entrapment in conflicts that no one wishes to perpetuate. Punishment becomes permanent not because it is effective, but because no path of retreat was designed at the outset.

Reversibility is therefore a strategic asset, not a sign of weakness. A tariff increase can be calibrated with sunset clauses or automatic review mechanisms, signalling resolve without locking both sides into indefinite confrontation. Financial sanctions can be tiered, with explicit criteria for removal tied to observable behaviours rather than vague assurances. Cyber responses can be structured as time-limited quarantines—blocking access or degrading performance for set periods—rather than as open-ended commitments to perpetual restriction. Each design choice embeds the possibility of retreat, ensuring that escalation is not a one-way journey.

Face-saving frames are just as important as the mechanics of reversibility. An adversary is more likely to de-escalate if they can present the retreat domestically as a strategic choice rather than a capitulation. During the Cold War, arms-control agreements were often couched as mutual steps towards stability, allowing leaders to defend compromises at home without appearing weak. In today's environment, narrative design matters: lifting sanctions might be justified as rewarding compliance with international norms, rather than as backing down. Providing adversaries with rhetorical cover does not diminish deterrence; it makes de-escalation politically survivable.

Measurement is the compass that makes climbing down possible. Without reliable indicators, decision-makers cannot know whether an adversary has moderated behaviour sufficiently to justify easing pressure. A sanctions regime, for instance, requires clear data on trade flows, financial transfers, or procurement anomalies to assess whether objectives have been met. Narrative conflicts demand sentiment analysis across audiences to track whether propaganda efforts are losing traction. Cyber conflicts need dwell-time metrics and incident reporting to judge whether hostile actors have pulled back. Without such measurement, states default to inertia—leaving sanctions in place or keeping restrictions indefinitely simply because no one can prove it is safe to remove them.

The habit of permanent punishment corrodes legitimacy as well as effectiveness. When sanctions drag on without visible purpose, they harden adversaries, alienate allies, and create humanitarian spillovers that erode moral authority. Similarly, long-standing cyber blacklists or export bans risk institutionalising hostility, making rapprochement politically unthinkable. By contrast, a system that demonstrates the capacity to lift measures when conditions are met strengthens credibility. It shows that power is exercised with discipline, not vengeance.

There is, of course, a tension. Too much emphasis on reversibility risks encouraging adversaries to wait out pressure rather than change course. Too little, and conflicts ossify into permanent confrontations with no exit. The art lies in designing ladders that are neither brittle nor endlessly forgiving—sturdy enough to signal resolve, yet flexible enough to adapt when behaviour changes. This balance requires constant rehearsal, not unlike military planning. States must anticipate not just how they will escalate, but how they will step back down, and under what conditions.

Case studies reveal both success and failure. The Joint Comprehensive Plan of Action (JCPOA) on Iran's nuclear programme contained elaborate snapback mechanisms for sanctions reimposition, but it also offered clear criteria for their removal. Its collapse illustrated the fragility of political will, yet its structure remains one of the clearest examples of reversible escalation design. By contrast, the United States' decades-long embargo on Cuba illustrates the opposite: a policy frozen in time, ineffective as leverage and corrosive to credibility precisely because no off-ramp was ever built into its architecture.

The deeper philosophical point is that deterrence without off-ramps is indistinguishable from vendetta. Power that cannot be withdrawn loses much of its persuasive force, becoming an exercise in punishment rather than influence. True strategic maturity lies in demonstrating that pressure is conditional, bounded, and subject to review. Such design not only makes conflicts more manageable but also strengthens legitimacy by showing restraint.

The unresolved question, however, is whether contemporary leaders—buffeted by domestic politics and the optics of toughness—will have the courage to institutionalise reversibility. In a world where escalation is often more visible than retreat, can states normalise the practice of designing exits in advance? Can restraint be sold to publics that equate permanence with resolve? The answers will determine whether tomorrow's crises escalate into deadlocks or yield pathways back to stability. The ladders exist; the challenge is whether we will allow ourselves to climb down.

Deterrence and democracy

When the Soviet Union placed missiles in Cuba, American households practised duck-and-cover drills while leaders debated nuclear red lines. Public fear was palpable, yet so too was public understanding of what was at stake. Citizens knew enough of the doctrine of deterrence to grasp why their leaders were acting with urgency, but not recklessness. Contrast that with more recent crises, where cyber intrusions or economic sanctions unfold behind opaque official statements, leaving citizens uncertain whether to worry, cheer, or ignore. The paradox is sharp: democracies gain legitimacy from public consent, yet they often design deterrence doctrines as though secrecy were the only shield.

Opacity may appear safer in the short term. It denies adversaries a clear map of thresholds and tools. But for citizens, secrecy breeds suspicion and panic. Rumours metastasise in the absence of credible communication, filling the void with speculation that can be more destabilising than the threat itself. Democracies that conceal too much risk losing what makes them distinct: the capacity to align national resilience with public will. When the social body is kept in the dark, deterrence becomes an elite game, unmoored from civic trust.

Transparent doctrine, by contrast, transforms deterrence from a technocratic formula into a civic project. Citizens who understand the conditions under which sanctions escalate, or the principles guiding cyber retaliation, are less likely to be blindsided by events. Clarity does not demand disclosing every tool in the arsenal. It requires articulating the rules of the game: what behaviours will be met with automatic responses, what red lines trigger coalition action, and what forms of escalation are deliberately avoided. Such communication narrows the space for panic and widens the foundation for consent.

Consider the mechanics of sanctions. Governments often announce sweeping restrictions but leave vague the benchmarks for their removal. Citizens and firms alike are left wondering whether the measures serve strategy or theatre. Transparent signalling could remedy this. By publishing clear criteria—such as specific compliance steps or measurable reductions in illicit financing—leaders convert sanctions into a visible tool of deterrence rather than an indefinite punishment. Citizens then see both the fairness and the purpose of the policy, reinforcing legitimacy.

Cyber conflict provides a similar lesson. When hospitals or municipal systems suffer ransomware attacks, public confusion is amplified by official silence. Did the attack originate abroad? Is retaliation under way? Are escalatory moves expected? In the vacuum, speculation fills the airwaves. Democracies could do better by providing structured updates that explain both uncertainty and intent: acknowledging the attribution process, outlining the thresholds for response, and clarifying protective measures. Such candour not only strengthens domestic resolve but also signals to adversaries that their tactics are understood and bounded.

Practical communication patterns make the difference between reassurance and alarm. One method is the use of "public playbooks": pre-published outlines of how governments will respond to categories of provocation, much like financial regulators issue stress-test criteria in advance. Another is the practice of joint drills—not only with allies but with the public. Just as Cold War air-raid drills prepared citizens for nuclear contingencies, modern exercises could rehearse civic responses to digital blackouts or disinformation waves. These rituals, if conducted with transparency and dignity, foster both competence and calm.

Critics will argue that transparency risks arming adversaries with a clearer map of thresholds. Yet the greater risk lies in eroding domestic legitimacy. A deterrence doctrine that cannot be explained without secrecy is one that cannot be sustained democratically. Moreover, clarity does not mean rigidity. Public doctrines can articulate principles while leaving the details of execution undisclosed. The point is not to script every manoeuvre, but to reassure citizens that actions are grounded in rules, not whims.

The deeper philosophical insight is that deterrence in democracies must operate on two audiences simultaneously: the adversary abroad and the citizen at home. Both require credible signalling, but the credibility is tested in different currencies. Adversaries weigh capability and resolve. Citizens weigh fairness, proportionality, and honesty. To succeed, doctrines must balance both forms of trust without collapsing into either secrecy or performative disclosure.

Examples of success exist, though they are rare. NATO's explicit commitment that an attack on one member triggers collective response has anchored decades of deterrence, not only by warning adversaries but by reassuring publics. In economic space, Japan's transparent food security policies—complete with stockpile thresholds and public reporting—have allowed citizens to see deterrence against coercive embargoes as part of national life, not an obscure policy domain. Both cases show how clarity stabilises not only international relations but domestic legitimacy.

Yet the unresolved challenge remains: can democracies sustain such transparency in the noisy churn of partisan politics and media cycles? Leaders fear that openness will invite criticism or exploitation. Citizens, meanwhile, demand honesty but often punish candour that reveals vulnerability. The tension is not easily resolved. Still, the alternative—strategies cloaked in secrecy and defended by rhetoric alone—risks greater instability. Democracies cannot afford to leave deterrence as a hidden art. It must be spoken, taught, and practised in public.

The future of deterrence will hinge less on the cleverness of sanctions or the sophistication of cyber arsenals than on whether citizens see themselves as participants in the project. A democracy that treats its people as bystanders in strategy risks losing both legitimacy and resilience. A democracy that treats them as partners, by contrast, gains a form of strength no adversary can easily erode. The question is whether today's leaders will have the courage to practise deterrence in the open—or whether secrecy will continue to undermine the very resolve they seek to project.

Chapter 12

Citizen Defences and Institutional Immunity

The great shocks of the early twenty-first century—from financial crashes to pandemics, from cyber blackouts to disinformation storms—revealed a quiet but consequential truth: states can only be as resilient as their citizens and institutions. Armies can deter invasions, treaties can align allies, but when the foundations of daily life are brittle—households unprepared for disruption, schools that do not teach scepticism, cities paralysed by dependency—the nation itself becomes fragile. It is not always the missile that topples a government, but the cascade of failures when systems and people are unready.

Consider the 2017 WannaCry cyberattack. In a matter of hours, hospitals across the United Kingdom saw computer systems locked and surgeries cancelled. The attack exploited outdated software, but it also exposed deeper weaknesses: procurement decisions delayed, contingency planning overlooked, digital hygiene neglected. No adversary fired a shot. Yet the disruption was profound, amplified not by the attack itself but by the absence of resilient routines. The lesson was stark. Resilience is not built in moments of crisis; it is cultivated daily—in how families manage information, how schools teach discernment, how bureaucracies learn, and how cities prepare.

This chapter turns the lens inward, away from the grand stage of geopolitics and towards the intimate, often overlooked arenas of resilience. We examine the household as the first firewall, where practices as ordinary as segmenting bank accounts, choosing media diets wisely, and backing up devices can, in aggregate, raise the national floor against economic coercion or disinformation campaigns. Strategy, in this sense, is translated into the mundane choices of daily life.

From there we move to education, where the cultivation of scepticism becomes a civic defence. Democracies cannot rely on secrecy to protect their citizens from manipulation; they must arm them with intellectual tools. Pilot programmes that teach source criticism, statistical thinking, and narrative mapping have shown measurable gains in resisting online falsehoods. Schools, then, are not just engines of literacy but incubators of strategic autonomy, producing generations less vulnerable to manipulation.

The role of cities is equally central. Municipal governments often sit closest to the infrastructures of resilience—water, energy, healthcare, communications. Their procurement standards, cyber drills, and supply audits can harden a nation more effectively than centralised theatrics in distant capitals. Case sketches show how city-led initiatives have absorbed shocks more gracefully than national agencies. The argument here is not against central authority but for devolved competence, where resilience is built layer by layer across society.

Institutions themselves must also evolve. Bureaucracies that ossify cannot adapt, but those that learn—through after-action reviews, red-teaming, and cross-sector secondments—can outcompete louder, more rigid adversaries. Such processes are not glamorous, but they transform organisations into living systems, capable of absorbing shocks and correcting errors before they metastasise. A government that learns is one that sustains legitimacy.

The chapter closes with a civic compact: transparency for trust, restraint for legitimacy, competence for consent. In essence, a blueprint for democratic resilience. It asks readers to consider resilience not as a technical add-on or a security measure but as the operating principle of free societies. Resilient citizens and adaptable institutions are not merely buffers against crises; they are the substance of sovereignty itself.

The question is not whether future shocks will come—they will—but whether societies will meet them with panic or poise. To answer that, we must look not to the arsenals of the state but to the habits of its people, the culture of its schools, the pragmatism of its cities, and the humility of its institutions. What follows is both a map and a call: to see resilience as the collective project of democracy, where every household and ministry, every classroom and council, contributes to a strength no adversary can easily corrode.

The household as the first firewall

When supermarkets in southern Europe emptied of basic goods in the first days of the 2008 financial crisis, the sight of families hoarding flour and fuel was not just a story of panic. It revealed how the smallest unit of society—the household—becomes the first point of contact with systemic shock. When households falter, nations falter. When they endure, nations can buy time, space, and stability. The paradox is that in an age of digital warfare, currency manipulation, and weaponised narratives, the decisive battleground may still be the kitchen table, the family inbox, the hard drive in the study.

This is not a romantic claim. It is a strategic one. A household with segmented bank accounts, curated media habits, and disciplined digital hygiene is not merely protecting itself; it is quietly contributing to national resilience. Aggregated across millions, such practices elevate the floor of national security. They do not eliminate crisis, but they reduce the ease with which adversaries can destabilise societies. Resilience at scale begins with competence at home.

Consider finance. During currency attacks, sanctions, or sudden liquidity shocks, households with diversified accounts—spread across institutions, and sometimes currencies—have a buffer against systemic freeze. The 2013 Cypriot banking crisis, when depositors awoke to find capital controls and levies imposed overnight, demonstrated how quickly savings can become hostages. Families who had segmented accounts abroad or across banks fared better, not only in preserving assets but in maintaining confidence. A nation of citizens trained to segment financial risk is harder to coerce through monetary disruption.

Information practices matter as much. Media diets are not a quaint academic metaphor; they are defences against weaponised narratives. In the Baltic states, Russian disinformation has long sought to exploit linguistic and cultural divides. Households that deliberately consume from multiple sources—national, regional, international—build a cognitive immune system. Exposure to plurality inoculates against capture by a single manipulative stream. Just as nutrition determines physical health, information intake determines civic health. The measure of resilience is not whether citizens believe the same story, but whether they can resist believing only one story.

Digital security brings the logic full circle. Backups, segmentation, and disciplined patching routines are not simply personal chores; they are national insurance policies. The WannaCry ransomware crisis showed how households and small enterprises became amplifiers of disruption when basic cyber hygiene was ignored. A family that maintains offline backups, separates sensitive accounts from casual browsing, and updates systems promptly is less likely to become a node of contagion. At scale, this transforms the national attack surface, turning millions of weak points into a distributed shield.

There is, of course, resistance to the framing of households as strategic actors. Many argue that the burden of national defence should not fall on ordinary citizens, that resilience is the job of governments and corporations. The objection is understandable but incomplete. In a world where attack vectors penetrate directly into homes—through phishing, supply chain disruption, targeted propaganda—the state cannot build firewalls high enough without participation from those inside. To refuse the role is not to eliminate it, but to leave it undefended.

Philosophically, the household firewall reframes the relationship between individual autonomy and collective security. Families do not act in concert, nor do they see themselves as extensions of strategy. Yet their aggregated routines generate systemic properties: liquidity buffers, information pluralism, digital hygiene. These properties determine whether a society collapses under pressure or absorbs the blow. In this sense, resilience is an emergent good, produced unintentionally but powerfully.

Schools and the pedagogy of scepticism

In the aftermath of the Second World War, Japanese schoolchildren were taught to examine newspapers not for grammar or vocabulary, but for propaganda. Teachers would lay two articles side by side—one from the wartime press, another from an international source—and ask pupils to identify omissions, exaggerations, and contradictions. It was not a lesson in history so much as a rehearsal in scepticism: a recognition that civic resilience is not secured by patriotic fervour alone, but by the ability to interrogate narratives. The insight remains striking. When societies equip their youngest citizens with critical habits, they are not merely enriching education; they are investing in long-term national security.

The paradox of our present moment is that information is both ubiquitous and unreliable. Children encounter persuasive claims long before they encounter the methods to assess them. They learn to scroll before they learn to doubt. Political debates over "fake news" or disinformation often place responsibility on technology companies or governments, but the most enduring line of defence begins earlier, in classrooms that deliberately cultivate scepticism as a civic virtue. The lesson is not cynicism—teaching pupils to dismiss everything—but discernment: an ability to parse sources, weigh probabilities, and map stories against evidence.

To see this logic in practice, consider Finland. For more than a decade, its schools have systematically embedded media literacy into the national curriculum. Pupils as young as seven are introduced to exercises in verifying sources, comparing headlines, and distinguishing between editorial content and advertising. The results are measurable: Finland consistently ranks among the most resilient societies in Europe against foreign disinformation campaigns. Pilot programmes in Sweden and Estonia have followed similar paths, each producing gains not only in comprehension but in civic confidence. A child trained to ask, *Who benefits if I believe this?* becomes an adult less easily swayed by populist tropes or hostile influence operations.

Statistical thinking is another underappreciated layer of sceptical pedagogy. Pupils are often drilled in calculation but rarely trained in inference. Yet the strategic stakes are plain. A society that can grasp the difference between correlation and causation, or recognise the distortions of small sample sizes, is harder to manipulate with selective graphs and out-of-context figures. Pilot schemes in the United Kingdom, introducing modules on basic probabilistic reasoning at the secondary level, show promising outcomes: students exposed to these curricula were significantly less likely to misinterpret survey data or sensationalised statistics in the press. Teaching pupils to think like informed jurors—asking *What is the quality of this evidence?* rather than *Do I like this conclusion?*—has consequences far beyond exam results. It raises the floor of public debate.

Narrative mapping adds a further tool. Stories are powerful precisely because they are coherent, not necessarily because they are true. By training pupils to map the structure of a narrative—who are the heroes, the villains, the causal chains—they can detect when an account is persuasive but incomplete. Programmes in Canadian schools have shown that even at primary level, children can learn to diagram narratives, spotting gaps or implausible links. Such exercises create not only literary awareness but geopolitical resilience: young citizens more attuned to when a foreign broadcaster or domestic politician is framing events in manipulative ways.

These examples illustrate a slow, steady inoculation rather than a one-off cure. Sceptical pedagogy does not aim to eliminate false beliefs in the short term but to build immune systems that work over decades. Like vaccination, its efficacy is most visible when a whole population shares in the protection. A few isolated classes in media literacy achieve little; systemic integration across schools makes the difference. The analogy is apt: herd immunity against manipulation depends on widespread exposure to the habits of questioning.

Critics sometimes argue that teaching scepticism risks breeding relativism—that pupils will treat all claims as equally suspect, paralysed by doubt. Yet evidence from pilot programmes suggests the opposite. Well-designed curricula do not encourage nihilism but discrimination. Pupils trained in source criticism were more likely to trust reputable outlets and official statistics, not less. The aim is not to strip away belief but to redirect it towards warranted confidence. The subtlety lies in showing that scepticism is not an end in itself, but a pathway to justified trust.

The stakes are more than academic. Authoritarian regimes have long understood that shaping young minds is a strategic imperative. Democracies must match that intensity, but through methods consistent with open societies: equipping pupils not with doctrine but with tools of resistance to doctrine. The very act of teaching scepticism models a democratic ethos—the humility to accept that authority can be questioned, the discipline to ground argument in evidence, the courage to revise beliefs in light of better reasoning. These habits, if nurtured early, spill over into professional life, journalism, science, and policy. They shape the strategic autonomy of a society as much as any stockpile of natural resources.

One can measure the cost of failing to invest in this domain. Consider the United States, where surveys show a third of adults struggle to distinguish between factual statements and opinions in news coverage. The downstream consequences are visible in polarised debates over vaccines, elections, and foreign policy. When sceptical training is absent, entire populations become vulnerable to manipulation that can erode trust in institutions and weaken national resolve. In this sense, education is not a peripheral cultural issue but a central element of security planning.

Strategic autonomy rests on the slow accretion of these civic habits. A society that educates its children to question and analyse does not merely protect them from manipulation; it expands the range of democratic choices available in times of crisis. Citizens capable of parsing statistics or interrogating narratives are less likely to panic, more likely to demand accountable responses, and harder to divide through propaganda. The pedagogy of scepticism thus becomes a quiet but decisive form of deterrence: raising the cost of influence operations and lowering the probability of internal collapse.

The challenge, of course, is that results take years to emerge. Politicians accustomed to short electoral cycles struggle to invest in long-run inoculation. Budgets for cybersecurity or border defence are easier to justify than funding for curriculum reform. Yet the societies that make the commitment—embedding source criticism, statistical reasoning, and narrative mapping into their schools—will find their dividends compounding over generations. The most potent national firewall may be invisible, distributed across millions of minds trained to resist manipulation.

The question that lingers is whether democratic states can summon the patience to build such resilience, or whether they will remain trapped in cycles of reactive outrage and hasty regulation. The pedagogy of scepticism asks for neither heroics nor grandstanding, only persistence. But persistence, when woven into classrooms, can transform the strategic posture of nations. The future of civic resilience may depend less on advanced algorithms and more on the quiet daily lessons where children learn, for the first time, to doubt.

Cities as resilience platforms

In 2017, when a ransomware attack paralysed hospitals and businesses across Europe, it was not a ministry of defence that first restored order but a patchwork of municipal IT teams, local clinics, and city-run emergency services. The episode exposed a quiet truth: the resilience of a nation often hinges less on the edicts of central government than on the competence of local authorities who know their infrastructure, their suppliers, and their citizens. In crises, cities are not merely service providers; they become strategic platforms.

This inversion of perspective—that the local is national security—runs counter to the familiar drama of centralised command. Politicians at the national level stage summits, publish white papers, and announce grand strategies. Yet it is city councils that procure the software, run the drills, and manage the data standards that determine whether essential systems buckle or bend under pressure. A resilient state is only as strong as its municipalities, and often their quiet competence is the decisive difference between disruption contained and disruption cascading.

Procurement offers the first, often overlooked, lever. When cities set minimum cybersecurity requirements for vendors, they raise the baseline for entire supply chains. New York City, for instance, mandates that software purchased by its agencies comply with secure development standards and undergo penetration testing. These local decisions reverberate far beyond the city itself, compelling firms to upgrade their practices if they wish to bid for contracts. In effect, municipal procurement becomes a distributed regulatory tool—incremental, unglamorous, but strategically potent.

Data standards extend this logic. City governments handle vast flows of information—transport schedules, health records, energy usage, emergency calls. When these are stored in interoperable formats with clear governance protocols, they enable rapid coordination in crisis. Tallinn, Estonia, has become a case study: its city-wide adoption of secure digital identity and interoperable registries has allowed residents to access services even during cyberattacks. What appears, on the surface, as municipal IT hygiene is in fact a foundation of national resilience.

Public communication is the third pillar. During the early months of the COVID-19 pandemic, trust in municipal authorities often exceeded trust in national ones. Cities like Seoul and Taipei, through transparent daily briefings, SMS alerts, and dashboards, managed to sustain public confidence while reducing panic. The lesson is instructive: citizens live their crises locally. National credibility is reinforced—or undermined—by how effectively city governments communicate with their residents in moments of uncertainty.

Practical exercises bring these elements together. Some cities now conduct cyber drills analogous to military manoeuvres. Los Angeles, for example, has staged city-wide simulations of ransomware attacks, involving not only IT staff but hospitals, schools, and utilities. The purpose is not theatre but muscle memory: ensuring that when systems go dark, officials know which redundancies to activate, which suppliers to call, which communications to prioritise. Similarly, city-led supply audits—tracking stockpiles of medical equipment, fuel, or critical spare parts—provide real data on days of cover, information that often proves more reliable than national-level inventories built on estimates.

The contrast with centralised theatrics is stark. National governments may announce sweeping initiatives, but unless competence is devolved—procurement officers trained, city IT systems hardened, local communication protocols rehearsed—grand strategies dissolve under stress. The strength of a federation or a union lies not in declarations but in the ability of its cities to absorb shocks without waiting for instructions from the capital. Resilience grows bottom-up, not top-down.

This raises philosophical as well as practical questions. If cities are resilience platforms, should they be treated as strategic assets in their own right, with powers and budgets to match? Or should they remain the silent executors of central policy? The tension is acute. Too much autonomy and national coherence may fray; too little and local innovation is stifled. Yet the pattern of recent crises suggests that devolved competence is the safer bet. Cities, by their very proximity to citizens and infrastructure, are better positioned to adapt swiftly to disruptions.

The deeper point is that resilience is not a performance but a practice. It is built in procurement checklists, coding standards, joint drills, and audit spreadsheets—activities often dismissed as bureaucratic. But precisely in their mundanity lies their power. Cities that excel at these routines create a floor of security upon which national strategy can stand. Nations that neglect their municipalities, by contrast, discover too late that glossy doctrines cannot compensate for brittle local systems.

The open question is whether political systems can reconcile their appetite for central spectacle with the quieter demands of devolved competence. Can they redirect resources from high-profile summits to low-profile procurement reform? Can they reward mayors for conducting unglamorous supply audits rather than unveiling monuments? The fate of national resilience may depend on such shifts. For when the next disruption comes, it will be local councils, city IT staff, and municipal communicators who stand between a nation and systemic fracture. The theatre of strategy ends on the capital's podium, but the reality of resilience is rehearsed—and tested—on city streets.

The bureaucracy that learns

In 1986, after the Challenger space shuttle disintegrated before the eyes of the world, investigators traced the tragedy not simply to a faulty O-ring but to a deeper institutional failure. NASA had heard engineers' concerns but filtered them through layers of managerial optimism and bureaucratic ritual. The disaster became a parable: an organisation that fails to learn systematically will repeat its errors, often with devastating consequences. The loudest voices in the room prevailed, but the patient work of reflection and adaptation was neglected.

The paradox of modern governance is that bureaucracies are often mocked for slowness, yet their true weakness lies not in pace but in their failure to *learn*. Institutions may be busy—issuing reports, holding press conferences, launching initiatives—but activity is not the same as adaptation. Loud bureaucracies accumulate slogans; learning bureaucracies accumulate wisdom. The difference is rarely visible in the short term, yet over decades it decides whether states withstand shocks or collapse under the weight of their own blindness.

At the heart of a learning bureaucracy lies the discipline of the **after-action review**. Originating in military practice, this deceptively simple routine asks three questions after every operation or crisis: What did we intend to happen? What actually happened? What can we do differently? When carried out honestly—without the defensive fog of blame-shifting—it transforms mistakes into assets. The British Army institutionalised this approach after bitter lessons in Northern Ireland; corporations from Toyota to Microsoft have adapted it for their own use. Governments, however, too often treat reviews as opportunities for scapegoating rather than collective learning, squandering the very crises that could sharpen their competence.

Alongside reflection sits rehearsal. **Red-teaming**, once the preserve of intelligence services, now serves as a diagnostic tool across finance, cybersecurity, and regulation. By appointing insiders to think like adversaries, institutions inoculate themselves against complacency. When Singapore's Monetary Authority commissioned red teams to stress-test its financial sector's cyber readiness, it exposed vulnerabilities invisible to routine audits. The value was not merely in fixing those flaws but in cultivating a mindset: assume your adversary is smarter than you, and prepare accordingly.

Rotation offers the third element of bureaucratic learning. **Secondments between regulators and operators**—placing civil servants temporarily inside the industries they oversee, and vice versa—bridge the knowledge gap that ossifies institutions. A regulator who has spent six months inside a telecoms operator understands, viscerally, how compliance burdens interact with engineering constraints. Conversely, an industry manager who spends time within a regulator's office gains an appreciation of the pressures of public accountability. Such exchanges replace sterile suspicion with informed dialogue, reducing the probability of both regulatory capture and regulatory irrelevance.

These practices, however, require more than procedural adoption. They demand cultural change. A bureaucracy that learns must value candour over ceremony, iteration over image. This can be uncomfortable in political environments where admitting error is seen as weakness. Yet the alternative—burying mistakes under rhetoric—creates fragility. The German government's sober post-mortems after its 2011 energy policy shifts, contrasting with the bombast of other states, illustrate how humility can coexist with authority. Learning, paradoxically, strengthens legitimacy.

The benefits extend beyond crisis response. Institutions that embed feedback loops in daily routines build resilience not by preparing for every imaginable threat but by ensuring they can adapt to the ones they fail to predict. In this sense, measurement and ethics—two themes developed elsewhere in this book—find their bureaucratic corollary. Measurement supplies the evidence base for after-action reviews; ethical discipline prevents red-teaming and secondments from becoming Trojan horses for capture or abuse. Learning bureaucracies knit these threads together into living practice.

Sceptics might object that bureaucracy, by its nature, resists change. But the record shows otherwise. Japan's post-war Ministry of International Trade and Industry reinvented itself multiple times, from guiding industrial policy to managing trade liberalisation. The U.S. Federal Aviation Administration, chastened by repeated accidents in the 1960s, became a world leader in aviation safety precisely because it institutionalised after-action review and data-sharing across airlines. The European Union's regulatory agencies, though often derided, have incrementally built sophisticated regimes in food safety and competition law by iterating through crises and feedback. Learning, though slow, compounds.

The question is not whether bureaucracies *can* learn, but whether they will be permitted and incentivised to do so. Political cycles reward noise over nuance, announcements over adaptation. Leaders may prefer the illusion of control to the humility of reflection. Yet the organisations that survive and thrive are those that embed modest routines—reviews, red teams, rotations—that gradually build a culture of realism. They are less likely to be surprised, less prone to panic, and more capable of steady course correction when the unexpected arrives.

The unresolved tension is clear. Can bureaucracies embrace the quiet disciplines of learning in an age dominated by spectacle and speed? Or will they continue to prioritise visibility over competence, rehearsing failure until catastrophe forces reform? The answer will determine not only the efficiency of administrations but the resilience of democracies themselves. For in a world where shocks are frequent and adversaries adaptive, the bureaucracy that learns will outlast the one that merely shouts.

A compact for democratic resilience

When the Icelandic banking system collapsed in 2008, the government faced one of the deepest economic shocks any modern democracy had endured. Banks holding assets worth ten times the country's GDP imploded almost overnight. Yet instead of descending into authoritarian emergency or populist chaos, Iceland improvised a compact between state and citizen: radical transparency in the release of financial data, restraint in the use of police and military power, and steady, competent rebuilding of institutions. Citizens may have disagreed bitterly with one another, but they recognised that the state had not hidden, overreached, or fumbled. Legitimacy survived, even when prosperity did not.

The lesson lingers. Democracies cannot avoid shocks—pandemics, financial crashes, cyber intrusions, disinformation storms. What matters is whether institutions can *absorb* them without destroying the trust that keeps civic life intact. Authoritarian regimes pride themselves on projection of strength, yet their brittleness is exposed the moment citizens lose faith. Democracies, by contrast, endure when they treat trust as their most renewable but fragile resource.

The compact proposed here distils resilience into three commitments: **transparency for trust, restraint for legitimacy, and competence for consent**. Each element is deceptively simple, yet together they form a template that any ministry, firm, or municipality can adapt. Unlike abstract doctrines or technocratic manuals, this compact translates strategy into practice at the level of civic life.

Transparency comes first because opacity corrodes from within. The COVID-19 pandemic showed the consequences starkly. Nations that shared data openly—South Korea publishing case-tracking apps, Germany releasing hospital capacity figures—preserved public cooperation even as restrictions tightened. Those that withheld information or massaged statistics faced suspicion that hampered compliance. Transparency is not about baring every secret; it is about demonstrating candour in matters that touch the public directly. The act of disclosure itself signals confidence in citizens' capacity to process reality, even grim reality, without panic.

Restraint is the second pillar, and it is often the most difficult. In moments of crisis, leaders are tempted to reach for sweeping powers: mass surveillance after terrorist attacks, censorship in the face of disinformation, emergency decrees to stabilise markets. Yet each overreach erodes legitimacy, feeding a cycle in which citizens comply out of fear rather than consent.

Democracies distinguish themselves precisely by their ability to act with *less* than maximum force. The most credible institutions are those that know where to stop, not those that prove they can dominate. Canada's measured invocation of emergency powers during the 1970 FLQ crisis—swift, temporary, and narrowly applied—remains a model of how to protect order without undermining liberty.

Competence is the third element, and perhaps the most prosaic, yet it underpins the other two. Transparency without competence is mere confession of failure; restraint without competence looks like paralysis. Citizens will forgive errors if they see an institution learning and adapting. They will not forgive performative busywork that masks incompetence. Competence here does not mean perfection but the capacity to respond reliably, scale proportionately, and correct course visibly. Taiwan's rapid development of digital systems to distribute masks in 2020—simple apps linked to pharmacy stock—showed how basic competence can prevent panic and build pride simultaneously.

Together, these principles form not an abstract philosophy but a working template. Ministries can adopt it through open data portals, proportionate use of emergency laws, and rigorous process reviews. Firms can mirror it by publishing clear risk reports, limiting coercive contract clauses, and maintaining high operational standards. Cities can enact it through transparent procurement, restrained use of policing, and competent service delivery. The compact is scalable precisely because it distils resilience into everyday practice rather than grand strategy.

Critics may ask whether such a compact is naïve in a world of ruthless adversaries. Can transparency coexist with security, restraint with deterrence, competence with the messy realities of politics? The answer lies in reframing resilience not as the absence of secrecy, force, or improvisation, but as the disciplined use of each within ethical boundaries. A democracy that hides selectively, wields power sparingly, and adapts visibly is not weak; it is strong in a way that brittle authoritarianism cannot imitate.

The compact also clarifies what citizens must demand of their leaders. Trust, legitimacy, and consent are not gifts from above but outcomes of a continuous relationship. When governments release information, citizens must resist conspiracy thinking; when leaders show restraint, citizens must not mistake it for weakness; when institutions strive for competence, citizens must hold them accountable without expecting omniscience. Resilience is reciprocal.

The deeper implication is that democratic strength does not reside in secret arsenals or rhetorical defiance but in a shared civic ethic. Institutions that honour this compact are less likely to overreact to shocks, and societies that live within it are less likely to panic when shocks arrive. Transparency, restraint, and competence may sound unglamorous compared to grand doctrines of power, yet they are the quiet infrastructure that allows democracies to outlast empires.

The tension, of course, remains unresolved. Can modern democracies, under relentless pressure from disinformation, polarisation, and geopolitical rivalry, hold to a compact that prizes patience over spectacle? Or will the temptation to overpromise, overreach, and overstage prove irresistible? The answer will decide whether democracies in the twenty-first century emerge as resilient stewards of trust or brittle performers on the global stage. The choice is still open, and therein lies the agency that prevents despair.

About the Author

Helena Marković writes about the quiet decisions that decide nations' fates. Raised between borders and languages, she came to distrust the simple story and to follow the plumbing of money, media, law, and code—where power actually runs. Her work sits at the crossroads of political economy and moral inquiry: how to exercise pressure without losing legitimacy; how to measure effects honestly when causation is designed to be hidden; how citizens can remain free in a world that competes without firing shots. Drawing on the history of embargoes from ancient sieges to modern sanctions lists, the jurisprudence of courts that shape markets, and the craft of engineers who keep the internet stitched together, she writes with the conviction that clarity is a civic duty. This book continues that project: to replace noise with structure and to give thoughtful readers tools for judgment rather than slogans.

www.ingramcontent.com/pod-product-compliance
Lightning Source LLC
Chambersburg PA
CBHW051354240926
51852CB00001B/25
9789390349029